NORTHERN
dreamers

OTHER *OUT OF THIS WORLD* BOOKS FROM QUARRY PRESS

Out of This World:
Canadian Science Fiction & Fantasy Literature
edited by ANDREA PARADIS

Trapdoor To Heaven
by LESLEY CHOYCE

Death Drives a Semi
by EDO VAN BELKOM

Interviews with Famous
Science Fiction,
Fantasy,
and Horror Writers

NORTHERN dreamers

by Edo van Belkom

Copyright © Edo van Belkom, 1998.

All rights reserved.

The publisher gratefully acknowledges
the support of The Canada Council
and the Department of Canadian Heritage
for the arts of writing and publishing in Canada.

ISBN 1-55082-206-3

Design by Susan Hannah.

Front cover image: photograph
of the aurora borealis as seen
from outer space.

Printed and bound in Canada
by AGMV Inc., Quebec.

Published by Quarry Press,
P.O. Box 1061, Kingston,
Ontario K7L 4Y5 Canada,
www.quarrypress.com

Photo Credits: Paul Rozario, pg 9; Allan Green Studio, pg 29; Beth
Gwinn, pg 39, 51, 149; Janet Duncan, pg 61; Susan King, pg 83; Merle
Casci, pg 105; Jenny Glicksohn, pg 115; Tom Robe, pg 127, 159, 235;
Barbara Turner, pg 169; M. C. Valada, pg 179; Carolyn Clink, pg 197;
Robert Laliberté, pg 211; Andrew Danson, pg 225; Roberta DiMaio,
pg 245, 254.

Contents

For my parents,
Frank and Romana van Belkom,
who taught me never to be afraid
of a little hard work.

Acknowledgements

This book wouldn't have made it into print without the help of a lot of wonderful people. I am indebted to them all: Bob Hilderley and Susan Hannah at Quarry Press; Rosslyn Junke and Jane Rowland at HarperCollins Canada; Michaela Cornell at Avon Books Canada; Amy Corely and Lisa Miscione at Putnam/Berkeley; Suzanne Hallsworth at H.B. Fenn; Janet Herron of the International Festival of Authors; John Rose at Bakka; John Dimou at Sci-Fi World; Matt Schwartz of Barnes and Noble; Robert J. Sawyer; Stanley Wiater; Jean-Louis Trudel; photographers Beth Gwinn and Susan King; and my wife Roberta.

This book took roughly a year and a half to complete. Out of twenty-two interviews in *Northern Dreamers*, ten were conducted in person, nine were done by e-mail, two were done over the phone, and one was done via Canada Post.

I'll leave it to the reader to figure out which is which.

The individuals captured and chained together in this collection of interviews are among the best and brightest talents in the speculative writing fields today. They share, among other characteristics, a passion for creating the fantastic and awesome, for taking humanity and adding an element of the extraordinary, tinkering with the question "what if" and discovering new worlds, new races, new ideologies, and new possibilities. Assembled here is a vibrant community that boasts an impressive list of major award winners and international bestselling authors in all three of the speculative genres — science fiction, fantasy, and horror. Their achievements are plentiful. William Gibson, for example, is the author of the most commercially-successful novel in Canadian history, *Neuromancer*, and scriptwriter for such major television and movie productions as *Johnny Mnemonic*, and *The X-Files*. Ed Greenwood, creator of the Forgotten Realms of Advanced Dungeon and Dragons, can boast that his most successful novel, upon its release, sold 75,000 copies between Christmas and New Year's Eve. Robert J. Sawyer has won several major awards for his science fiction, not only in Canada, but in the United States, Japan, France, and Spain, while his work has been translated into Italian, Russian, German, Dutch, Polish . . .

So who are these international superstars? Speculative fiction writers are an assorted lot of creatures, as unique and mesmerizing as the characters and worlds that appear on the pages of their works. They are individuals such as Ed Greenwood, who, despite enormous success of the Forgotten Realms, is still content to work full-time as a librarian. Or Lesley Choyce, author of *Trapdoor to Heaven* and editor of the highly acclaimed anthology *Ark of Ice*, who surfs in the

North Atlantic ocean in the middle of winter, apparently immune to ice and cold. Or Nancy Kilpatrick, who not only writes about vampires, but embraces the dress and lifestyle of the Canadian Goth scene and is a member of both the Gothic Society of Canada and the SIN Society of Montreal. Or Spider Robinson . . . well, now, that's a very long and truly bizarre story . . .

The immense success of these individuals is even more impressive when one considers the lack of regard speculative fiction is given in Canada. Despite the obvious talent within its borders, there is not one major Canadian publishing company with a commitment to science fiction, fantasy, or horror; the media has been accused of being dispassionate and ill-informed; and critics have been accused of reviewing books that they believe Canadians should read, instead of reviewing the books that Canadians do read. These factors, taken together, make it clear why, almost exclusively, the writers in this book have been forced to publish outside of the country with such American publishers as Tor and DAW. So why do these artists stay? Or more accurately, why did they come in the first place?

One of the strangest features of this collection is that, out of twenty-two writers interviewed, the vast majority were not born in Canada. Most, by strange twists of fate and eerie coincidence, arrived in Canada by choice. So why flock to a meteorological-challenged icecube of a country to write in a genre that is under-appreciated? Perhaps the relative youth of the nation, its open spaces, and the wide expanse of its oceans allow their minds to run free to new worlds and new possibilities. Or perhaps their status as aliens in a new country has given them the insight to write as aliens in strange new worlds. Or perhaps, just say maybe, they're here because of some great cosmic notion — brought together by a supernatural body beaming inspiration directly through the northern lights. Hey, anything's possible in the world of speculative fiction. But no matter why these Northern Dreamers made the journey, this book demonstrates that they have arrived and are commanding the world's attention. In the domain of speculative fiction, these writers are the pioneers, leaders, and supreme masters of the realms in which they travel.

Nancy Baker

Nancy Baker is an oddity among northern dreamers. While writing genre horror fiction (and more specifically, the horror sub-genre of vampire fiction), she has been published exclusively by a large mainstream Canadian publisher, Penguin Canada. The result of this strange coupling has enabled her to be called "the dark star of Canadian vampire writers" in *Maclean's*, Canada's national weekly newsmagazine, as well as appear on the cover of Toronto's *Eye* entertainment weekly under the garish headline, "Blood Sucking Freaks!"

Born in 1959, Baker blames her life-long love of horror and fantasy fiction on the first horror story she can remember, *The Tale of Squirrel Nutkin*, by Beatrix Potter. She dabbled in rock and roll (writing lyrics and singing in basement bands during her university years) before switching to writing fiction.

In 1988 she published her first story, "The Party Over There," in *Rod Serling's Twilight Zone Magazine*, and followed it up the next year with the publication of "Exodus 22:18" in the same magazine. Her next short story sales didn't come until years later when "Cold Sleep" was published in the first *Northern Frights* anthology in 1992, and "Consent" was published in the Horror Writers of America anthology *Deathport* in 1993. After the sales of her short stories and before the sale of her first novel, Baker worked various jobs in the magazine industry, ultimately becoming the marketing manager of *Canadian Living* where most of what she wrote was along the lines of — "FREE BONUS! BUY ONE, GET TWO FREE!"

Eventually, Baker made her mark on the Canadian horror scene with three vampire novels. Set in Toronto, *The Night Inside* was published in 1993, has been translated into five languages, and was a finalist for the 1994 City of Toronto Book Award. *Blood and Chrysanthemums*, a sequel to *The Night Inside*, was published in 1994, and moves between Toronto's Queen Street goth scene with its "wannabe vampires" to the picturesque surroundings of Banff, Alberta, where vampires feed on elk blood. In 1996, Baker published *A Terrible Beauty*, a modern reversal of "Beauty and the Beast" in which a young man is held captive by a seductive female vampire.

EDO VAN BELKOM: How long did you work on your first novel, *The Night Inside*, before you felt it was ready to submit to a publisher?

NANCY BAKER: It was about seven or eight years, but I was working long hours at a stressful job and I did not write religiously. I tended to write in very short spurts over the year. I would go on vacation and write, or I'd spend Sunday afternoons at Harveys writing because I came home every night at nine o'clock and writing the novel was the last thing on my mind.

VAN BELKOM: Was it a question of finding the time, or are you one of those writers that has to be inspired?

BAKER: Well, it's a combination of those things. It was a question of time and energy because I was putting so much mental energy into my work, I really didn't have a lot left to devote to writing. I would have said that I needed to be inspired, but the subsequent two books I wrote were under much less stressful circumstances and I've been fairly disciplined. Like now, if I'm writing a book and I know I have to have it done, I'll write a chapter a day or so. I'll sit down at 9:30 and start writing and go until I'm done whatever I'm doing that day.

VAN BELKOM: How much of your time is spent researching before the actual writing process?

BAKER: Depends on the book. With *The Night Inside*, there was virtually none. With *A Terrible Beauty*, there was some in terms of reading for ideas about painting, which was really what I was looking into. And some stuff in terms of development of a big house in the middle of nowhere because I had to think of a good reason why it was there. But with *Blood and Chrysanthemums* there was a good six months of research before I could even start writing the book, before I could even write an outline, because I had to do so much research into Japanese history and culture in order to determine what kind of characters I would be dealing with and what events could drive the story.

VAN BELKOM: Did you find it satisfying to do the research or was it a lot of work that made you vow not to do that kind of thing again?

BAKER: It was very interesting. I enjoyed it in some ways. I know far more Japanese culture than I put in that book. I could have written five or ten books based on what I found out. But certainly, when you're dealing with the real world, you have an obligation to be realistic about things. You just can't run around portraying other people's cultures and not make a legitimate attempt to be true to them. I was dealing with it in a vague fashion in many ways because the structure of that part of the novel was essentially Fujiwara telling you short stories about his life — which were not necessarily entirely true. That structure allowed me to play a little more with detail than I would have if I were writing a straight historical novel. Also my copy editor, a wonderful woman named Mary Adachi, has a degree in Japanese literature so I knew that I had to have things right.

VAN BELKOM: Your writing career started off with plenty of promise when your first short story was published in *Rod Serling's The Twilight Zone Magazine*. Could you tell me how that came about, and what effect it had on your writing at the time?

BAKER: They were running a short story contest which I thought would be much less stressful than submitting a story to the magazine. You just enter the contest and if you don't win, you don't win. I didn't realize at this point that previous winners of this award were people like Dan Simmons . . . So I entered one year and got a nice note back saying it wasn't quite what they wanted.

The next year I wrote a story called "The Party over There," which I entered and heard nothing. Finally the magazine showed up and I opened it and found that I got an honorable mention. Whoa, this is pretty cool. Next I got a letter from the editor, Tappan King, saying here's the things we liked and didn't like. He suggested I might want to change the title and the ending. (Laughs) I don't think so. I'm sorry, but the title and the ending is what this story is about. So, I did nothing. And then, two months later I got a call from Tappan King who asked why I hadn't sent my story back. I didn't want to change it and he said maybe you don't have to change it, maybe it just needs to be a little deeper. I thought about that for a while, so I changed a couple of things — but I didn't change the title or the ending — and I sent it back and they ended up buying it for the "TZ Firsts" program. They also had a contest for their "TZ Firsts." I think I ended up fourth, but the winner was Elizabeth Hand who has gone on to a successful writing career. I didn't mind losing to her because I thought her story was the best.

VAN BELKOM: I've looked through the magazine and lot of people who placed well in that contest haven't been heard of since so you must take some satisfaction in having launched your career with that sale.

BAKER: It was really great to have it affirmed that I could write, because I hadn't done a lot of writing at that point. I was working and busy with my magazine career and I wrote, but I didn't really take it seriously so it was a great affirmation that I wasn't completely untalented. I subsequently sold another story to them, but I'm not a very prolific writer — I think I've written five short stories in my life — so I very quickly switched to novels because I couldn't possibly make a living out of writing short stories.

VAN BELKOM: Making a living aside, why so few short stories when the initial ones met with such success? Do you look at it solely in terms as making a living as a writer or that you get few ideas that are worth your time?

BAKER: I think it's really that I'm not prolific and I don't get a lot of ideas. It just happened that all the ideas that I've had in the last five or six years have been novel ideas. And I think you reach a saturation point of what you read of other people's writing. I always read the Year's Best anthologies. That's primarily where I did my reading in terms of short fiction, and I always thought that unless I could write a short story that was as good as this, then why bother. I have a high "so what" factor. I think of an idea and say, "yeah, so what." Is there going to be something in that story that I've never seen before? And a lot of times I go, "No, not really," so I don't bother.

So it's a function of the way my mind works in terms of ideas. It was never really a career decision. I'd be happy to write more short stories and sell them if I could actually think of one to write.

But *The Night Inside* started as a short story that just kept getting longer and longer and longer . . .

VAN BELKOM: You've talked elsewhere about men reviewing you

poorly. Do you think it has to do with the female characters in your books being assertive, independent, and strong-willed. Do you think some men find that hard to accept while women cheer that kind of thing in their fiction?

BAKER: I would sure hope we'd gotten over that. It's really only been an issue with *A Terrible Beauty*. I have noticed that there's been a fair bit of criticism of, for instance, the writer C.J. Cherryh, by men — that all her male characters are wimps — whereas women tend to like her male characters. So maybe there is a gender thing on that book in particular because the male character is cast in the passive role. I mean, in "Beauty and the Beast" there is a certain role assigned to Beauty and there's a certain role assigned to the Beast. In this case the male is being the Beauty character so he cannot suddenly get a gun and decide to shoot the Beast. It isn't going to work that way. But I would hope that men reading genre fiction have gotten over that. So much of science fiction and fantasy is being written by women, so much of it has strong female characters, that if you were to say I don't want to read that stuff you'd be cutting yourself off from a lot of really good work that's being written today.

VAN BELKOM: You published two stories, but there wasn't anything that would indicate that you would turn to vampire fiction when you started your novel career. What was it about vampires that drew you toward them?

BAKER: Part of it was that was the idea I had, and not having so many ideas that I could afford to throw one away. I never set out to become a vampire writer and I don't think I will be writing vampire novels for the rest of my life. I started out as a fantasy writer, and that is in many ways my first love, and the default of my brain. If my brain is casting about for ideas, it defaults to fantasy, but I've yet to conquer the world-building issue so I'm working on it. I had an idea involving vampires and a way to approach vampires that I didn't think I'd seen before. I'd read a lot of vampire stories and I'd always loved horror fiction, so I thought this is something I could take a go at.

And I never, in all the years I was writing it, realized that vampire fiction was becoming so popular. It really wasn't until the end when I was thinking of selling it that I realized every second book on the shelf was a vampire novel. Then I thought, I'm never going to sell this thing because it'll be over by the time I get there.

VAN BELKOM: What about afterwards?

BAKER: I had a contractual obligation to write *Blood and Chrysan-themums*, which is not to say I didn't love the book. It was a very hard thing to write. I struggled a great deal with it. But I'm proud of it in many ways. I think some of it contains the best writing I've ever done. It was a really interesting experience. But what I really didn't want to do was write *The Night Inside 2*. I wanted something completely different from *The Night Inside* and *A Terrible Beauty* ended up being something completely different as well.

But I think there are only so many things you can say about vampires, and unless I've got something to say about it, why am I writing this book? So I'll see.

VAN BELKOM: So it's a safe bet that the next book out won't be a vampire novel?

BAKER: All bets are off because I said I wouldn't write another vampire novel after I wrote *Blood and Chrysanthemums*. I don't have any objection writing another Rozokov novel, but I have yet to think of what happened to them that would be so important that I would want to tell the story. It would have to deal with an issue that hadn't been dealt with in the first two. The first one dealt with becoming a vampire and what the moral issues are in that, and the second was how you live together as vampires, so the third one would have to be about something — and I don't quite know what that thing is.

I could even write a sequel to *A Terrible Beauty*, and I do have some ideas about that, but again I've got to work them out.

VAN BELKOM: You say you started with vampires because that's the idea you had. Were you aware of the whole vampire/Goth sub-culture while you were doing the book or was this something you became aware of after the book was published?

BAKER: I knew it was there, obviously. I tend to associate it with the Queen Street scene (in Toronto) because bars like Sanctuary were starting up at the time I was writing the book. But I didn't go to them, I wasn't part of it. I just dealt with it as another aspect of the world that Ardeth was looking in on with her nose pressed against the window, and then suddenly she was this thing that they all want-ed, and that was part of her reconstruction of herself in this image.

When she turns into a vampire she doesn't know how to deal with it, so she reconstructs herself as this media/goth image because that appeals to her. Then in the second book, she deals with that again and realizes it is only a very fractional reflection of what it would really be like to be a vampire.

It's a very romanticized image.

VAN BELKOM: There's a lot of music in your work. Bar bands and music in general plays a large role, certainly not a predominant role, but it's there enough times to be noticed.

BAKER: Well, in my late teens and early twenties I wrote lyrics. I was in a basement band — we never got out of the basement — and so I really wanted to be a musician. When it became apparent that this was unlikely, I switched to writing fiction, but the music still had a big influence on me and I still enjoy the chance to somehow or other fit that world into my fiction because it still attracts me. And I spent so much time writing all those songs that I had to find a way to put some songs into my stories. It happened that ideas like "Exodus 22:18" and "The Party Over There" had to do with music and bars and nightclubs and stuff — that whole thing was part of my life for so long I couldn't just abandon it.

VAN BELKOM: You were into the club scene and basement bands, but how does someone so into that end up living in Markham, which is a town that looks like Stephen Spielberg decided to build it as a movie set.

BAKER: I grew up here and spent my teens here. And it was the place I always had to get away from, so I lived in Toronto for a number of years. But then I got married, and I married someone who works in Markham. We lived in downtown Toronto for a few years, but it was getting to be a long commute for him, so it was only fair that we move and try it here for a while. Then, when I decided to quit my full-time job, I didn't have an excuse for not living in Markham anymore. But this part of the city I quite like because it's a thirty-five-year-old subdivision and it has a bit of history to it.

VAN BELKOM: Now that you're freelancing full-time, do you feel there's pressure on you to produce or come up with ideas?

BAKER: I have an idea that I'm working on . . . It needs to move along faster than it is, but it's not at the point where I need to worry about it monetarily because I have other work that is reasonably steady. And I'd really rather not write a book because I needed the money. It hasn't been a problem because I quit about the time I was going to write *A Terrible Beauty* anyway, so I went right into *A Terrible Beauty* and that was great.

But ask me in a year from now. If I haven't written another book by then, I might be panicking.

VAN BELKOM: You're somewhat unique in Canada as a genre writer being published primarily by a major Canadian publisher. Did it come as a surprise when your first novel sold to Penguin Canada?

BAKER: It was a complete surprise. I had expected that I would probably end up selling it to a US paperback house, but I had been to a University of Toronto writers workshop and Cynthia Good, who's the editor of Penguin, was speaking there, and she said, "We like to publish popular fiction, we'd like to publish horror." So, about eight months later, when I finished the book, I thought well, why not? I can write to her and say I was at this workshop, I've been published before, and would you be interested. The worst she could say is no, but they ended up saying yes we'd like to look at it.

I sent it off and waited six weeks, eight weeks, twelve weeks, until I finally phoned them and said, "Did you get it?" And they went, "Yeah, and we like it."

So, I was really surprised, and it's turned out to be a great relationship because they do such beautiful books and they treat me very well.

VAN BELKOM: Is their enthusiasm still at that level? Or do you feel that you're either gaining momentum or losing steam?

BAKER: I don't know, certainly they were very enthusiastic about *A Terrible Beauty*, and they seem to be committed to the books, and they've sold the film rights and foreign rights, so I hope they're making money. My theory on this is both of us should be making money.

VAN BELKOM: You mentioned foreign editions. There have been a lot of foreign editions, especially of your first novel. How much did the publication of your subsequent novels depend on the sale of all of those other editions?

BAKER: Well, possibly the terms of the sales for the second two had something to do with the number of foreign rights sold for the first one, but the first one was not sold dependent on the foreign rights, it was sold separately. Any foreign rights sales were gravy to them, I guess. Or money to them anyway.

VAN BELKOM: Are the good people at Penguin encouraging you to produce, or asking you "What's next?"

BAKER: They keep in touch but they don't pressure me too much. I'm sure if I don't start coming up with something they'll want to know, at least for their own plans. We have a good relationship and if I wrote something they didn't like I wouldn't be offended if they felt it didn't fit in with their publishing plans. Having been in the marketing business myself I know that you have to make money. I hope that we'll be able to continue to work together and I would always go back to them first with any new book.

Lesley Choyce

esley Choyce is "out there," in more ways than one. First of all
he's the most prominent writer of speculative fiction on Canada's
east coast. Second, he is a former national surfing champion who
enjoys seeking the isolation of the open sea off Nova Scotia's Lawrence-
town Beach where he makes his home. And even in a genre that's
already on the edge, Choyce has still managed to remain on the fringes,
writing and editing not only science fiction and fantasy, but also
young-adult novels, poetry, autobiographical essays, and popular history.

Choyce was born in Riverside, New Jersey in 1951 and studied at
East Carolina University, Rutgers University, Montclair College, and
The City University of New York. After several visits to Nova Scotia,
he moved there in 1978 and shortly after started up a small publishing
company called Pottersfield Press. He became a Canadian citizen in
1983.

Pottersfield has the distinction of publishing one of the very first
Canadian SF anthologies, *Visions from the Edge* (co-edited with John
Bell), featuring speculative fiction from Atlantic Canada. A later SF
anthology, *Ark of Ice*, included the work of such prominent Canadian
mainstream authors as Margaret Atwood, W.P. Kinsella, and Timothy
Findley. Another Pottersfield SF publication was the collection *The
Woman Who Is the Midnight Wind*, the first book by Toronto's
Terence M. Green. In addition to publishing, Choyce also hosts a literary cable talk show, *Choyce Words*, which was initially broadcast on
cable across the Maritimes, but eventually got national exposure on
the Vision Network.

As a writer, Choyce's most successful works have been in the
mainstream with books like *The Republic of Nothing*, and young adult
titles like *Good Idea Gone Bad*, which won the 1994 Ann Connor Brimer
Award.

Some of his science fiction stories, which have been published in
a wide variety of literary and other magazines as well as several volumes of the *Tesseract* anthologies, were published in his 1986 collection *The Dream Auditor*. Ten years later he published the "metaphys-
ical murder mystery" *The Ecstasy Conspiracy* and his first true SF
novel, *Trapdoor To Heaven*.

EDO VAN BELKOM: You moved to Nova Scotia in 1979. How much of a factor did the Vietnam War and what you call America's "Gluttony of Progress" have to do with the move?

LESLEY CHOYCE: That was well after the Vietnam War, but I think the first really positive images of Canada as a better, saner alternative to the United States got stuck into my head during the Vietnam War. I graduated high school in 1969 and was very interested and involved in the protest movement and that sort of thing. I never did get drafted, and I never really did come all that close. My brother almost did and I was planning to get him into Canada. I don't think he had the ability and personal motivation to pull it off, but I think I did, and I was going to make sure he didn't go into that war.

So, anyway, I remember TV images of guys running for the Canadian border and Canadian immigration people actually hauling them across and keeping the American authorities back and that was part of it. And when I moved to Canada, Reagan had just been elected and it looked like it was going to be at least ten really unhappy years for me.

Canada seemed like a semi-Utopia.

VAN BELKOM: Now that you've lived on the east coast for nearly twenty years, do you feel that you're more of an East Coast Canadian than an American from New Jersey?

CHOYCE: I'm more of a Nova Scotian than I am an American. I'm also more of a Nova Scotian than I am a Canadian; that's for sure. By the time I moved here Nova Scotia came first. It happened to be in Canada and that was a happy marriage. But yeah, my identity is pretty tied in with geography.

And I think there's some connection between living on the margins and writing science fiction which fits nicely for me being in Nova Scotia and not back in New York where I used to teach or even in Toronto. I've got a little window where I can stick my head above the clouds and take a breath of fresh air and go at the world in a different way.

Maybe if I was in New York or too close to the publishing capitals I might get too caught up on what's going on and who's doing what and be influenced by that, and so far I'm not.

VAN BELKOM: You've written or edited some forty books since the late 1970s. How much of that output would you consider to be speculative fiction?

CHOYCE: I guess in the neighborhood of ten percent. It would all depend on how you want to define that term. I think that if I had found more of a comfortable niche in that area I would have done more of it, but I don't think I've ever really been all that commercially successful at it. Even in the world of science fiction, I've been pretty much on the fringe and kind of had my own agenda that didn't necessarily fit in with commercial stuff.

That might have bothered me at some point, but now I'm happy with it. So it still seems a struggle and even with this last book, *Trapdoor To Heaven*, the publisher and I were both stumbling about trying to decide if it was science fiction or fantasy. And since it was a combination of both, what do we do with it? How do we get it into the bookstores so that it doesn't scare off people who are used to reading mainstream Lesley Choyce novels like *The Republic of Nothing*. And then are real SF people going to read this because it doesn't really fit into that category either? The whole world of science fiction is still a mystery to me in terms of the categories and how you market that kind of stuff.

VAN BELKOM: Bob Hilderley, your editor at Quarry Press, told me that you persuaded him to have the words "science fiction" taken off the cover of *Trapdoor To Heaven* and replaced by the words "new fiction."

CHOYCE: I don't know if it's as bad in Toronto, but what happened with that book in this region was that it never made it onto the "local author" rack, which is where you can sell books very well, whatever they happen to be about. But I couldn't convince bookstores that it was mainstream fiction, so it never got onto that rack. It got spined into a massive wall of American science fiction, but it wasn't the right size or color as all the other books and virtually got lost there and nobody bought it. So, I think my fears proved correct on that.

VAN BELKOM: Your short story "The Loneliness of the Long-Distance Writer" opens with the lines: "Even now I sometimes have my doubts about being a writer. I mean, it's not like I have a big audience. There is a grand total of four readers in this solar system who see my work."

Does it ever seem that way for you?

CHOYCE: Yeah, but I'm comfortable with the idea that if I can do what I'm trying to do well and find an audience that genuinely cares about what I'm doing, then I'm on the right track with my motivation and my agenda. Now, in some ways that makes me a fool, but I guess I don't mind that too much now that I've written and published a whole bunch of books. I think I can do things like the YA (young adult) novels that are maybe more commercial, but if I really want to go out on a limb and do something in the great imaginary playground — where I think all fiction should be — I can do something that's kind of off-beat, off the wall and not like anything anyone's expecting.

VAN BELKOM: You certainly must have a love of science fiction and fantasy, since your Pottersfield Press has published quite a bit of it, particularly the anthologies *Visions from the Edge* and *Ark of Ice*, and Terence M. Green's collection, *The Woman Who Is the Midnight Wind*.

CHOYCE: Yeah, all books that I'm really quite proud of.

VAN BELKOM: So is science fiction something that's close to your heart?

CHOYCE: It is. But it all goes back to limitations again. In the world of mainstream fiction you do kind of come up against a wall in terms of what you can do, so as soon as you jump over it into speculative fiction all kinds of doors start opening up. I want to go into those rooms, I want to go into that territory and see where it can take me.

I started out writing really bad science fiction as a teenager, but I was writing bad poetry and bad everything . . . I was trying to emulate the writers that I was reading during my teenage years — Heinlein and Asimov.

Even now I write a lot of stuff that I toss, or store. One way or the other it doesn't go out, just keeps my wrists limber and my brain jogging along, and then something will click in that's worth having other people read.

VAN BELKOM: How well did the SF books Pottersfield produce sell in comparison to the other "mainstream" books you've done?

CHOYCE: *Ark of Ice* did very well and I was really happy with that anthology. And Terry Green's book, *The Woman Who Is the Midnight Wind,* of which we printed about 1,500 copies, sold out.

Visions From the Edge, the very first one we did — and of course this was very early on in Pottersfield Press — was so off the wall in terms of categories that nobody knew what to do with it, but it was still a wonderful experience. I think that at the time it came out it was only the second anthology of Canadian science fiction published and it was a specialized one — we were on a real kick back then where everything had to be Atlantic Canadian — and of course when it came out people had a really hard time trying to get their head around to the idea of writers from the 1930s writing stories like "The Living Galaxy" that takes place 200 million years in the future. But it did actually sell slowly over the years, and I always got a kick out of orders that came in from libraries in the Soviet Union and Japan.

VAN BELKOM: Which is the favorite of your SF books and why?

CHOYCE: I guess, *Trapdoor To Heaven.* It's the most ambitious, not necessarily the most successful, but the most ambitious — the idea of trying to write a novel that takes place over 25,000 years, blending together ideas about reincarnation and time travel, and trying to do the self-contained story mode and yet create a mesh for it all to hang together.

VAN BELKOM: Do you have a favorite genre of writing, or do you find yourself unable to write too much of one thing for too long before having to move on to something different?

CHOYCE: If I could find the right audience — and I don't know if this is the exact opposite of what I said earlier — I would probably write my brains out at science fiction, but I don't think that's going to happen. So I think that where I want to be is writing novels and I want them to be somewhat literary but not too esoteric, and I want them to be somewhat commercial.

VAN BELKOM: With so many books to your credit, does it sometimes become hard to convince people of the literary merit of your work? I'm thinking primarily of Daniel Richler when he interviewed you for TV Ontario.

CHOYCE: That was an interesting interview because he seemed to be angry at me over the fact that I was writing a lot of books and that I was having a good time at it. I wasn't suffering, I wasn't agonizing over something. And yeah, if I'm writing that many books they must be coming quickly and they can't possibly be all that good. I don't buy that at all. I think I can write a couple of books a year. They're not all going to be great but I think some of them are quite good.

It's just a different writing process for me so that I'm happier when I'm in the midst of writing a novel than when I'm not, so I might as well just keep doing it. In truth, books that appear have usually been kicking around for two or three years because they overlap. I'll write a novel and then just stash it in the drawer for six months to a year and not touch it, and then I'll rewrite it two or three times and then it goes out. And in the meantime I've already begun another novel.

VAN BELKOM: How did being the interviewee in that situation compare to being the interviewer on your talk show, *Choyce Words*?

CHOYCE: Well, on *Choyce Words* I try to be a really nice guy and I try to make sure that whomever I'm interviewing has a platform to say some interesting and important things that they want to say. As I remember about the TV Ontario thing, I felt — as I often feel whenever I go to Toronto — a little bit of an oddity. You know, "Here's this Nova Scotian eccentric, he surfs in the winter and writes all these funny books. What do we make of him?"

I still feel a great distance from the center of Canadian culture as it spirals around Toronto.

VAN BELKOM: In addition to being a writer, poet, and publisher, you're also a Canadian surfing champion. How does surfing complement the other sorts of things you do?

CHOYCE: Well, I was. I'm a has-been. I was champion in 1993 and since then I've been knocked down to number three.

Surfing is a great escape, it's a meditative activity. It's an adrenalin pumping thing as well. When I'm sitting out on my surfboard and especially when I'm totally alone, there's a great sense of space and openness.

When I'm surfing, it's like — cliché, cliché — being tuned in with the forces of the planet and somehow trying to tap into the energy of waves. I think of the writing process in the same way.

Maybe I'm not creating any of these things at all, I'm just tapping into some great cosmic flow of ideas that every once in a while I can connect with.

VAN BELKOM: Didn't you combine your love of surfing and science fiction in a story called "Some Waves Start Cold?"

CHOYCE: That was a science fiction story that appeared nowhere else except for *Surfer Magazine*. That had to do with global warming and glaciers falling off into the fjords of southern Alaska.

I had taken a ferry ride from Alaska to B.C. and noticed this glacier on the coast, and I saw this big chunk of ice falling into the sea and this perfect wave rolled on out to sea instead of in, and I thought, "Whoa! What a great thing. If you could be sitting there at the right time and catch this thing as its going out to sea." So in the story I've got this surfer — after these weather wars have happened and screwed up surfing everywhere — trying to find some of the last good waves available, which are the ones created by the chunks of glacier falling into the ocean.

VAN BELKOM: Is there anything you'd like to write, but haven't got around to yet?

CHOYCE: I'd like to write a number of science fiction novels in the young adult area, although there's such a thin line when kids are reading science fiction they're already into reading the best SF available to adults. But all the YA publishers I've dealt with have been reluctant to open up into that realm. I'd like to have a little more of an American audience because I grew up there and I'd like to see if some of these novels connect down there. But all the dealings I've had with American publishers suggest my writing is too parochial. Too Nova Scotian or something, but that wasn't your question.

VAN BELKOM: Well, I was going to ask that question. You've published so much in Canada, have you made the attempt to sell in the US and therefore reach a bigger audience?

CHOYCE: I've made the attempt and I guess I pretty much failed. From what I can tell there isn't a lot of interest down there. I had one YA novel get translated into Danish, *Skatefreaks og Graesrodder (Skateboard Shakedown)*, and there's one being translated into French coming out in Quebec, and then I've been to Japan trying to make inroads into selling rights in Japan, which was fascinating, although the publishers I did talk to were most interested in

Trapdoor To Heaven rather than anything on the mainstream side of things.

VAN BELKOM: You've said that you don't work at anything, just have fun with your life, but with all of the things you do, surely some of it must be considered hard work?

CHOYCE: It is. It's a nice little lie that I tell every once in a while because it refers to the best part of the process. Rewriting is a real pain in the ass. I've never liked it, but I do it.

I want this magic thing to happen and I'm sure all writers do. You sit down and write this story with all the rough edges and all the joy and fun you can pack into the rough draft, and you hand it to some genius editor who just takes this scribbled mess and fixes it all up and then it gets published. There's the dream. Now I can't do that and nobody can do that because so much of what needs to be fixed up has to do with the writer sorting out the hodgepodge of thoughts. So the rewriting is difficult and painful, but necessary.

And that's the craft.

Michael Coney

L ike many writers, Michael Coney held a wide variety of jobs before settling down into a career as a science fiction writer. Born in Birmingham, England, in 1932, Coney later qualified as a Chartered Accountant and immediately began rebelling against this sober image, even to the extent of running a pub for several years. "I had no experience of pubs," he says, "except as a consumer. But the brewery figured that this, plus the CA designation, was their guarantee of a solid, reliable citizen." Coney managed the Maltster's Arms in South Devon, then got a position managing a hotel and night club in Antigua, West Indies.

It was during this time that Coney began writing SF, publishing his first novel, *Mirror Image*, in 1972. That year was also the one which Coney came to Canada with his wife and two children. After traveling cross-country he settled in British Columbia and worked for some years with the province's Ministry of Forests as a management specialist. The experience with the Ministry helped Coney produce his sole work of non-fiction, *Forest Ranger, Ahoy!*, a history of the Forest Services' boats. But non-fiction was only a small portion of Coney's output, as his first novel was followed by *Syzygy* and *Friends Come in Boxes* in 1973 and eight more titles by the end of the decade: *The Hero of Downways*, *Monitor Found in Orbit* (collection), *The Jaws that Bite*, *The Claws That Catch*, *Hello Summer Goodbye*, *Charisma*, *Brontomek!* and *The Ultimate Jungle*.

In the 1980s, Coney continued with *Neptune's Cauldron* and *Cat Karina*, followed by the connected novels *The Celestial Steam Locomotive* and *Gods of the Greataway*, and the eccentric Arthurian fantasies *Fang, The Gnome* and *King of the Sceptre'd Isle*.

The 1990s saw publication of a pair of humorous adult fantasies set in a very British Columbia-like setting: *A Tomcat Called Sabrina* and *No Place for a Sealion*. He's also been busy writing numerous well-received stories and novelettes, such as "Tea and Hamsters," first published in *The Magazine of Fantasy and Science Fiction* in 1995, and a Nebula award nominee.

In addition to publishing in the US, Britain, and Canada, Coney's work has also been published in France, Holland, Yugoslavia, Japan, Russia, Sweden, Italy, Spain, and Germany.

EDO VAN BELKOM: You've lived in Canada for more than twenty years and almost all of your work has been published while you've lived in Canada, but I still think there's a strong perception of you as being a British writer. Has that been the case?

MICHAEL CONEY: I've been asked that question many times and I still don't know the answer; after all, I've written enough short stories set in Canada and the States. It must be something about the style. Unless I'm writing in the present day I try to avoid current North American slang or issues because of their inappropriateness for a tale set in the future. Maybe this strips my style down to a timeless, perhaps mildly pedantic Standard English which people deem to be British. This doesn't apply to my humorous novels, such as *Fang, the Gnome* and *King of the Sceptre'd Isle*, where I made no pretense of authenticity and, instead, had fun with wild anachronisms. And my current crop of humorous short stories such as "Werewolves in Sheep's Clothing," although using both British and American idioms, are set in Southwest England.

On the other hand the answers may lie in my inability to write Canadian stories as such. The truth is: I don't really know what a Canadian story is. When I wrote a series of stories for *The Magazine of Fantasy and Science Fiction* set on Vancouver Island I thought they were Canadian. But no: I was told they were British stories set in Canada. Currently I have a story in *Tesseracts 5* called "Belinda's Mother." It has snow, Indians, possibly even caribou, and it was deliberately written to sound Canadian. We'll see what people think of that.

But then I've just completed a novel entitled *I Remember Phallahaxi*. It's set in Southwest England, thinly disguised as an alien world, and why not? It's the story that counts, and current political boundaries and cultures have nothing to do with science fiction, to my mind.

VAN BELKOM: Your work seems to have had a particularly receptive audience in the UK. Do you have any explanation for that, other than you being born and raised there?

CONEY: Yes, my stuff goes over well in the UK, but my biggest market has always been France. I don't think it has anything to do with my place of birth. It's simply that I established a name in those countries before I was published in North America; and when I *was* published in the States, I was lost among a few hundred other SF writers.

VAN BELKOM: You've said that you don't do more than a brief two-page outline of your novels before you begin. Is the process for short stories the same, and have you ever written yourself into a corner, truly not knowing what happens next, or how to get your characters out of a certain predicament?

CONEY: I've prepared a much more extensive outline for my last few novels. The difference is the computer. I used to find the typewriter incredibly tedious so I was reluctant to alter anything once it was down on paper. And above all, I couldn't be bothered to type out any kind of extensive synopsis. Now, with word processing, I can write my outline, expand it without having to retype, and shuffle the events and characters around until I've got them the way I want them. Large sections of the synopsis eventually become part of the story itself, without having to key it all in again. I'd have given up writing long ago, if the PC hadn't been invented.

I always construct the ending of a novel or short story first. Since the characters are always progressing toward this ending, they don't get boxed in. Take "Werewolves" as an example. I already knew the characters; I'd used them before. The story's climax would contain a rationale for the werewolves and a chase scene. Obviously that had to be written first; if it didn't work, then the whole story would be a dud. So naturally I planned out the climax, then went back and wrote the beginning and the middle.

It all comes of reading a lot of detective stories.

VAN BELKOM: So you tend to equate writing to an exploration or an adventure. Has that always been the case?

CONEY: Yes, it has, particularly with my earlier two-page outlines. Even now, as the outline is expanding into a novel, I find myself contemplating adventurous refinements along the way to entertain the reader. *I Remember Phallahaxi* has a gigantic mining machine bursting from a cliff face and devastating the primitive village on the beach below. Exciting stuff, but how to make it plausible, and necessary to the plot? Well, I'd planned to kill off a character and to show the grief of his son, and to have the hero discover something about them both. All I needed was the setting. And there it was. Rather than have the guy die in bed with black-clad mourners grouped around, boring as hell, why not make it an action scene? The mining machine was due to run amok anyway; I was getting tired of it.

But I never know all that is going to happen when I sit down to write the novel. Small refinements and additions occur to me along the way, and I keep a note of these to incorporate in the final version. I'm sure most writers do the same. It all comes in the plotting, the shuffling around of characters and their motivations, and the potential for excitement in the world you've built.

VAN BELKOM: Have you tried your hand at other genres besides SF and fantasy? Mystery, or romance, perhaps?

CONEY: I've written a mystery novel without finding a publisher. I don't blame the publishers for that; maybe it was a lousy story. I had a short story in the May 1996 *Alfred Hitchcock's Mystery Magazine* called "Catnap." It's dark humor with a new twist on an old problem — just a one-off thing. My SF stories always have a strong mystery element, so if I removed the SF content from my planning stage I'd feel there was something missing.

Likewise romance. I wrote a Harlequin-style novel but they told me my heroine was "too tough." Well, I thought they wanted them tough these days; they always say so in their instructions. Where the novel really failed, was in the use of the familiar Harlequin trigger phrases: the strong square chins and the fluttering hearts. I'd decided to write the real story first and sprinkle all that stuff on later, like garnish. But I didn't sprinkle enough; I felt it was wrecking the story and insulting the readers' intelligence. And Harlequin spotted me for a faker, and they were right.

I once wrote a romantic short story about the jealous reaction of a wife to a husband's memory of an old flame. The point of the story was that the wife had nothing to be jealous of; it was simply a beautiful memory, irrelevant to her husband's present situation. Three women's magazines rejected it with cruel abandon. I loved that story because it had happened to me in real life. So I rewrote it, introducing an SF element. It took on a new dimension which —

dare I say it? — convinced me of the richness of SF's potential compared with any other genre. As if I needed convincing. *F&SF* bought the story, called "Sophie's Spyglass."

So I have good reason to stick to SF.

VAN BELKOM: What was it about SF that made you want to write it, and how did you get started?

CONEY: I started writing SF because it was what I read, back then. So far back, in fact, that I didn't know it was SF. I only knew that my favorite Conan Doyle story was "The Lost World," and I enjoyed Rider Haggard and H.G. Wells, and so on. They didn't call those books SF, so how was I to know? Much later I was subscribing to the British magazine *New Worlds* at the time of the New Wave. Remember the New Wave? One month they sent a questionnaire asking readers what they thought of the stories. I wrote in to say I hated the stories — those that I could understand at all — and what had happened to good old SF like Wyndham and Asimov wrote, and who was this J.G. Ballard anyway? And I told them I could do better myself.

Having said that, I gave it a try. I dashed off garbage for two years, then sold a story. It was no less garbage than the others, but it proved to me that *it could be done.* I took a great deal more care with my writing after that, and sold most of what I wrote.

VAN BELKOM: In 1986, you published a story in *The Magazine of Fantasy and Science Fiction* called "Memories of Gwyneth" under the name Jennifer Black. Why the pseudonym?

CONEY: Jennifer Black? She never wrote anything else. I was experimenting with different points of view in my characters at the time, and it occurred to me to try a different writer's point of view. So I tried to write from a woman's point of view; not an easy thing for me because I'm not sure how it differs from a man's, except when it comes to buying clothes. When I'd finished the story I somehow shrank from putting my name on it. And when "Memories of Gwyneth" appeared in *F&SF*, I challenged a friend — who knows my writing almost better than I do — to identify my story in that issue. She failed after several attempts.

But that didn't mean the story read as though it was written by a woman. It means, I suppose, that it read as though it wasn't written by me.

VAN BELKOM: You managed a pub in England and a hotel in Antigua. How did this experience help or hinder your early writing efforts?

CONEY: Running a pub is not conducive to writing. There's too much to do and too much to worry about. In our days at the Maltster's Arms (which incidentally is the same pub Keith Floyd the TV chef bought more recently) profit margins were low and we could only afford assistance on Friday and Saturday nights. All kind of weird things happen when you run a village pub, but before you've had time to incorporate them in a story, the next crisis looms.

The Antigua hotel was different. We had outside funding and an efficient staff. I wrote several novels and short stories in our three years there.

VAN BELKOM: When you left Antigua. You could have settled anywhere in the world. Why Canada? Why British Columbia?

CONEY: A fellow can go crazy living on an island only twenty-four miles across. There's no intellectual literary stimulation. By the time my contract with the owners was up, I was desperate to get away. But I didn't want to go back to England; it was to escape the problems of the Old Country that we'd gone to Antigua.

A lot of the hotel guests were Canadian, and they painted a glowing picture of their homeland. We'd already visited Toronto and the Muskoka area a couple of times — in the winter, to get away from the endless goddamned sunshine and palm-fringed beaches. So when the time came, Canada seemed to be the place to try next.

We stayed with friends in New Jersey and Vermont, made our way to Toronto, then flew west because we figured we'd seen enough of the east, pleasant though it was. We bought a car and trailer in Calgary, drove over the Rockies and down through BC to Vancouver, where we went through the immigration process. It was quite simple in those days. It was raining in Vancouver, as usual, so we took the ferry to Victoria, and stayed.

That's why we're here. There was no conscious decision. It was just the end of the road, literally.

VAN BELKOM: Do you prefer writing novels to short stories, and do you have a preference between SF and fantasy?

CONEY: For many years I preferred writing novels because of the broader canvas. Then a couple of years ago I started writing short stories again because I had this sudden fear that I'd lost the knack. But they sold well, and I enjoyed writing them. I've even managed to write a couple of short stories to order, something I'd always refused to do before. Now, with confidence regained, I have no particular preference.

I much prefer SF to fantasy. I find it almost impossible to write fantasy because, for me, everything must have a rational explanation. Even my two Arthurian novels were science fiction: I invented scientific explanations — albeit far-fetched — for every fantastic aspect of the myths. I have to do that, otherwise I'd be disbelieving my own stories while in the throes of writing them.

I suspect that real fantasy writers believe in God, or at the very least, acupuncture. Nothing wrong with that, but it's not for me.

VAN BELKOM: Your books have some of the most interesting titles in SF. *Friends Come in Boxes,* and *The Jaws That Bite, The Claws That Catch* are classics. Have you had trouble getting your titles into print, and if so what are some of the more outrageous titles that didn't make it.

CONEY: Those titles you mention, they were dreamed up by Don Wollheim. He rejected my own titles every single time. And he was right of course. Except that his original title for my *Girl with a Symphony in her Fingers* (the title used in England) was *The Jaws that Bite, the Claws that Snatch.* It took a frantic call from me to get it corrected just before it went to print and branded me forever as a Philistine. I think Don was thinking of the Bandersnatch.

Since Don dropped me my titles went into decline — because subsequent publishers always used my original titles. I rather liked *The Celestial Steam Locomotive* and *Cat Karina,* and possibly *Fang, the Gnome,* but as for the others . . . Well, I could have done with some suggestions from dear old Don.

VAN BELKOM: Several years ago you changed your name from Michael G. Coney to Michael Greatrex Coney. First of all, is that really what the G. stands for, and second, why the change?

CONEY: My full name is Michael Greatrex Coney, to my everlasting shame. It's worse for my sister, who also bears that wretched middle name that caused me so much trouble at school. It's not easy to assure virginal schoolgirls of your honorable intentions when the boys are yelling "Sexy Rex" after you.

My writing name is Michael Coney; the initial G. should not be there. I don't know how it started, but it keeps creeping onto book covers and unbalancing the composition. I've learned to make it a big issue when publishers get into cover design. That doesn't always work. As recently as 1990, Press Porcépic put

MICHAEL

G.CONEY

on the cover of *Phallahaxi Tide*. Am I alone in thinking that looks weird?

Okay, so I used Greatrex for *Fang* and *King*. That was because I saw them as a completely different kind of book from my usual SF, and I wanted to distinguish them in some way. Added to which, Greatrex struck me as the kind of name an Arthurian writer might have. So, just the once. Never again.

VAN BELKOM: You've established your own publishing company, Porthole Press. What was the reason for that, and what can you say about the experience of publishing in Canada?

CONEY: Porthole Press was initially formed for the publication of my local boat history book, *Forest Ranger, Ahoy!*, over which I wanted full control. The company went on to publish a number of local history and child safety books until I sold it in 1995. What can I say about it all? Well, it was fun for ten years and I enjoyed designing and putting other people's books together. Distribution was the big problem; it always is for small outfits. Financially I did no more than okay; as with writing, there are much easier ways of making money. The company never had the kind of regular publishing schedule to qualify for government grants; I just published books when something came up that interested me. Now the company is sold I feel some minor regret, but mostly relief. It's been an interesting experience, like the pub and the hotel, but it's time to move on. I'm building an extensive model railway in the room that used to be full of unsold books. *Model Railways, the Creative Hobby of Today.* That's what they say on the cover of the monthly magazine I take, and who am I to contradict them?

Charles de Lint

While Charles de Lint's book-length debut was a traditional high fantasy, he followed it up with a string of novels that injected fantastic elements into the mainstream and as a result created a new sub-genre for himself — urban fantasy. But despite being credited as a pioneer in the realm of urban fantasy, de Lint has never been content to do just one thing and has, at one time or another, written just about everything in the speculative field, from science fiction to horror, from poetry to columns and reviews.

His first novel, *The Riddle of the Wren*, appeared in 1984, and following its publication, he quickly gained the reputation of being a prolific author with some ten books published before the end of the decade: *Moonheart*, *The Harp of the Grey Rose*, *Mulengro*, *Yarrow*, *Jack the Giant-Killer*, *Greenmantle*, *Wolfmoon*, *Svaha*, and volume three in Philip José Farmer's Dungeon series, *The Valley of Thunder*.

De Lint began the 1990s with volume five of the Farmer series, *The Hidden City*, and continued publishing at a torrid pace, averaging two to three books per year, including hardcovers, paperbacks, and chapbooks published by small presses like Axolotl and his own Triskell Press. Major releases include *Drink Down the Moon*, *The Dreaming Place*, *The Little Country*, *Into the Green*, *The Wild Wood*, *Memory and Dream*, and *Trader*. Under the pseudonym Samuel M. Key, he has penned three horror novels: *Angel of Darkness*, *From a Whisper to a Scream*, and *I'll be Watching You*. Always a prolific short story writer, de Lint has three collections in print, including *Spiritwalk* and two collections of stories set in the imaginary city of Newford, *Dreams Underfoot* and *The Ivory and the Horn*.

His non-fiction work has included entries to encyclopedias, critical essays, columns, and reviews for newspapers and magazines, including *The Ottawa Citizen* and *The Magazine of Fantasy and Science Fiction*, for whom he writes a monthly column. In 1995-96 he served as Writer-in-Residence at the Ottawa and Gloucester Public Libraries. He has been a professional musician for more than twenty years playing in bands that specialize in traditional and contemporary Celtic music.

Charles de Lint was born in the Netherlands in 1951. A Canadian citizen, he currently makes his home in Ottawa.

EDO VAN BELKOM: I suppose in this type of interview situation, you've heard the word "prolific" plenty of times before.

CHARLES DE LINT: It's an understandable perception. When I started seriously writing fiction in the late 1970s I had been writing for seven years so I had a lot of backlog by the time the first books were published. Some of the books were crap and they're never going to see print, but I was writing a book and a half a year so when I started getting published it looked like I was writing an awful lot. In fact, I was writing at the same speed I had been for a long time.

VAN BELKOM: You're well regarded within the fantasy field, but have you come up against any barriers in regards to being accepted by the mainstream in Canada.

DE LINT: I don't know about in Canada. Once mainstream readers read my work they often like it. In fact it strikes them as particularly fresh because it's the real world and it has a little quirk to it. I'm constantly getting people coming up to me at signings or writing me letters saying, "I don't read fantasy or books with those kinds of covers, but someone bought me one and I loved it, and I went out and bought all your other books." That happens with great frequency.

VAN BELKOM: Do you ever get it the other way, people dismissing you because you write fantasy?

DE LINT: I don't get it to my face, but I'm sure that stigma is there. You can see my books do better in chainstores and SF bookshops than they do in independent bookshops because independent bookshops, I'm assuming, are for more literary minded people and they seem to judge things by the lowest common denominator, so genre fiction gets judged by the worst that's produced in the field as opposed to the best.

VAN BELKOM: You've been called a fantasy "pioneer" for your attempts to combine traditional fantasy with the modern world. Are you comfortable with that label, or have you just come to accept it?

DE LINT: "The Father of Urban Fantasy."

VAN BELKOM: Is that another one?

DE LINT: When I first started publishing there was next to no one doing what I'm doing. Even now, a lot of people who do what's considered contemporary fantasy still aren't doing what I'm doing because what I'm doing is basically writing mainstream novels that are very concerned with contemporary people, how they relate to each other, and how they relate to the problems in a contemporary life, and I spice it up with a fantasy element. A lot of what I read that is marketed as urban fantasy or whatever they want to call this stuff just seems to be high fantasy transplanted into a contemporary setting, which isn't the same thing.

I can understand some of the problems of where to put me because I've written that stuff as well. I've written traditional high fantasy, secondary world fantasy, I've written horror novels, science fiction, but that's just because I like to do different things. But the main body of my work is what I just described to you — written with a very mainstream sensibility. And I don't mean I'm trying to get away from fantasy. That has nothing to do with it. It just means that's where my interests lie. My interest is here and now, and how strange and magical events or deep mysteries affect people here and now.

VAN BELKOM: When you were starting out, was the fact that you were writing something that was a little bit different much of a roadblock?

DE LINT: It was only a roadblock in that I got put into the genre of fantasy. Which was my own fault because my first novel was a high fantasy, my second, *Moonheart*, was not. The problem came after *The Riddle of the Wren* when there were four books in a row that were really contemporary books. But the publisher didn't really know what to do with them, so they just marketed them as fantasy books, and because of that, I ended up being considered a fantasy writer. So marketing has been a problem all along.

VAN BELKOM: Is that what happened to *Jack the Giant-Killer?*"

DE LINT: Yeah, *Jack the Giant-Killer* was totally bizarre. I don't necessarily expect good art on my books because a lot of fantasy artists don't have fine art sensibilities. You can't expect them to do a fine art style, and a lot of them don't seem to have any concept of anatomy, or have done any figure drawing. So I'm not expecting that, but I am expecting them to be appropriate.

Now, Thomas Canty is a wonderful artist and he has a beautiful sense of design and does great artwork, but that cover (on the original edition) in no way reflected what was inside the book. So after the hardcover came out I was discussing that with Ace and they said, "Oh yeah, we understand that and we're going to fix it, we're going make it much grittier for the paperback." And that's how I got something that looked like a post-holocaust fantasy (on the paperback edition).

Canty isn't one of the artists I'm saying doesn't have the ability to do fine art rendering, but unfortunately the original cover didn't give you the idea what the book is about. And that's the most important thing, to give the reader an honest idea of what the book is about. So someone who is really keen on high fantasy isn't going to be disappointed the book is set in Ottawa.

VAN BELKOM: Is there any point in your career that you look upon now as a big break or a turning point?

DE LINT: I was probably writing the novel before *Moonheart* (which never got published) where I was attempting to do something in a contemporary setting. The interesting thing was I loved fantasy, and I wanted to write fantasy, but I thought that fantasy could only be Tokienesque, so my first few books were secondary world fantasies. But I wasn't reading a lot of fantasies, I was reading lots of contemporary novels and my wife MaryAnn said to me, "You love contemporary books, why don't you write that and add fantasy to them?" And I said, "No, it just wouldn't work." Because nobody had done it. But of course, when someone tells you something you start thinking about it. So I wrote a book, very long, longer than *Moonheart* actually, and it didn't work. But by writing that book I knew how I could make it work. So I wrote *Moonheart* after that and that was the big turning point for me.

VAN BELKOM: Early in your career you did a couple of novels for Philip Jose Farmer's The Dungeon series. Did you enjoy that sort of work, or was it just a case of helping to pay the bills?

DE LINT: A combination of both. I'm not one of those people who frowns on shared world or franchises — I don't really care, because it's people's own choice if they do them, it's people's own choice if they read them. My reason for doing the first one was that I had loved Farmer's work for a long time and I had so many books in inventory with Ace that anything I was going to write was going to take a couple of years to come out anyway, so I thought it was a good chance to do something else. To see if I can write something in his voice, or a combination of his voice and my voice and see how it turns out. I had a lot of fun.

I had a certain hole in my schedule, but when that opening came up, the first two in the series hadn't been written yet. So I went ahead and wrote the third book — it was the first book written — and then by the time the others started getting turned in they wanted someone to do the fifth book and that was a case where they came to me because I'd done a timely job on the first one. So I agreed to do the second one. It wasn't as much fun to do because I had already done it once, and basically I was almost doing the same thing again because you had to have the characters at one point and you had to lead them somewhere else in the end. You could do whatever you wanted in the middle but it's the same bunch of characters and you couldn't really change them very much. The second one basically bought me my first computer.

I don't regret it because it was still sort of fun to do, but doing those books made me realize I didn't want to write any books where the characters didn't change. And I would say that the biggest challenge for writers in a franchise universe is that the characters can't change.

VAN BELKOM: Many of your stories and novels take place in the imaginary town of Newford. Was the creation of Newford a conscious decision, or did it just grow while you were writing the stories?

DE LINT: The reason I used that setting for those stories was that I wanted to write about something that wasn't like Ottawa, that was a big urban sprawl. Ottawa is a very pretty city, but I had stories I wanted to tell that would be set in Chicago or in the Bronx or East LA. I'm uncomfortable writing about places if I don't have a lot of hands-on experience about them. Even my high fantasies, when I write about a certain kind of landscape at least I know the landscape. It might be a magical land, but I know the landscape. It wasn't a conscious decision to do Newford. Someone just asked me to do a story and I thought I'd set it in one of those sprawling places I was thinking of, I just wouldn't give it a name or say where it is.

And then I got asked to do another story by another editor and I thought, well, that was fun, maybe I'll use some of that repertory company and do another story. And after four of five stories I realized that it was something I was having fun with so I gave the place a name and made myself a rough map just to figure out where everything was. I started making a concordance, but I gave that up and now I'm just flipping back through old books looking for references myself.

So it just grew from that, and even the Newford collection wasn't my idea. I was selling two books to Tor and they said they wanted a collection of Newford stories and it was the first time I even realized there were enough stories for a collection. And now I'm in the process of negotiating a new unwritten novel and a third Newford collection.

VAN BELKOM: Are there enough stories for another collection?

DE LINT: There will be when it's time to turn the book in. They are all written; it's just a matter of having them appear in their original anthologies. And I'll have to write something new for it as well.

VAN BELKOM: You published three horror novels under the pseudonym Samuel M. Key, and some things under some other names. First of all, is their any significance to the name Samuel M. Key and what was the reason behind its use, and the use of the others?

DE LINT: I had a lot of inventory at Ace and I wasn't going to see something coming out for ages and it made sense to have a different name. And the first one was also quite dark and different so I thought I'll separate it from me by getting a pseudonym.

The jokey answer to why Samuel M. Key is that it fits on the same shelf with Koontz and King. The even jokier reason is that I have a little stuffed monkey that I've had since I was a kid and it's on top of my desk with a rolltop desk and typewriter of his own. A friend of mine, the late Ron Nance, used to joke that Sam actually wrote all my books. So Sam is the name of the monkey: Samuel M. Key — Sam The Monkey.

VAN BELKOM: And the other names?

DE LINT: I was publishing a magazine with Charles Saunders. We always paid everybody who contributed to our magazines, but we didn't have to pay ourselves and that made it cheaper. So sometimes we'd need little filler poems and stuff like that, but I didn't want to have the same name all over it so I just made up a name and stuck it in. So, my one real pseudonym is Sam Key.

VAN BELKOM: Were you happy with the decision to use a pseudonym?

DE LINT: Yes and no. I was happy the books got out, because when you're writing you want your books to come out. You don't want them to sit on the shelf somewhere. The down side of using a pseudonym is that the more times your name gets used, the more people know it. So I'm sure there are people out there who read Sam Key books and who maybe enjoyed them and would like to read more and are now wondering what ever happened to Sam Key, not realizing there are twenty or so other books out there by the same guy.

VAN BELKOM: Are there any other Sam Key books on the way?

DE LINT: No, Sam doesn't earn nearly as much as I do, and I don't have time to write any more. It's a time thing. I put as much effort into those books as I do my own, but now it's got to the point where I'm writing slower and it's just not feasible.

VAN BELKOM: And now you don't have the backlog anymore.

DE LINT: No, I'm the other way now. I'm selling books before they're written so I don't have any time for any extraneous projects.

VAN BELKOM: You've won some of the smaller awards, been nominated for many of the bigger ones. What's your whole outlook towards awards and the awards process considering you've been on both sides of the coin as member of several awards juries and as a nominee?

DE LINT: As a member of awards juries, I know there is a lot of politicking involved. If there are five of you trying to decide which the best book is, you might say, "Okay, if you vote for this book, then I'll vote for that novella." I think books that are nominated and win are worthy things, but I don't like the idea that they are the "best." I like what Dean Koontz did with the Bram Stoker Award making it for "Superior Achievement." In other words, they're not better than anything else, it just means that what you did was really good and we're going to commend you for having done it. Lots of times the books I think are the best books of the year don't win. But it's all personal and subjective, and if you get too wired into that you're going to drive yourself crazy. If you win great, if you don't win, does your life change? Not really.

That's not why I write anyway. I don't write to win awards or to get fame and fortune. I do write to make a living — and that's a bigger award than anything else. I've been able to make my living for fourteen years now doing something I love to do. I mean, awards can't even compare to that.

VAN BELKOM: Despite a flourishing fiction writing career you continue to write opinion and review columns. Does that sort of writing serve as a break from fiction writing, something to write "instead of" fiction rather than "in addition" to it?

DE LINT: It just comes from liking to shoot your mouth off. I used to work in record stores for years and I loved getting people to try things they've never tried before. I got into writing reviews of books simply because there were books I was excited about and I wanted people to read them and hopefully get the same excitement.

You'll notice if you read my column in *Fantasy and Science Fiction* that I don't really write bad reviews. It's not that I'm Mister Pollyanna, although I have a pretty positive attitude about things, but the reason I do it is twofold: first, I don't like to waste time by giving space to a bad book; second, I don't review a book that I haven't read all the way through because why should I waste the time just to write a bad review? And bad reviews are so easy to write. It's so much harder to write a good review.

VAN BELKOM: In 1995 you were Writer-in-Residence at the Ottawa and Gloucester Public Libraries. What can you say about that experience?

DE LINT: It was very time consuming. That's basically it. I think it's a worthwhile thing to have a Writer-in-Residency program, and every city should have one because there are a ton of people out there who could really use the information. As the person doing it, I basically didn't get any work done for six months. I probably went about it wrong, because everyone else I talked to who has done those things actually did work of their own while in the program. I never did that once, I never had the chance. I had so many manuscripts to deal with, so many people to see; I just spent all my time dealing with other people's stuff so I got way behind.

VAN BELKOM: In addition to being a writer, you're also a professional musician and have incorporated your music into many of your stories and novels. What's the relationship between writing and music for you and how much of a role does music play in your work?

DE LINT: It's part of my life. I'm a music junkie. I was doing music the whole time I was writing. I worked for years in record shops, played in bands. I still go to sessions. The band still plays the occasional gig — two or three times a year at the most. It is a very nebulous thing. I listen to music while I'm writing and I have a kind of soundtrack going in my head all the time anyway.

It's nothing I can specifically point to, but I know that having done as much music as I've done has given my writing a certain flow that I might not have had otherwise. Just like doing fine art has given me observational skill in my writing that I might not have had otherwise.

VAN BELKOM: Some of your novels have fiddle tunes in the back of them. Were they actually written for the books or were they something that you'd already written and thought you had an opportunity to get some of your music published?

DE LINT: No, they weren't there because of the opportunity. It was the kind of thing that's fun to have in a fantasy, like an appendix with some extra stuff. The first book to have tunes in it was *The Little Country* and the tunes were all supposedly written by the character Janey Little. Some of them were specifically written with that in mind, some of it was stuff that I had hanging around that was appropriate to that.

Then I wrote *Into the Green*, and the publisher asked if I had more tunes I could put into the back because they thought that since the character was a harp player it would be kind of fun to have a set of tunes in that book as well.

VAN BELKOM: You've written in all of the speculative fields, but is there one you enjoy more than another?

DE LINT: I think it's pretty obvious that it's the hybrid of fantasy and mainstream that I enjoy the most. My theory of writing is that I write the books I'd like to read that nobody else has written yet. I have to be excited and interested in it myself and that's what makes it click. If other people like it, great. But if other people don't like it, then at least I've had that good experience.

VAN BELKOM: Even though your latest novel, *Trader*, is a fantasy, judging by its packaging I get the impression that either you or your publisher, maybe even both, are trying to move you out of the speculative genres toward a more mainstream audience. Is that true?

DE LINT: I've been struggling with this literally for years with my books. I've always been pushing for that and now Tor has decided that maybe it's a good idea. So we'll see what happens.

It's not that I want to leave fantasy, or I don't care about the fantasy readership, that's far from the case because they've been very loyal, and I really appreciate their support. I just know there is a large readership base in the mainstream that would also enjoy my work. I don't know how far the fantasy readership can grow because most fantasy readers like the secondary world type of fantasy and they're not going to find it in my books. I can find a larger readership in the mainstream, so I'm hoping that the fantasy readers that I have will stay with me. The books certainly aren't going to be written any differently.

Candas Jane Dorsey –

Despite publishing a relatively small amount of speculative fiction since becoming a full-time freelance writer and editor in 1980, Edmonton's Candas Jane Dorsey has still had a tremendous impact on Canadian speculative fiction.

Born in 1952, she debuted on the Canadian SF scene in the early 1980s, and in 1986 won the Pulp Press International Three-Day Novel Writing Contest for *Hardwired Angel*, which she wrote with Nora Abercrombie. Her first short story collection, *Machine Sex And Other Stories*, appeared in 1988 from Victoria's Porcépic Books. A story from the collection, "Sleeping in a Box," won the Casper Award (now Aurora) for the Best Short-Form Work in English, and the collection was subsequently reprinted in 1990 by The Women's Press, London. Others stories have appeared in anthologies such as *Getting Here, Writing Right, Tesseracts, Ark of Ice, Alberta ReBound, Solaris*, and *The Norton Anthology of Science Fiction*. Non-fiction has appeared in The *Edmonton Journal, The Globe and Mail, Quill and Quire, Books in Canada*, and *The New York Review of Science Fiction*. In 1994, Dorsey produced *Dark Earth Dreams*, a short story collection published as a book-with-audio-CD. Her first novel, *Black Wine*, was a hardcover from Tor in 1997 and won the Crawford Fantasy Award shortly after its release.

In addition to fiction and non-fiction, Dorsey has also published several books of poetry: three volumes published by blewointmentpress in the 1970s and a more recent title, *Leaving Marks*, published by River Books in 1992.

As an editor, Dorsey co-edited (with Gerry Truscott) the third volume in the *Tesseract* series of Canadian speculative fiction anthologies in 1990 and guest-edited the special SF edition of the literary magazine *Prairie Fire* in 1994. Currently, she is editor/publisher of River Books and Tesseracts Books, both imprints of the Books Collective, which Dorsey owns jointly with several other Canadian writers, editors, and academics. As a supporter and champion of Canadian speculative fiction, she is a founding member and past-president of SF Canada (the Canadian association of professional SF writers) and a founding member of SFWorkshop Canada Ink. In addition, she's a former president of the Writers Guild of Alberta.

EDO VAN BELKOM: You have a writing style that would be just as well suited to mainstream fiction. What turned you on to science fiction and made you want to write it?
CANDAS JANE DORSEY: I don't really differentiate between mainstream and science fiction and apply one style to one and another to the other. I think style is part of the story that needs to be told. However, in general, I think I have some attitudes toward storytelling that influence style and voice. I don't believe in, to use Delany's phrase, "burdening the reader with unintegrated chunks of information," whether that information is exposition, characterization, or description. Stories have within them the requirements for what must be put in and left out, and anything beyond that is gratuitous verbiage. This doesn't mean that there isn't a lyrical or poetical potential in the language I choose to use, but to be lyrical or ornamental just for the sake of a good sound is not important to me — all parts of a story must be integrated. This happens organically as stories grow, whatever the order and method of growth is.

I also don't set out necessarily to write "science fiction," "fantasy," or whatever. I write the story that needs telling, and if I must use a science fiction or fantastic "trope" to do so, if that framework suggests itself, if that setting seems to have the requisite atmosphere or that concept the requisite relevance, then I use them.

I grew up in a family of book readers. The kinds of books ranged widely, but fantasy of all eras was part of the fare, as was science fiction — but it held equal pride of place with biography, adventure, mystery, "serious literature," poetry, and so on. The "genres" and differentiations were impositions later in life, intellectual things I had to learn, rather than just the difference between emotional, stimulating, pleasant, or enthralling (funny, fun, smart, and moving are perhaps better, simpler words) versus dull, boring and stupid. In my family a book and its writer were respected, and those books which spoke to our experience or our sense of the mystery — or of humor — were quoted, reread, and made part of our lives. They were our friends, and not discriminated against on the basis of color or creed.

I learned to talk genre in order to get by in the world.

VAN BELKOM: Your collaborative novel *Hardwired Angel* was written with Nora Abercrombie as part of the Three-day Novel contest. What was that experience like, writing a novel in three days?

DORSEY: It was silly and a great deal of fun. Nora is a beloved colleague whose humor and intelligence are formidable. The first day we started by going out to breakfast at Uncle Albert's Pancake House, a venerable Edmonton institution, then set up our Kaypros (tells when that was — 1986) back to back on my dining room table, and our friends brought us food and sat around watching. The first day it was Myrna Kostash with gazpachio and veggie pasta, the second day my father with Kentucky Fried Chicken, and the third day Nora's mom with lime Jell-o, gum, potato chips, and soda pop — which about sums up the tenor of the experience.

The whole thing was a bit like a hands-on workshop in novel writing. I learned a lot about the process that weekend, though for some of the things it was years before I could apply them to a "real" novel. We learned — by doing — about thru-line, plot/subplot, the importance of action and dialogue — and to just keep writing, no matter what. We never shorted on sleep and Nora (who is married) had regular sex, which led to us joking about why I was the one to write the sex scenes. We lost one chapter to an incorrect backup and a friend retyped it into the computer from the hard copy while we kept working.

I'd just come home from the first SFWorkshop Canada Ink in Peterborough, organized by Judy Merril, and that's where some of the energy came from. I told Nora we had to do it, it would be fun — and it was, but we certainly didn't expect to win.

My greatest disappointment about the book was that the cover was so ugly, and the typeface on the cover unreadable. We had hoped they would put a trashy cover on it and sell it in bus depots and we'd get rich. No such luck.

The thing haunts us in both positive and negative ways. Negatively, it keeps getting referred to as if it were a real book, which is frustrating to both of us, who know if we were writing a real book it wouldn't happen in three days (indeed, it *hasn't*) — but on the positive side I am working with a producer right now who wants to develop a movie from it and a TV series around the character. Interestingly, the most collected of my short stories is "(Learning About) Machine Sex" which is about the same character. It was written (except for the first two pages) afterward and set before *Hardwired Angel* in time, and is much more from the heart. It's funny to compare them — the story is not a puff-pastry, but the three-day novel certainly is a bit of fluff, and it is set in the same universe.

Phyllis Gotlieb in *The Toronto Star* reviewed the three-day novel and noticed that it had some feminist and ironical points of view — that pleased me, because, though it was, in many ways, fluff, there are certain things I believe in that I didn't want to betray even in something fluffy.

VAN BELKOM: You've had plenty of success with your short stories in Canada, winning an Aurora Award for "Sleeping in a Box" and publishing the collection *Machine Sex*. However, you've made few appearances in American short fiction markets. Why is that?

DORSEY: I'm lazy about sending stories out, and I write very slowly. Also, when I am working on a novel it's hard to move my thoughts over to other, shorter stories. And my last excuse — it's my story, and I'm stickin' to it! — is that since we bought Tesseract Books I have had many more demands on my time than I ever thought when I went into it. But I would like to work on some short fiction again — I've got a lot of beginnings on the back burner — the problem is that I have a novel to deliver this year . . .

VAN BELKOM: Despite a lack of short fiction published in the US, your first novel, *Black Wine*, was published in hardcover by Tor, a major American publisher. Did it come as a surprise when the novel sold there?

DORSEY: No, I wouldn't say I was surprised. I have more ego than that! I had met David Hartwell, and when I named several of my favorite books over the few years previous to our meetings, he had edited most of them. So I knew that this was an editor who would understand my work. He asked for the novel while we were talking over the contract for my pieces being reprinted in the Northern Stars anthology he and Glenn Grant edited — he seemed pleased to hear I had a book ready to send out. So in a way, it was like the book found its proper home quite easily.

VAN BELKOM: The term "Feminist SF" has been used to describe

Black Wine, usually alongside a mention of the works of Ursula K. LeGuin. Are you comfortable with that term, or does it even matter to you?

DORSEY: Several answers spring to mind. On a personal level, Ursula LeGuin has been very supportive, and that is great. We have a very pleasant collegial acquaintanceship — though when I say that I think from my point of view, given the relative lengths and scopes of our careers, the more correct analogy is that when I stand at the feet of the giant she graciously recognizes me. And she is indeed one of the most gracious people, in support of other writers, and has actively spoken for my work, for which I am so grateful. Since I admire her and her work, both individual pieces and as a body of work, I don't have any trouble with the comparison — I feel flattered. On a purely self-serving level, such comparisons sell books, which is also fine by me!

I liked Gary Wolfe's preamble to his review in *Locus*, where he says something about how people are being narrowminded if they think that feminist SF is stories about "angry women on horseback" stories. There are a number of really tremendous "angry women on horseback" books, and a few which aren't tremendous, but what is loosely called "feminist SF" overall is much wider, and seems to tell the kind of stories in which I'm interested. I am interested in stories about the tiny increments or moments (the "creaking rusty hinge") in which large changes take place. I am interested in the dynamics of power and powerlessness. I feel that if speculative fiction does its job, it speculates as much about the social order as it does about new tech-toys — not surprising, as they are closely related. Each new technology creates a social vortex into which many things are drawn, and people's lives are changed thereby.

And in the broadest (pun unintended — no, maybe I *did* intend it!) sense of the word, I am, after all, a feminist . . .

VAN BELKOM: *Black Wine* won the Crawford Award. Could you say a little about the award and what it felt like to win it?

DORSEY: The Crawford Fantasy Award is given by the International Association for the Fantastic in the Arts, a group of academics and SF writers/editors/practitioners which meets yearly at (surprise) the International Conference on the Fantastic in the Arts in Ft. Lauderdale, Florida. I was told that the sponsor of the award was to remain anonymous, but I saw in *Locus* that the donorship is attributed to Andre Norton. The most interesting thing for me was how quickly after the book's official release date the award came. It just slid in under the eligibility guidelines, I guess. I had just been reviewed in the local paper by someone who said "This book will win awards!" and there it was, a prophecy fulfilled less than a week later! I was of course thrilled, even more so because I was *forced* to leave Edmonton in mid-March and go to Florida, where lizards dart across city sidewalks, and where I had a chance to stand at night in summer clothes with my feet in the warm ocean and watch an eclipse of the moon. Not how it would have been at home at that time of year. The atmosphere at the conference is very nurturing to writers: these academics understand that we write the stuff which their analyzing gives them tenure! So in all ways it was a very positive experience.

Coming home to the novel I'm working on was easier too. Since they were created by the same process, I could say, given the reviews and the award, "Well, it worked for the last one, maybe it'll turn out okay for this one too!"

VAN BELKOM: In addition to your experience as an SF writer, you've also done considerable editing of SF in Canada. Do you enjoy it?

DORSEY: I find that the editing of a book, assisting the writer to make it the best possible book she or he can, is a really exciting process. It's very different from creating one's own book — it is all about getting into the author's style and understanding the book from that point of view, and is definitely not about trying to make the author write it as one would have done — but I feel that being a writer and understanding the process has helped me be empathic about what the writer is going through. I must say that the best editors I've run across, whether they also write or not, have that empathy big-time — but most of them have written *something*, whether fiction, criticism, or whatever.

And maybe there is just a little bit of a chance that a writer-editor is occasionally *more* heartless: the "if I had to rewrite mine, and I lived, you can rewrite yours and live: quit whining" scenario!

Now, that's about book editing. Anthology editing is a different kettle of fish. I like it, but there is usually a time when I feel I have died and gone to hell. Surprisingly, the worst part is not reading the bad submissions. It's choosing between the best at the point where nothing in front of you is bad and you *still* have to cut half or three-quarters of the stack out to fit the page length. I find those decisions heartrending.

Editing *Tesseracts 3* with Gerry Truscott (who by the way is an editor I admire very much, and whose work on my book ten years ago taught me an immense amount about the positive aspects of the writer-editor relationship), I felt that at least that pain was shared; but editing the *Prairie Fire* anthology in 1993–94, I faced the full anguish all by myself . . .

VAN BELKOM: For years you helped organize the Canadian SFWorkshop Canada Ink? What were they and how did they work?

DORSEY: They were peer workshops for professional writers. The first was organized in 1986 by Judy Merril on the model of the Milford workshops she had started when she lived in Milford. This was just following her editorship of the first *Tesseracts* anthology, and drew on people she'd found through that process. The workshop had eight people and a few partners came along: there were John Park, Michael Skeet, Rhea Rose, Ursula Pflug . . . I know I'll get in trouble for not mentioning everybody, because it was a great workshop. Terry Green came up from Toronto to do a session with us . . . It was in Peterborough. The next ones were on Karma Road in Toronto, in Edmonton coinciding with the first ConText, and so on. They were all organized as peer workshops by people who believed in the model: myself, Michael Skeet, and later the Cecil Street writers in Toronto extended the tradition with weekends at Hart House. Monica Hughes, Michael Coney . . . well, we've had quite a cast, over time.

VAN BELKOM: You're one of several members of the Books Collective, publishers of Tesseract Books. What role do you play with that group?

DORSEY: I was one of the founders of the collective in 1992. We had two imprints at that time, River and Rowan Books, both also collectives; I am part of River Books also. We were publishing on a smaller scale before Tesseract Books came up for sale. When Gerry Truscott heard it was for sale, he called me and reminded me of my fantasy to buy it. I called up a lot of people across the country who could help, and together we formed the Tesseract Group, in its way another collective. After that it seemed logical to bring it in to the Books Collective, which we had already characterized as a strategic alliance of small publishers to share tasks and resources for distribution and marketing. From there, it has developed into a good organization with a strong reputation for attractive, high-quality books.

VAN BELKOM: What can you say about your experience publishing an SF line in Canada?

DORSEY: Well, like editing: I love it, but there are also times when I feel I've died and gone to hell!

Publishers in Canada are an endangered species. If you had twelve or so pages I could explain the economics in detail, with charts and diagrams, but the bottom line is that living next to the US is bad for us. We have to match the price points of books produced on a much larger scale, which already creates a deficit for each title published, and then we have to shoehorn a hole in the marketplace to insert our books. Given that the US has 78 per cent of our book market, and other countries another 10 per cent, that leaves only about 12 per cent for all Canadian books. Now, at the moment, with the level of capitalization we were able to obtain at the time we bought the press, which hasn't increased of course, we can put out four books per year. This is far from 12 per cent of the speculative fiction market, so the problem is clear.

On the other hand, we make fine-looking books, to the limit our budget allows, and the content is superb, so we are keeping a Canadian voice alive in speculative fiction in a big way. And you have to remember that from the *Tesseract* series as a whole, as well as other small press single titles in fantasy and science fiction, grew a good chunk of the US interest in Canadian writers, which culminated in the *Northern Stars* anthology, much of which was drawn from the *Tesseract* anthology series and Lesley Choyce's great *Ark of Ice* anthology. Now Tor, for instance, is publishing me, Yves Meynard, Terry Green, and others whose work first appeared from Canadian so-called small presses. It's clear that small press feeds big megapublishing, and I'd say that's how roughly half the Canadian writers currently being published abroad got there. So in addition to the books themselves, which are tremendously satisfying, there is a sense that we are a necessary part of the ecosystem.

VAN BELKOM: Do you sometimes get the feeling that Tesseract Books is Canadian science fiction rather than just a publisher of a unique line of books. Is there a sense of responsibility to the genre working for the collective?

DORSEY: I guess I started in on that prematurely in answering the last question. I must say that I don't feel we are Canadian science fiction; there have been many other single titles published by other small press, there are new small presses starting in Calgary for English language SF, and the scene in Quebec is incredibly fertile and active. But I do feel we have been and are an important part of making Canadian SF strong and keeping it in the readers' eye. We've had a strong role in translating francophone SF as well, which I feel is vital. We need to understand each other's voices in this country to keep going, and there's too little cross-fertilization of ideas, voices, styles in the mainstream. We actually do better in Canadian SF/SFQ at reading each other's work than the mainstream on average, in my opinion anyway, but that's partly because of a few fluently bilingual translators who work a lot of volunteer hours to add to the official translation efforts!

VAN BELKOM: Are the *Tesseract* anthologies profitable enough to continue on indefinitely?

DORSEY: That depends on the bookstore buyers, and then readers, doesn't it? We're planning to continue as long as we can pay the printer . . .

VAN BELKOM: Will there be another novel soon from Candas Dorsey or will we have to wait as long as we did for *Black Wine*?

DORSEY: I'm supposed to deliver the one I'm working on now to Tor before the end of the year (yikes!). After that, there's another one crowding my mind, wanting out. There is also another speculative short story anthology looking for a home, as well as a non-fiction book on sex, gender, and pop culture. I have a mainstream book of short fiction hanging around on the back of my desk — I am so lazy about sending it out . . . I'm just now developing a film treatment which a producer is starting to market, and she's got me working on a TV series pitch too. All of this in my spare time (that's a joke, by the way!)

I do write slowly, but part of the wait for *Black Wine* was the other stuff I do which takes time away from my writing. The positive critical response and the Crawford Award coming so quickly have been powerful motivators to give my own writing higher priority. I feel very encouraged about my work these days.

Dave Duncan

Dave Duncan states in his bio that "Even as a child, I wanted to be a writer," but despite that wish he was in his mid-fifties before that childhood dream was finally realized.

Born in Scotland in 1933, Duncan was educated at the University of St. Andrews, where he received a Bachelors of Science Degree in Geology. He came to Canada in 1955, settling in Calgary (marrying in 1959), where he began a thirty-year career in the Canadian oil industry as a geologist and a geological consultant.

In 1984, after several unsuccessful attempts at writing in the 1970s, Duncan sat down at his computer to see if he could write a novel. He says it was done "more or less on the spur of the moment, thinking it would be a fun thing to try." But once he began writing, he quickly became hooked and started stealing time away from his work as a consultant in order to find the time to write. In all he produced the equivalent of five books, garnering some interest from publishers, but no contracts.

When the oil business collapsed in 1986, Duncan found himself out of work for the first time in three decades. However, just two weeks after his final consulting project, Del Rey called from New York and offered to buy *A Rose-Red City*. Soon after that, a veritable flood of science fiction and fantasy novels followed, twenty three all tolled in a ten-year span. The majority of Duncan's output has been fantasy with four series encompassing the bulk of his work. They include *The Seventh Sword* series — *The Reluctant Swordsman, The Coming of Wisdom, The Destiny of the Sword*; *A Man of His Word* series — *Magic Casement, Faery Lands Forlorn, Perilous Seas, Emperor and Clown*; *A Handful of Men* series — *The Cutting Edge, Upland Outlaws, The Stricken Field, The Living God*; and *The Great Game* series — *Past Imperative, Present Tense, Future Indefinite*. Other solo fantasy novels include *The Reaver Road, The Hunter's Haunt*, and *The Cursed*. Under the pen name Ken Hood he has published *Demon Sword*.

Duncan's science fiction novels include *Shadow, Strings, Hero!* and *West of January*, which won the 1990 the Aurora Award for best long-form in English.

EDO VAN BELKOM: What was the reason behind your coming to Canada in 1955?

DAVE DUNCAN: That's an easy one. I had just taken a degree in geology and there were no jobs for geologists in the UK. I wanted to work in soft rock, meaning petroleum, and Canada seemed a good choice. Anyone who suggested in those days that Scotland would one day be a major oil exporter would have been certified daft and chained to a post.

VAN BELKOM: You've said in other interviews that your writing career picked up just as the oil boom in Alberta was coming to an end. Do you think you would have done so much writing had the oil industry thrived in Alberta?

DUNCAN: That's a lovely might-have-been. I suspect I would have still made the shift, but not as soon. I enjoyed geology and it was very good to me, but after thirty years I needed a change. I found writing great fun — and still do. I had already been stealing some time from my consulting business to indulge in writing, so probably I would have eased out of one career and into another. Remember Frost's poem about the road in the woods?

VAN BELKOM: How much did your work as a geologist in the oil business help prepare you for a later career as a fantasy writer?

DUNCAN: Quite a lot, surprisingly. At least I get the scenery right, and I could mention some writers who do not! Most of my work consisted of identifying places that seemed likely to contain oil or gas and then persuading my employer, and later my clients when I was a consultant, to acquire leases and prospect there. Of course the result was often a dry hole, but not always. I never found any Prudhoe Bays, but I have never written any bestsellers, either. I met with about as much success in my first career as I have in my second. I still have a tiny trickle of oil royalties coming in.

In the eleven years it has managed to survive without me, the oil business has become much more scientific in its use of computers and geophysics. In my day there was more art and imagination involved. When I changed careers, I kidded my geological friends that I was merely switching from one form of science fiction to another, and there was a grain of truth in that. Obviously my dreaming can be much wilder now, even when I write hard SF, but the "what if?" principle is the basis of science just as much as of speculative fiction. If an ancient river valley is buried a thousand meters underground and you have to chase its trail across the landscape based on the records of a scattering of existing wells and analogies with modern drainage systems, you soon learn to exercise your imagination. You also learn to stick your neck out and play hunches.

I can't stress too much that being a full-time writer is a lonely job, requiring dedication and self-direction. I learned those skills as a consultant. I knew what it was to be without a boss to take problems to, what it felt like to wonder, "What do I do next?" or "Do I keep on beating my head against this or should I give up and try something else?" I learned how to run my own office, keep my own books, handle my own correspondence, stay cheerful and keep rowing without having a bosun standing over me with a whip all the time. The old advice of not giving up your day job is based on more than just maintaining income. If you can't be a loner, you can't be a writer, or at least not a novelist. Movie and TV work is more of a team effort, of course.

VAN BELKOM: While you were working as a geologist, did you ever seriously consider a career as a writer, or did that always seem to be a pipe dream?

DUNCAN: I never wanted to be a professional writer. As a kid I wrote stories . . . let's say I *began* stories, imitations of any book I'd read that impressed me. But I never considered writing as a career.

There's a saying in the business that I am sure you know: They who want to be writers won't; they who want to write will. I actually saw this happen long before I'd heard that adage. My brother, visiting us from Scotland, remarked that he would really love to be a writer. I, in my innocence, retorted that I didn't think I would, although I would quite like to write a book.

If you want to assume that my later career was then forged in the fires of sibling rivalry, go right ahead. We'd have been in our forties then, both of us.

I did take a creative writing course about 1970 or so, but I had absolutely no success. I was trying to write short stories, a technique I have never mastered. I gave up because I could not afford the time in those days.

So the urge to write was there, but the idea of making a living at it never appealed until I had it thrust upon me.

VAN BELKOM: So you're basically a self-taught writer?

DUNCAN: I learned a great deal from my first editor, Veronica Chapman of Del Rey, but that was after she bought my first book and I got there on my own. In many ways this was a disadvantage, because I had to reinvent the wheel several times, but creative writing courses can be dangerous for newcomers. Anyone who wants to write genre fiction must beware of professors who insist on teaching "literature." (One I know of automatically fails any student who turns in work containing plot. A few months of that will destroy whatever talent the student possessed.)

Come to think of it, I've never had much formal training in anything. My degree in geology was in hard rock, not the soft rock geology of the oil industry. I cannot claim I was self-taught in that, because I had some wonderful scientists to work with in my first few years, and they taught me on the job, but my degree was very little use to me. I once took a post-grad course in geological mathematics and metamorphosed into a computer consultant. I'd never had any training in computers, but oil companies were paying me as if I were a lawyer, so I either knew what I was doing or I was stringing a wonderful line of fantasy. I even had a brief stint as an entrepreneur when I founded a computerized data service. It didn't do very well, so I sold it at a nice profit and vowed never to have employees again.

VAN BELKOM: You write both science fiction and fantasy. Do you see any major differences between the two genres and do you have a preference?

DUNCAN: Which is yin and which is yang? I define fantasy as speculative fiction with supernatural elements and science fiction as all the rest else by default, but there are other criteria. SF is more idea-driven, masculine, less dependent on characterization. Fantasy tends to be feminine, more poetic, and depends more on characterization. SF looks forward to problems solved by technology; fantasy looks back to when the problems did not exist, or when they were solved by people. Obviously these are generalizations subject to many exceptions. Women write some tremendous SF and the top-selling fantasy writers are men.

Plausibility has nothing to do with it. Telepathy, FTL space-ships, time-travel are all as impossible as fifty-ton flying dragons but are included in SF by convention (although they can appear in fantasies). Both fantasy and SF can be either upbeat or downbeat. When you apply more than one criterion, though, you end up with some arguable classifications. Because of my technical background, I tend to write very SF-ish fantasy. (Am I allowed to claim that I also write fantastic SF?) Which do I prefer writing? Well, SF takes more work to get the facts right. It doesn't sell as well, so it doesn't pay as well. That makes it a poorer proposition all round. And a writer should always write what he would like to read. I enjoy both genres as entertainment, but I have a bias toward fantasy.

VAN BELKOM: Why? What's the appeal of fantasy?

DUNCAN: It has to be many things to many people, because it has an extraordinarily varied readership. I have fans who are kids, seniors, stockbrokers, dentists, and politicians that I know of. Of course fantasy can be meaningful, but most of it is just a tropical vacation from a Canadian winter. Fantasy is to fiction what espresso is to coffee, or crack to cocaine. Fiction creates an orderly world as an anodyne to the chaos and meaningless suffering of real life. In stories things make sense. The evil perish, the good prosper. Morals may be drawn.

Fantasy is fiction with no holds barred. Events are not merely foreshadowed, they are prophesied. Good is good, bad bad, and never the twain get confused. Hero and heroine live happily ever after. Other genres may sandbag you with a dissertation on child abuse or gender discrimination but in Middle Earth that is not allowed. All you need worry about there are dragons and evil gods, never a car payment or crotchety aunt. Fantasy has a unique appeal in that it satisfies our subconscious yen for the mythic hero, the uniquely important person, rightwise-born king of all England, Teacher, possessor of innate powers, the Chosen. In SF the people are often mass-produced. I don't mean by the writers, although that happens, but by their technological society. If the Black Blob kills the captain of the *Enterprise*, Starfleet Command will just send out a replacement, but when Arthur dies, Camelot dies with him. That individual importance strikes a bell in this morbidly overcrowded and too-homogenized world. We all want to matter for what we are, not what we do, because most of us don't get the chance to do anything of any significance. I can name SF books where characters have this kind of uniqueness, *Dune*, say, or the *Dragonriders of Pern*, but they read like fantasy.

VAN BELKOM: Will there be much more science fiction from you in the future?

DUNCAN: At the moment I have my plate full with other genres, but I do have a couple of unpublished SF novels on the shelf, so maybe one day I'll work them over and send them out into the cruel, hard world. I also have some promising ideas about Helium 3 and a virtual detective.

VAN BELKOM: Why do you say you write SF-ish fantasy?

DUNCAN: Well, SF is often based on a "What-if?" premise, and I enjoy inventing new forms of magic. This often makes my plotting as logical as the hard stuff.

In *The Cursed*, I posited magical powers as a disability resulting from a disease. The various types of magic were linked to the seven "fates" which in turn were derived from the seven planets by a new astrology. The magics were also so personal and subjective that there was not one scene in that lengthy novel that could be used as a subject for cover art, the magic had no visible consequences. That's SF in fantasy drag.

VAN BELKOM: Your *Seventh Sword* series has been the best-seller of all your works to date. Do you know why that's been the case, and if so, have you consciously tried to do it again?

DUNCAN: No dammit, and yes you bet! I wish I did understand the appeal of the *Seventh Sword*. I would certainly repeat the success if I could, although never at the price of rewriting the same story over and over with just the names changed (like You-Know-Who and Yes-Him). I wrote the original version solely to amuse myself, with no real thought of publishing it. Perhaps that sense of just-having-fun is what comes through, although the work subsequently metamorphosed through several complete rewrites and grew from a single book to three. In the first book, *Reluctant Swordsman*, Wally blunders around in a world that makes no sense to him and made no sense to me either, because I was making it up as I went along. Nowadays I would plan it more. Perhaps that's it. I still think the ending of that trilogy was the most satisfying wind-up I ever achieved and most readers seem to find it appropriate. A few go ballistic.

VAN BELKOM: When you start a project, do you think in terms of a series, or do you work on solo novels that grow into series?

DUNCAN: I always know at the beginning what the ending will be, and that means I know if I'm writing a novel or a saga. An exception to prove the rule is my next fantasy, *The King's Blades*. I wrote a stand-alone novel, which Jennifer Brehl bought for Avon and liked so well she asked if it could be a series. I agreed because the Loyal and Ancient Order of the King's Blades can, like Arthur's Round Table, generate more adventures very easily. So the first book was renamed *The Gilded Chain* and The King's Blades became the name of the series, but this will not be a SERIAL like, say, *The Great Game* or *The Seventh Sword*. It will be a collection of discrete stories set in the same sword-and-sorcery world with some recurring characters.

VAN BELKOM: In an interview in *Locus*, you mentioned that one of your more prominent themes is alienation. How does using that theme in your books relate to your own situation as a writer and Scotsman living in Canada so many years?

DUNCAN: Writers of fiction are often loners. We may not all be Somerset Maughans — brooding in the shadows making notes on people — but it is easier to see a group from the edges than the middle. And writing is not a team sport. How writers manage collaborations is utterly beyond my ken. In my case, I had a very lonely childhood, then left everything behind and came to a new country to start over when I had just turned twenty-two. For more than twenty years now I have been self-employed, working alone. This harrowing history is a convenient excuse for my consummate boorishness and total lack of social skills. My wife will tell you.

Alienation is almost a cliché in *F&SF*, where the setting has far more importance than it does in mainstream. In any story the writer's second task (after staging a good opening) is to inform the reader of the where and when as subtly as possible: "As I wheeled my Studebaker onto Sunset Boulevard . . ." If the world does not exist or is even impossible, this becomes a major challenge. A common solution is to employ an alienated protagonist who has to be told everything, like Bilbo Baggins, and who sees everything through strangers' eyes. I find such characters come easy to me — Shadow, Wally Smith, Knobil, Rap, and especially Vaun in *Hero!* who was so alienated that he didn't even know what species he belonged to. If you want an alienated heroine, there's Gwin in *The Cursed*, traumatized by bereavement. Perhaps I relate to them because of my personal history. I don't know how one would prove it.

VAN BELKOM: You obviously enjoy writing a lot, but almost all of your production has been novels, or even multiple novels. Why do you think you've not written more short fiction, even earlier in your writing career?

DUNCAN: I did. It didn't sell. Novels and short fiction are different media and not all writers are equally competent at both. Short fiction doesn't pay a living wage, which reduces the incentive for this old dog to learn that particular new trick. That isn't the whole story, because movies pay much better and I have never tried to enter that field. I find I never read short fiction, so I can't expect to be able to write it. I am amused that the dust jackets of my books all claim that I have written "numerous novels and short stories." I keep asking for that to be corrected, but it seems to be a stock phrasing that publishers can't delete. I imagine some gnome in the typesetting department keeps putting it back in.

VAN BELKOM: The word prolific has been used to describe you many times, but are you really that prolific a writer, or have others forces been at work in your career to make it seem that you write at a blistering pace?

DUNCAN: I average a little over two books a year, which is not abnormal for fulltime writers of genre fiction. Charles de Lint is much more prolific, not to mention Barbara Cartland, Alexander Dumas Sr., and many others. I have written a book in less than two months; I have dragged others out for years, although not working on them continuously. The amount of time spent does not seem to correlate to quality of product. Novels run between 60,000 and 120,000 words, so two a year is much less than 1,000 words of polished text a day. A fast typist could do that in 15 minutes, which leaves lots of time over for thinking. I'm a two-fingered man on the keyboard, but I don't think I'm working miracles at two books per year.

VAN BELKOM: Which of your books or series is your favorite, and which is the one you like least?

DUNCAN: Tough. I usually like the next one best, hope springing eternal. So I guess the answer is *The Gilded Chain* and *A Prize for Achilles*. The first is more traditional sword-and-sorcery than anything I have tackled before, and the second is an historical novel, a major break away.

I am not ashamed of any of my books, but I have regrets about some of them. For instance, *West of January*, which won the Aurora Prize, has some crude sex and violence in it. Were I ever to rewrite it, I would change those scenes. They may explain why that is the only one of my books that has not generated a single "foreign" (meaning offshore) sale.

VAN BELKOM: Despite all your success, you seem to have trouble attracting the attention of critics and reviewers in Canada. Any explanation as to why that might be? Do you even care?

DUNCAN: First, let's look at the record. I must pay tribute to Southam's *Calgary Herald* and its long-time book editor, Ken McGoogan. Ken has interviewed me several times and devoted a generous review to every one of my books. He could not do more to support local writers and we are all very grateful to him. *The Edmonton Journal*, 300 km. away, has been more selective in its support of me, naturally, but I have no complaints about it. I have also been interviewed a couple of times on CBC radio, only on local channels.

Apart from that, in the last eleven years and twenty-one books, I count one review in *The Toronto Star*, one in *Quill and Quire*, and one in *The Victoria Times-Colonist*. Nothing in *The Globe and Mail*. This contrasts with the consistent support American media give me, including *Locus*, *Publisher's Weekly*, *Kirkus Reviews*, *Library Journal*, *SF Chronicle*, *Kliatt*, *Analog*, *Booklist*, etc. What gives? Partly this disparity must be blamed on my publishers, who have always been American and may not have bothered to push me very much in

Canada. Nor am I the sort of guy who hypes himself a lot.

Mostly it is because Canada is not a viable market. Canadian writers and publishers struggle to survive on small presses, small print runs, and (above all) government grants. A Canadian who sells south of the border has obviously sold out to the Yankees, and there is something indecent about a Canadian writer earning a living wage without relying on government money. If he sells his books in a dozen countries worldwide, then he is out of control and positively dangerous.

Mind? Of course I don't mind! Why ever would you think I do? I console myself with thoughts of Janette Oke, who has sold more than TWENTY MILLION copies of her novels. I have never met the lady, but she used to live in Didsbury, Alberta. I understand she has recently moved to Calgary. She outsells me or even Margaret Atwood many times over, but no one ever reviews her books, because she writes "Christian" fiction. Prophets have no honor in their own country, I guess. Sadly, Canada's newspapers don't know much about books. They just know what they think we ought to want to read.

James Alan Gardner

James Alan Gardner has had several different writing careers, each one of them an unqualified success. First, he's an award-winning technical writer, a career he began shortly after obtaining a Masters degree in Applied Math from the University of Waterloo. From 1980 to the present, he has written technical manuals and other support documents for the university as well as numerous software companies in the Waterloo area. In 1989, he became an "author" for the first time by writing the technical manual *From C to C: an Introduction to ANSI Standard C* (Harcourt Brace Jovanovich). That book was followed by *Learning Unix with MKS Tools* (Howard W. Sams), and *A DOS User's Guide to the Internet* and *Internet Anywhere* (Prentice Hall).

Second, he's an award-winning playwright, another career begun at UofW, this time in the late 1970s, where he wrote or co-wrote plays for a variety of university theatre productions, as well as for other groups like Simcoe Little Theatre in Simcoe, Ontario. One of his plays, "The Collaborators," won first prize in the 1990 Canadian National One-Act Playwriting Competition.

Third, he's an award-winning science fiction writer.

This third writing career, like the first two, got its start on the campus at UofW. Several of his plays featured SF and fantasy elements, and one of his first SF stories, "The Phantom of the Operator," was published in the UofW's *Courier* magazine. That story, published in 1984, was followed six years later by his first professional SF sale, which just happened to be another award winner. "The Children of Crche" won the grand prize in the *Writers of the Future* contest in 1989 and was published in Volume Six of the contest's anthology series. Next came "Muffin Explains Teleology to the World At Large" in *On Spec*, the winner of the 1991 Aurora Award for Best Short Work in English. More stories soon followed in such major publications as *The Magazine of Fantasy and Science Fiction*, *Amazing Stories*, *Tesseracts*, *The New Quarterly*, and *Asimov's Science Fiction Magazine*. A Clarion West graduate (1989), Gardner debuted as a novelist in the SF field with *Expendable* in 1997, which was followed a year later by *Commitment Hour*, both from Avon Books.

Born in 1955 in Bradford, Ontario, Gardner currently lives in Waterloo with his wife, artist Linda Carson, and splits his time evenly between technical writing and science fiction.

EDO VAN BELKOM: What first drew you to the SF and fantasy genres?

JAMES ALAN GARDNER: When I was a kid, I was a comic book fanatic . . . and comic books are one of the tried-and-true entries into both SF and fantasy. The books I read were also SF or fantasy; maybe it was just the nature of our local library, but the only kind of books I ever found in the kids' section (in the early 1960s) were SF, fantasy, or mysteries. I read them all.

The first stories I wrote (when I was 10 or there-abouts) were science fiction spy thrillers . . . sort of a cross between Thunderbirds and The Man From U.N.C.L.E. Thank heavens they've been lost in the mists of time. But I can't think of a time when the genre wasn't as natural to me as breathing. Once in a while, I've written "straight" fiction (not SF/fantasy/mystery), but it's not as tangible to me. Straight fiction (especially so-called literary fiction) always seems so formulaic; it seldom keeps my interest, either reading or writing.

VAN BELKOM: You wrote and produced several plays — both humorous and fantastical — before you began writing and publishing your short stories. Is the theater your first and favorite medium, or was it just the one that suited your writing best at the time?

GARDNER: The theater wasn't my first medium — I've been writing stories forever, and I even attended the Banff Writers' Workshop (taught by W.O.Mitchell) before I wrote my first stage pieces. However, writing for theater is a great way to learn a lot in a short period of time.

First of all, it's reasonably easy to get produced. In a town of any size, there are usually several amateur the-ater groups around, and I've always found them open to doing new work, even if it's only a workshop production. I started out writing for the FASS Theatre Company, a group at the University of Waterloo that puts on a musi-cal comedy every year. Soon, a group of people from FASS started a summer theater group where we wrote our own scripts, not to mention a number of weekly series for the campus radio station and even a show on our local cable TV channel. If I wrote a script, someone would mount a production . . . which is very different from the print publishing world, where it's much harder to break in.

Second, theater provides immediate feedback for what works and what doesn't. You have actors and a director to give you their responses, and you soon have an audience responding too. The response is very visceral: the audience's body language makes it completely obvious when a passage has captured them and when they're bored. (The viewers may not know when they're bored, but it's obvious to you.) Of course, when you're writing comedy, you also get the thrill of hearing people laugh . . . and the agony of seeing them sit like lumps when the jokes bomb.

In addition to scripted theatre, I did a lot of improvisation in the early 1980s. That also teaches important lessons about constructing narrative on the spot, and the eternal value of reincorporation in creating a story. Improv also cured me of any fears I had, starting out a scene without knowing where it would go. I've never written from outlines and often don't have much idea of where I'm going next when I write a story or novel . . . but I have faith that I'll be able to keep going, keep on pushing into the future, without falling off a cliff. I discover the story as I go along and create the structure through reincorporation of earlier story points, rather than aiming toward some known destination.

I should say that even while I was writing play scripts, I was working on prose too. In 1978, for example, I was chief scriptwriter for FASS, for our summer theater show, and for several consecutive radio series; but I was also working on a novel and actually finished the first draft. (The novel is sitting in a trunk now. Some day I may dust it off and try to sell it, but there are a number of other book ideas in the queue ahead of it.)

VAN BELKOM: You were the Grand Prize winner of the Writers of the Future contest in 1989. Were you concerned about the contest's connection with Dianetics and the Church of Scientology when you entered?

GARDNER: No. The judges for the contest my year were people like Larry Niven and Frederick Pohl. I had confidence that if they were willing to participate, the contest must be completely on the up and up. And I must say, the contest organizers never breathed a word about Scientology in all my dealings with them. Some of the contestants were worried that they were setting us up for some kind of hard sell, but nothing like that ever happened. I would wholeheartedly recommend the contest to any unpublished writer who is looking for somewhere to send a story.

VAN BELKOM: What was winning that contest like? Did you feel it gave your fledgling career a boost, or was it something that just heightened people's expectations?

GARDNER: There's very little overt recognition of the contest within the SF community . . . which I think says more about the community than the contest. I had a good time meeting writers like Niven and Pohl, not to mention Algis Budrys, Dave Wolverton, Kris Rusch, and a number of other people who came to the awards ceremonies. I also got to know the other contestants my year — people like Bruce Holland Rogers who won the Nebula this year. For a fledgling writer, meeting such people and talking with them about writing (and the publishing business) was a valuable experience, even if I didn't have editors suddenly knocking down my door and asking me to send them work.

VAN BELKOM: Winning the Writers of the Future contest enabled you to attend Clarion West in the summer of 1989. What were the benefits of attending the workshop when you were already a working writer and had just won a significant SF award?

GARDNER: In the SF community, there is much more respect for Clarion and Clarion West than for Writers of the Future. Before I went to Clarion West, I never got anything but form rejections from professional magazines. Afterward, I never got anything but personal messages, even for stories that I wrote before going to Clarion. (Sometimes the personal messages were rejections, but still . . .) I think Clarion is a magic word that moves up your status in the slush pile; something clicks in the editor's mind and he or she feels you have to be taken seriously. My first truly professional sale was immediately after I came back from Clarion — I sold *Fantasy & Science Fiction* a story that I wrote at Clarion (virtually unchanged from my first draft, by the way, so I'm afraid I can't say it was feedback from the workshop that made the difference).

As with Writers of the Future, the most important benefit of

Clarion was being surrounded by people for whom writing was an important and valuable thing to do. It gives you commitment, not just to the hard work of writing but to the harder work of writing well. Of course, I also met many people who helped me in various ways — Orson Scott Card, Karen Joy Fowler, Connie Willis, Lucius Shepard, and Roger Zelazny, to name a few. Did I learn anything specific? Well, Roger told me how to write a fight scene, and Lucius gave me some important keys to writing description; those two things stand out in my mind. On the other hand, all of the instructors (and all of the students too) gave invaluable support just by being there, by taking us all seriously, by showing us how they worked and thought through a story.

I suppose Clarion might not be for everyone . . . but I was very lucky in my teachers and in my fellow students. I know that I'm a much better writer because of the experience.

VAN BELKOM: You've been a technical writer for years, producing computer manuals and technical documents for a variety of companies. How do you manage to juggle your time and energy between technical writing and science fiction?

GARDNER: These days, it's pretty simple: I write fiction in the mornings and computer stuff in the afternoon. Since I write the fiction first, there's no difficulty changing gears for the technical writing. It might be harder the other way around.

Back when I needed a full-time job (when I wasn't making enough money from writing to cut back my day-job), I wrote at night and on weekends. I still write on weekends unless something else gets in the way.

VAN BELKOM: How much do the two forms of writing differ? Is it the sort of thing that almost requires that you use two different sides of your brain?

GARDNER: Technical writing has to be completely ego-less; the reader is always right. That's a useful attitude to carry over into fiction, but only to a point. Ultimately, you write fiction for yourself and technical work for other people. Does that mean that I use two different sides of my brain? I don't know. In fiction, I'm writing about a totally different subject matter, but I'm still constructing sentences, still typing, still trying to present things in a sensible way.

One reason why the two forms of writing aren't so far apart is that I'm opposed to stupidly formal technical writing. There's still a lingering tradition that computer documentation has to follow a stilted "corporate" style . . . heavy on the passive voice and certain awkward phrases that supposedly sound business-like. Writers who take such an approach haven't figured out the ego-less concept yet; they're trying to make themselves sound important by assuming a pompous tone of voice. My computer writing is much more casual, because I think it's clearer that way.

Even if fiction and computer writing do use different parts of the brain, they use similar tools and similar discipline: you have to sit down at the keyboard and type for long periods of time. People want the two forms of writing to be wildly different, but at heart, many of the differences are simply cosmetic.

VAN BELKOM: What do you like to do when you're not writing?

GARDNER: For the last four years, I've been studying kung fu (Shaolin five animal style). I go to class two or three times a week, and practice at home or outside when I get a chance. Does it make me a better writer? Well, I know I can write better fight scenes now. It also gets me out of the house where I meet people who aren't writers or working with computers. That's certainly healthy.

I've also been playing role-playing games for more than ten years. It's an interesting form of storytelling that is occasionally useful in writing, in the same way that improvisational acting experience makes it easier to push forward into the future of a story, even when you have no predetermined plot outline.

VAN BELKOM: The inspiration for the Explorer Corps in your novel *Expendable* has to be obvious to anyone familiar with the SF genre, and even to those whose only knowledge of SF is *Star Trek*. Nevertheless, perhaps you could explain the genesis of Festina Ramos and the Explorer Corps.

GARDNER: As I said, I spent several years writing for FASS at the University of Waterloo. In 1977, we did a parody of *Star Trek* and someone (I can't remember who) suggested that we should have a running joke of calling for a red-shirted crew member to keep coming on stage and getting killed in classical Trek fashion. In the script, we referred to this character as the expendable crew member, and we kind of took it for granted the actor would be male . . . but when the director cast the show, the part was given to a woman (probably because we had more women than men show up at auditions that year).

Now something that I used to do (and still do sometimes) is start writing in someone's voice — call it an exercise, or a form of brainstorming when I don't have anything better to write: pick a character and just let that character talk. Sometime in about 1980 I was doing that, and happened to pick the expendable crew member from FASS. Something along the lines of "Oh yeah, you think it's so funny, just call in a character to die because she's expendable. You want to know why I'm expendable? Because I'm ugly. Because I have a huge birthmark on my face . . ."

That was completely unplanned (and certainly had nothing to do with the woman who had played the part in the show). But the words just started blurting out. In very little time, I had produced a diatribe from the character, explaining the cruelty of the world and her place in it. This had nothing to do with the *Star Trek* universe any more — the circumstances that this voice described were very different. In fact, after a page or two of the voice coming up to speed, I wrote something that was very close to what ended up as the first 100 pages of *Expendable*. The writing took place over the course of a few weeks, but the voice kept flowing and I kept typing. I really didn't think it through at all — just pure character improvisation.

So the flow kept coming right up to the point where Festina, Yarrun and Chee get to the planet and go incommunicado . . . then it stopped and I had no idea what came next. I tried several directions, but none of them worked; so the 100 pages ended up in a drawer for a while. Now and then I brought them out and took a stab at carrying on . . . but I never came up with something that clicked.

Time passed. By the fall of 1995, I had published a number of short stories and had written two novels that were good but didn't get sold. I wanted to start another novel; so I took out *Expendable* again and promised myself I would work on it until I got it moving again. There were a few false starts and dead ends, but eventually I found my momentum again and finished the book in about nine months.

VAN BELKOM: Will there be more "Explorer" novels, or something set in the "League of Peoples" universe?

GARDNER: My next novel is called *Commitment Hour*, and it takes place in the same universe, but with none of the same characters. That book is scheduled to come out in April 1998. I'm currently writing a third "League of Peoples" novel which does bring back Festina Ramos from *Expendable* but centers on a new lead character and features planetary politics rather than exploration. I don't want to find myself stuck in doing "more of the same" for every book, but I'm happy to keep playing with the universe itself. There are so many stories that can be told there, and stories that can run the gamut from comedy to action to tragedy. I'll keep trying out different directions with each book for a while. . . but of course there are other books I want to write that have nothing to do with the League.

VAN BELKOM: Are you still writing short stories and plays these days, or is all of your time for fiction writing spent on writing novels?

GARDNER: I haven't written plays in quite some time — the last bout was two years ago, when three other writers and I created a series called "Comedy Under Construction." The idea was simple: we got together Friday to talk about skit ideas, wrote like mad fools all day Saturday (usually producing three to four comedy skits each), then put on a workshop production of the show on Sunday with a group of very cooperative actors. After four binges like that, we pulled out the best scenes from the lot and turned them into a full comedy production. (Some of the scenes were really quite good.)

As for short stories, I've written a couple in the past two years, but for the most part I'm spending all my time on novels. Like most writers, I find I have to spend proportionately longer on a short story than I do on a novel . . . except, of course, for the wondrous few that come burning into my mind and demand to be written in a white heat of two or three days. Those have been the only kind of short stories I've done recently — the ones that basically write themselves and won't let me write anything else until I've got them out of my system. I like it that way; it means the short stories have a purity and intensity to them that's a nice holiday from the long-haul writing of a novel.

William Gibson

Although difficult to prove, a strong case could be made that the bestselling Canadian novel of all-time is not a work of Canadian "literature" but a work of science fiction.

The novel, *Neuromancer*, was written by American expatriate William Gibson and first published in 1984, winning the Hugo, Nebula, and Philip K. Dick awards. It has been continuously in print ever since with its tenth anniversary commemorated by a hardcover reprinting.

Neuromancer and some of Gibson's early stories published in *Omni* magazine ("Johnny Mnemonic," 1981; "Burning Chrome," 1982; "New Rose Hotel," 1984) laid the groundwork for the cyberpunk movement. Cyberpunk is a kind of SF sub-genre that's set in a computer-driven, high-tech near-future and features low-life protagonists interacting in hard-boiled detective type plots.

Gibson's early stories were later published in the landmark 1986 collection *Burning Chrome*. That same year, the second book in what was to become The Neuromancer Trilogy, *Count Zero*, was also published. Two years later, the series came to a close with the publication of *Mona Lisa Overdrive*. Gibson's next novel, *The Difference Engine*, took him in another direction, this time into the past. The novel, co-written with Bruce Sterling, revolves around the premise that Charles Babbage's attempts to build a computer in the early 1800s actually succeeded. In 1993 Gibson produced another solo novel, *Virtual Light*, a near-future thriller set in California. Published in 1996 *Idoru* takes place in the future Japan that was only glimpsed at in *Virtual Light*.

Gibson has written several screenplays, but only *Johnny Mnemonic*, a film based on his short story of the same name, has made it to the screen, starring Canadian-born actor Keanu Reeves and boasting the highest budget of any film then shot in Canada.

Gibson was born in Virginia in 1948 and moved to Canada in 1968 after being rejected by his local draft board. He first lived in Toronto, but moved to Vancouver in 1972, where he met his wife Deborah and obtained a B.A. in English from the University of British Columbia. The father of two has lived in British Columbia ever since.

EDO VAN BELKOM: You began by writing short stories, many published in *Omni*, before moving on to novels. However, one of your more recent works was the poem "Agrippa." Will there be any other short works in the future, or was that just a special case.

WILLIAM GIBSON: Writing short fiction requires a different kind of muscle. It's like sprinting. I probably started with that because it's the traditional entry level activity for science fiction writers. After having spent years and years writing novels, I've tried to do short stories and I just don't know how to make it all fit in to a twenty-seven page manuscript anymore.

VAN BELKOM: Before you published in *Omni*, at least one of your stories appeared in a fanzine. Was it a case of lack of confidence in your own work, naiveté about the market, or did you think the stuff was too different from what was being published at the time?

GIBSON: It was lack of confidence and naiveté. I went from this one semi-professional publication to submitting to what were the top markets at the time, but I was forced to do that by other writers. My initial impulse was to hide it under a bushel and avoid rejection, and I was very fortunate that I had people who came along who beat me up and twisted my arm and made me send stories to *Omni*.

VAN BELKOM: Did you think they were crazy at the time?

GIBSON: No, I knew they were right because that was basically what it said in all the "How to Market Science Fiction" checklists. They said send to the most lucrative market first, and when it's rejected there send it to the next most lucrative market.

But the first time I just wouldn't do it. Actually the first piece of fiction I wrote, I had turned in in lieu of an essay for a science fiction course at UBC. I got like a B+ or something, and then the instructor said, "You should submit this for publication." And I said, "Okay," and submitted it to *Unearth*, which was this fabulously obscure magazine.

VAN BELKOM: I've seen copies of it.

GIBSON: Well, they printed millions of them apparently. It is currently a kind of fake rarity because they couldn't get it together to distribute very many, but I understand that somewhere in California there's a garage full of that particular issue.

VAN BELKOM: I've also seen a fanzine with a cartoon by you. It was of a martial arts expert sharpening up his hand underneath a pyramid. Did you do many of those kind of cartoons?

GIBSON: No, that was when I rediscovered the subculture of science fiction when I was an English major at UBC. I was sort of back, post-60s as an adult student. And I was amazed to discovered that the stuff that I'd known about when I was a teenager was still going on and that it was even happening locally. I think what happened when I first ran into it was that I said, "Oh, yeah, I know what you guys are doing," and I drew them cartoons and wrote some little things and then forgot about it.

VAN BELKOM: *Neuromancer* recently celebrated its tenth anniversary with a hardcover reprinting. Looking back, are you sometimes amazed by the success of the book?

GIBSON: Well, I certainly didn't expect it when I wrote it. I know that what I expected was very much the opposite. I thought it was going to be the kind of paperback original that was never reprinted again. My secret ambition for it was that it would attain some kind of odd cult following in England or France where I knew there were at least two-dozen people who liked the same kind of science fiction I had liked as a teenager.

It surprised me, although there were hints early on that it was going to have an unusual career. I couldn't recognize them at the time because it was all very novel to me. I thought, "Oh yeah, this is how people respond when they see an SF novel in manuscript." I had nothing to compare it to. Now, looking back, I can see that in some weird way it was some kind of marked card.

VAN BELKOM: You collaborated with Bruce Sterling on *The Difference Engine*. What was it like to work with a collaborator and what did you think of the end product?

GIBSON: That's sort of like asking what it's like to be married, because it's different in every case. That book had a very organic genesis. Bruce and I discovered that we were writing it sometime after we began, in a sense, to write it. We'd been talking about Babbage and having this sort of ongoing dialogue with imaginary bits of what might have happened. This was going on for about a year when one of us — I forget which one it was — said, "Wait, wait! This is a book." At that point we argued about which one would do it because neither of us wanted to undertake it.

It's the only one of my books that I go back to with any regularity and read with a kind of pleasure. I don't have that with my solo novels. *The Difference Engine* really feels to me as though I didn't write it and neither did Sterling. It's by some third character whom we've never met and, by the end of the book, we were both slightly frightened of.

VAN BELKOM: You couriered the manuscript bits back and forth, is that correct?

GIBSON: Yeah, we really didn't have any option. There was no Internet at the time. We purchased these primitive, weird, slow, little modems and attached them to our Apples and actually attempted, by long-distance phone, to modem bits of it back and forth, but it was such a cranky, inaccurate process that FedEx won as technology. So we became early FedEx advocates.

VAN BELKOM: Of all your works, were you surprised that *Johnny Mnemonic* was the first to be made into a film?

GIBSON: Not so much. Almost everything I've ever written has been under option for film at one time or another. It's sort of like those old-fashioned pinball games where marbles fall down and they either strike nails or go into holes. So I've been watching a whole field of marbles bounce down this endless and very boring board for years. *Johnny* finally made it through, but it was five years in its genesis.

VAN BELKOM: I read an article in *Premiere* magazine that outlined the troubles the production had getting going.

GIBSON: I don't remember that one too clearly, but I'm sure we were being very diplomatic and outlining only a fragment, or one level, of production difficulties.

VAN BELKOM: Were you happy with the end results on that film?

GIBSON: The film that was released bears almost no resemblance to the film we shot. And given that, I thought, "Yeah, it's okay."

The film that was released is something like what you would have seen if the distributor had taken over post-production of David

Lynch's *Blue Velvet* and made a whole-hearted, but very misguided attempt to turn it into straight, irony-free thriller.

VAN BELKOM: I watched it recently in preparation for this interview and it seems like a straight action-adventure movie.

GIBSON: What we shot was nothing like that, which accounts for the very odd tone of the piece. The screenplay, as published, is pretty much what we shot. One of the reasons I let them publish that was I wanted it to be able to prove my good intentions regardless of what was finally released. The screenplay is a very different piece of work. It was meant to be a sort of semi-comic, or in any case, very ironic movie that in a way was about B science fiction films as much as it was about anything else. And we really went to a lot of trouble to get what we wanted, and we pretty much had what we wanted when we turned it in to TriStar.

But it wasn't what they wanted.

VAN BELKOM: In addition to the screenplay for *Johnny Mnemonic*, you also did a screenplay for *Alien 3*. Will there be more screenplays, or after those two experiences, will you be more than happy to stick to writing novels?

GIBSON: No, I've written eight or ten screenplays to contract over the years. I think that being a novelist and being paid for it is just about the best job I could have, and being a Hollywood screenwriter and being paid for it is easily the worst job I've ever had.

VAN BELKOM: Will you continue to do that worst job, though?

GIBSON: Well, it depends on the project. It's a very perverse activity for me. Most of the people I know do screenplay work because they can't earn a living writing novels. When I do screenplay work my accountant gets pissed off with me because I don't make as much money. I make a much better living as a novelist, so screenwriting is always a very twisted thing for me to do.

At first I wanted to do it just because I was very curious about how movies are made. Now I've certainly satisfied that curiosity, but every once in a while someone comes along with something that is just intriguing enough and I'll say, "Okay, I'll do just one more."

VAN BELKOM: You've seen a lot of the world and lived plenty of different places. What was it about British Columbia that made you want to settle there?

GIBSON: My wife. My wife was born in Vancouver and we moved

out here in 1972. The sixties were over, or what I had thought of as the sixties were definitely over, and there just didn't seem to be much going on. And at that time Vancouver was a kind of back-water, it seemed to me. There really wasn't much going on here, it was just kind of a good place to heel up and lick one's wounds. In the meantime it has become sort of post-modern Pacific-rim and an endlessly expanding urban scene.

I'm very happy living here. I've slowed down and it's speeded up and some kind of parity seems to be in effect.

VAN BELKOM: You've lived in Canada for half of your life now, but you've said you don't consider yourself to be Canadian — or American, for that matter. At one point will that change, or will it ever?

GIBSON: I don't know if it ever will change. I probably wouldn't be very comfortable, at least initially, moving back to the States because it's not the place I left. It's changed, and I don't know how to get medical insurance, and I've become uncomfortable living in cities where the majority of the population is armed — I find that really an odd way of doing things. I certainly identify with the state of being Canadian, but I don't quite feel like I am. I don't have the memories that my wife, for instance, has. The Canada she remembers — which no longer exists either — I don't have any access to except through her stories of it. I'm probably becoming the kind of Canadian that people become if they stay here long enough. It seems to take a while. I always liked the idea that Canada had the cultural mosaic rather than the melting pot. I thought it was really cool that they didn't require that you had the flag tattooed on your butt or whatever, which is really the American way.

VAN BELKOM: Would you have left the United States if it had not been for the Vietnam War?

GIBSON: I doubt it. Although it's awfully difficult to separate those two. I mean, that was America, or it seemed that way at the time. The war was sort of a prominent issue in something else that was going on. The war was happening because America was whatever it was that America was. Without the threat of imminent military ser-vice I don't think I would have had the motivation to leave. It's really hard to motivate eighteen-year-olds to do anything, let alone abandon the country of their birth and go and live where it snows in the winter.

VAN BELKOM: I realize that there's probably no such thing, but what's a typical writing day like for you?

GIBSON: I wake up very early and drink coffee and read the papers and drive around buying danishes and things. Then I come down to my office, check the incoming faxes, answer a few letters and things, and then try to write something. If I'm having a really super productive day I'll try to write something until lunch time, have lunch, go back and try to write something until dinner time. That's perfection really; it doesn't happen that often. When I'm not officially on vacation, I try to come down and do something in a writerly direction.

When I'm finishing a book, in the last couple of months of finishing a book, I work compulsively and very hard and get quite mental and disagreeable and hard to talk to, mainly because I'm anxious to get it over with, and at the same time I'm trying not to hurry it. It's one of those "because it feels so good when I stop" routines toward the end.

VAN BELKOM: You seem a very private person and are somewhat difficult to get a hold of. At what point in your career did you realize that you were becoming so famous that it was having an effect on your lifestyle?

GIBSON: It hasn't had that much of an effect on my lifestyle compared to what you have to put up with if you are a middle-rung pop musician. So, my recognizability factor continues to be much lower than say, Billy Idol's, who is actually a fairly obscure figure these days, but he would be hassled more in public than I would.

One of the effects it had, though, was that I — without really thinking about it — started going to fewer and fewer science fiction conventions because those were the places I would be hassled. I could no longer go there and be a citizen of the convention, I had to go there and be William Gibson. So that took away the fun of it; but I'm still not famous enough that I have trouble being William Gibson on the street, so that's good.

VAN BELKOM: On your most recent visit to Toronto to promote the hardcover release of *Idoru*, you did plenty of interviews, but I got the impression people were more interested to hear what you had to say about the future, rather than about your new book. Does that frustrate you?

GIBSON: Actually I think it frustrates them more than it does me because I spend a lot of time trying to disarm the idea that I'm a prophet. I'm not entirely innocent there because publishers market science fiction writers as these predictive engines or futurists and there are lots of science fiction writers who are happy to be seen that way. But for whatever reason that's always bugged me. To the extent that I'm any sort of theorist or critic of science fiction, I would be one of those people arguing that science fiction is actually always about the present or about the period in which it was written.

VAN BELKOM: You've already begun to touch upon my next question which is: you talk about the commodification of subcultures like punk and grunge, but do you sometimes feel that William Gibson is being commodified as some technological prophet?

GIBSON: I participate to whatever extent to my own commodification. It's just what we do as a culture. It's pretty much becoming the main thing we do as a culture, or at least that's what Idoru is arguing: that maybe we're doing it a bit too much. But I think that's why I write about some of the things I write about. When I started writing I was only guessing.

VAN BELKOM: They were pretty good guesses.

GIBSON: Well, I was guessing about the mechanisms of popular culture, and if you look at Count Zero and Mona Lisa Overdrive and what's going on in the background, there's a sort of extrapolated, near-future version of Hollywood written with a certain surety, as if I knew what that stuff was actually like. I didn't, but my experience subsequently showed me that I was right. I got the tone of it. One of the reasons I got involved with other media was that I was really curious to see whether it was as I had envisioned it. It was always weirder than I could have envisioned, but still pretty much like what I had envisioned.

VAN BELKOM: You've been called "the father of cyberpunk" and have been credited with foreseeing and shaping the Internet, maybe even inventing it. Perhaps you could explain here, as a sort of matter of record, which parts are reality and which are myth?

GIBSON: You've got two topic headings. One is "cyberspace" and one is "cyberpunk."

Cyberspace, I coined. I made that word up to describe something in my fiction that does sort of resemble what the Internet and the World Wide Web are becoming at this point. And that's probably the only classical science fiction move in my entire body of work. But it was a really good one, because it was as though I had simultaneously invented the rocket ship and space. "He didn't just invent the rocket, he invented the whole concept of space travel!" That's not literally true of course, because there were all sorts of precursors in science fiction to what I did with cyberspace, and for some reason people just don't recognize them. I mean everything from Ellison's "I Have No Mouth and I Must Scream" to Vinge's *True Names*. There's a body of work there that's never been recognized, but I was certainly aware of it. When I started doing those early cyberspace stories, I remember thinking, "This is kind of cool, but it's just too obvious." This simply isn't going to amaze people. This idea had been around in larval form in a lot of other stories.

VAN BELKOM: Do you think that if you hadn't picked up on it, somebody else would have eventually?

GIBSON: I think that someone would have. I know that the people who were inventing virtual reality and the World Wide Web were doing it actively at the same time I was writing those stories. They had their visions they wanted to realize in the lab and then market. So, yeah, this stuff would have come along in any course. I think that someone would have been writing science fiction about something like this, but I don't know if the punk side of the equation would have come into it.

Cyberpunk was not my coining. It was sort of a journalistic bumper sticker applied from outside the group of supposed practitioners. I don't know what I would have called it, but I wouldn't have called it that. I might have called it cyber-populism or something which wouldn't have been nearly as catchy.

But I don't know if anyone else would have come up with that particular union of, I suppose you could call, personal computer technology and Bohemian attitude.

VAN BELKOM: With all of your critical and financial success, you don't have to write anymore if you don't want to. What is it that keeps you writing?

GIBSON: That's a good question. I think if I just absolutely stopped writing right now I could coast for a while, but I'm sure there still is some financial pressure there somewhere.

I think someone once said that writers are these tails that are dragged around and wagged by the bodies of their work, and I think there's some truth to that now. I don't feel as though I'm on any particular literary mission myself so much as I'm completing a movement I began twenty years ago — simply because it hasn't been completed. I don't know if you ever get to a point where you say, "Okay, that's it. I'm done writing now," or whether it just goes on and on until it peters out, but it feels to me like I'm still doing what I was doing before, except I'm doing the late 1990s versions of it.

VAN BELKOM: Are there still some goals or plateaus you want to reach that you haven't attained yet?

GIBSON: Oh yeah, certainly. I'm never set, although I can't tell you what they are, only that I'm never satisfied with these books. If I'm very, very satisfied, they would be about seventy-five per cent of what they might have been. The book I'm working on now is the end of some aspect of my work — I'm not sure what to call it — and the next one I think will be very different, but I haven't a clue what that will be. I keep feeling that there's a kind of book that hasn't been written that I want to write now, in the same way that when I wrote *Neuromancer* there was a kind of book that hadn't been written that I wanted to write in 1983. That was really the impulse there, the sense that there was something missing that was needed in the world. When I wrote *Neuromancer* I knew it had to be sort of like *The Stars My Destination* and sort of like Robert Stone's *Dark Soldiers* and sort of like a Velvet Underground album. I had a whole list of things it had to be sort of like, and if it all went together it would become one of those seamless pop artifacts that sort of resemble everything and nothing at the same time.

VAN BELKOM: Do you have a list for what this next book should be?

GIBSON: I'm sure I do, but not as consciously yet. It's something I spend a lot of time wondering about. Wondering about that one has become a big part of what I do.

Phyllis Gotlieb

here was a time that Phyllis Gotlieb was Canadian science fiction. That's because when she began publishing short stories with "A Grain of Manhood" in *Fantastic* in 1959, and continued through the 1960s in magazines such as *If* and *Amazing Stories*, she was the only one in Canada doing so.

And more than thirty years later, the Canadian science fiction and fantasy community has grown up around her to the point where she is just one of many. But while there's more Canadian science fiction writers than ever before, Gotlieb is still active as ever, publishing a new collection, *Blue Apes* in 1995, and a new novel, *Flesh and Gold*, in 1998.

Gotlieb was born in Toronto in 1926, married Calvin (Kelly) Gotlieb (a computer science professor and member of the Order of Canada) in 1949. She earned an M.A. in English language and literature from the University of Toronto in 1950 and raised three children while working towards becoming a poet and science fiction writer.

She began publishing poetry and science fiction around the same time, but earned notoriety as the "housewife poet" on the basis of an early poetry chapbook, *Who Knows One*, in 1961 and a 1964 collection from McClelland & Stewart called *Within the Zodiac*. It wasn't until the publication of her first novel, *Sunburst*, in 1964 that she began to make her mark in SF. Gotlieb continued her duel career, publishing both poetry and science fiction at irregular intervals. Her 1969 poetry collection *Ordinary, Moving* was a Governor General's Award nominee and was followed by two more collections, *Doctor Umlaut's Earthly Kingdom* in 1974 and *The Works* in 1978.

Although *Sunburst* was very well received, Gotlieb followed it in 1969 with a mainstream novel, *Why Should I Have All the Grief?*, and it was another seven years until the publication of Gotlieb's second SF novel, *O Master Caliban!*. In the 1980s she published five books: three novels about sentient cats — *A Judgment of Dragons, Emperor Swords, Pentacles, The Kingdom of the Cats*; the novel *Heart of Red Iron*; and a collection, *Son of the Morning and Other Stories*. In 1987, she also co-edited the second volume in the *Tesseracts* series of Canadian SF anthologies with Douglas Barbour.

EDO VAN BELKOM: It's been said by several people, that for a time you were Canadian science fiction. Did it ever feel like that?

PHYLLIS GOTLIEB: No, it just felt like being the alien. I was more like that person who wrote that questionable stuff, that Buck Rogers stuff, and it impinged on my general career as a poet or a respected literary figure.

VAN BELKOM: But while you were writing science fiction you did have quite a career as a poet. Do you think you would have gotten more notice as a poet if you hadn't been writing science fiction as well?

GOTLIEB: I might, but then I couldn't only write poetry. I needed prose the way you need bread sometimes and cake another time.

VAN BELKOM: The period in which you were the only SF writer in Canada, was that in the seventies or eighties?

GOTLIEB: I became a member of SFWA in 1965 when Damon Knight started it and you paid three bucks a year. I was one of two: there was William Bankier of Montreal, but he went into crime and detective stories or something like that. So, for a long time I was the only Canadian writer of science fiction in SFWA, and it was pretty lonely. I didn't know anybody else and a lot of my friends were poets who I'd met through tours as a poet or who were poets in college.

VAN BELKOM: Did any of that change after the publication of *Sunburst*?

GOTLIEB: No, not at all. Nothing changed. I never felt as if I had a science fiction community around me, so it's much better now. I think it probably started with Judy Merril coming in and stirring things up and that encouraged a lot of other writers to begin.

VAN BELKOM: There does seem to be a community now, one that practically grew up around you.

GOTLIEB: Some of them are young enough to be my grandchildren and I'm the oldest one. And that sets me apart more than I'd like. It puts a space between me and the others.

VAN BELKOM: There is a group of peers, but now there's generational gap.

GOTLIEB: My children are all in their forties and all the other writers are in their thirties and forties. Rob Sawyer I think must be in his thirties and he's done very well for himself; I never had my first novel published until I was thirty-eight. I was a very, very slow developer. I'm a very slow writer. It can take me three or four years to write a novel. I just finished a novella of over 16,000 words that took me a year and a half, so for a good part of the time I feel that, because I'm so slow and because I don't belong, I feel like I'm writing out into the darkness.

VAN BELKOM: I don't think you're the only writer who thinks their work is written and sent off into the void.

GOTLIEB: Well, I think I've got writers grump or something, the same as every other writer.

VAN BELKOM: I think it's safe to say that your career has been split: you've had a career as a poet and another as a science fiction writer.

GOTLIEB: I had a feeling that after a while the poetry would leave me as I got to be middle-aged, but instead of leaving me it got to be more science fictional and I wrote poetry on fantasy and science fiction subjects. And then it got into my novels, like the one that just got accepted (*Flesh and Gold*). The heroine is a poet, only she has scales and looks something like a dinosaur, a great big thing that writes these teeny weeny poems of nine syllables.

I invented a new form for her — I kind of like that.

VAN BELKOM: Some critics have said that you do a lot of clever word play in your poetry. Have you found that poetic style creeping into your fiction?

GOTLIEB: Oh yes. I feel it enlivens the fiction. Some of my critics have felt that I was just too clever for my own good . . . I don't think some of those people quite know how to read.

VAN BELKOM: In addition, they say that your work is cerebral.

GOTLIEB: There's others who think it's too sentimental and all that or too morbid or something.

VAN BELKOM: So when you get such a wide range of views, what's your assessment of reviewers and those who take a critical eye at your work?

GOTLIEB: In 1988 there was a Boreal (French Science Fiction

Conference) I attended, led by Élisabeth Vonarberg. There were a lot of French critics there and they did a lot of talking about how the job of the critic was to lead the writer in the way he should go, and I said I was damned if I was going to let anybody stand between me and my vision.

VAN BELKOM: Would it be fair to ask you which you enjoyed more, the poetry or the fiction writing? Each must have their own set of highs and lows, but which had the better highs and the lesser lows?

GOTLIEB: Well you could get a good high on poetry in a short time. It was something you put together word by word and it was an essence of the joy of creation, but the stories were things that nourished you like bread. It was an essential, the kind of thing I thought I needed to grow on.

VAN BELKOM: Did you always feel you needed to write? You talked about how you couldn't only write SF, that you needed to have poetry for yourself.

GOTLIEB: I write science fiction for myself, too, by putting all the care into it in a different mode than I do with the poetry.

VAN BELKOM: But did you always have the need to put the words down on paper?

GOTLIEB: Yes, from about age ten.

VAN BELKOM: Did you always want to be what you became.

GOTLIEB: Yes, yes. It took me an awful long time to do it, though. And I still feel like I'm learning. I remember the story about the Japanese artist Hokusai who was dying at eighty-nine and said, "Why do I have to die so early when I'm just learning."

VAN BELKOM: Did you have to push yourself? You said you were a slow developer. Was it because you weren't ready to sit down and do it, or were you afraid that you might fail?

GOTLIEB: My parents thought I was weird. My mother thought I'd never get married because I was so weird. In school I was the weird one. I went back for my fiftieth high school reunion and someone said to me, "Well you did what you wanted and you stuck to it." I never got a tremendously great academic record, either there or in university, because I had gone through everything before anybody else got to it.

VAN BELKOM: What drew you into science fiction?

GOTLIEB: I had a very bad period of general depression and I thought I'd never write again. My husband and I had just gotten married and he knew I had done a lot of writing and he said, "Well, why don't you try science fiction," him being a scientist.

And I said, "Oh I don't know anything like that," although I knew of science and was interested in it as a child. So I was interested and my husband said he would help me out if I needed it, and gradually I learned that I didn't have to write about science all the time.

VAN BELKOM: Did you not read SF as a child? Do you have any recollection of reading and loving comics or the pulp magazines?

GOTLIEB: My father was a theater manager and at the entrance to the building there was a candy store that sold *Black Mask* and *Doc Savage* and *Amazing Stories* and movie star magazines and comic books. At that time they didn't have returns — they just junked them — so I got to keep them. I read them all.

VAN BELKOM: Having read them all, and I assume reading voraciously in your youth, was that one of the reasons you were hesitant about writing SF?

GOTLIEB: Oh no, I had hoped to grow up and write detective stories, actually. I loved pulp literature. I went to the Saturday matinee — we were too poor to belong to a synagogue, and my father had to work on Saturday because my uncle was his boss . . . a real tyrant — and I went to the Saturday matinee the way other people would go to synagogue. I was a devotee of popular culture. I wanted it. And I never thought of myself as literary in the slightest degree. I wanted to write all about adventures and excitements.

VAN BELKOM: Having this wonderful experience of the genres in your youth, were you disappointed later when you were writing science fiction and there was this generally negative outlook on science fiction and science fiction writers?

GOTLIEB: Canadian culture was based on the Canada Cow, not so much now, but Canadians wanted to have a culture, a high culture rather than a popular culture which was what one got from the United States. And I think they tended to be snobbish, for all we had was Captain Canada, instead of Superman. I never meant to become only a genre writer. The poetry coming back was a surprise to me, because as soon as I started to try and write science fiction, the poetry came back, so I could write what was essentially high culture stuff and at the same time write genre fiction as well.

VAN BELKOM: But even in the science fiction field you would be looked upon as a more literary writer.

GOTLIEB: Yes, I can't help it. The love of words extends to it and I can't help being "exquisite." And I have about 350 people who love my work, so I never had really good sales.

VAN BELKOM: Have you ever wanted to write some whiz-bang adventure story and it always turned into something else?

GOTLIEB: All my stories are the whiz-bang adventure story I'd love to be reading.

VAN BELKOM: Apart from writing science fiction, have you participated in the other aspects of the genre, like conventions and Worldcons?

GOTLIEB: I mainly go to local cons. When I go to other ones they don't hardly know me. I like Ad Astra because it's homey. I only went to the Worldcon when it was in Toronto, and that was in the seventies.

I think I would be lost at some of them. I was amazed when I went to an authors/editors meeting in New York and people came up to me and say, "Oh, Phyllis Gotlieb, I just loved this or that."

VAN BELKOM: Well you've been at this long enough that people should know your name.

GOTLIEB: It's been thirty-six years, so yes.

VAN BELKOM: After thirty-six years writing science fiction are you able to be more critical of your own work in terms of what your strengths and weaknesses are as a writer?

GOTLIEB: Everything has been a learning process. I used to write awkwardly, sentimentally. I had a very good lesson when *Sunburst* was accepted as a serial by Cele Goldsmith at *Amazing*. It was originally 64,000 words and she wanted me to cut it to 60,000. Now I didn't know what to cut because I write very tight and I wanted every word to live.

But at that time there was a fad for "Swifty" jokes — you know, "I'm bored," she said piercingly, "I'm tired," she said flatly — because all the *Tom Swift* books had all those adverbs. So I started cutting out adjectives and adverbs and that was a wonderful lesson that many writers today would do well to learn.

And then the other thing that I learned was that when I had it published as a book, the editor wanted me to add 5,000 words because it was too tight and they thought it was hardly understandable and I had to put in material to pace it better.

VAN BELKOM: The collection that's just been published, *Blue Apes*, is your second collection, and has four stories from your first collection, *Son of the Morning*. Was the inclusion of those stories your idea or the publisher's?

GOTLIEB: Partly mine, partly Gerry Truscott, who was editing. He and I both thought they were stories that should be in there because they're so representative.

VAN BELKOM: So you've done others stories and you've just chose not to include them?

GOTLIEB: No, I haven't done many stories. I don't think I've done more than twenty-five stories all together. I'm slow. And, of course I'm a depressive too, so that doesn't make it easier.

VAN BELKOM: Do you wish you could write more, or faster?

GOTLIEB: Oh, to just sit down and go *tickity-tackety-tickity* on the keyboard would be the most wonderful dream. But I just sit there and sit there, and I'm lost in some kind of dream and I wake two hours later and if I find I've done 150 words, boy that's just wonderful. The most I ever did when I was really hot was maybe 4,000 words in a month.

VAN BELKOM: So that would explain the number of stories; but you must have had more ideas than you knew what to do with.

GOTLIEB: Uh-uh-uh (shakes head). No. I'd think of something then think, "Oh, but so-and-so did that." Then I'd get a wonderful idea and think, "Oh my god, you got that out of such-and-such a story." I'm very sensitive. It was H.L. Gold that forced that sensitivity on me because, for him, every single thing had to be an absolutely new idea. I started sending stuff to Galaxy in 1950 and it took me nine years of trying, from the first idea to the publishing of the story. And it wasn't Gold that accepted it. He found an agent for me but didn't accept my first story.

VAN BELKOM: Did you ever have a period where the will was there to write, but you had nothing to write about and you thought that you'd used it all up?

GOTLIEB: Yes, I had that before I wrote *Flesh and Gold*. And a \part of that was from it being so difficult to sell. It's not exactly encouragement, but I work well with a deadline. There's nothing like a deadline to speed me up.

VAN BELKOM: You did co-edit one of the *Tesseracts* volumes. What can you say about that experience and the kinds of stories you were receiving? Was there anything about the Canadian experience that you could shed light on?

GOTLIEB: Well, we tend to write more civilly, that's all I can think of. And then, of course, I read all the French stories in French, and French writers tend to write a lot longer, so there was a whole lot of 10,000 word stories. So that was a unique experience for me. And they have wonderful fantasy ideas which you just can't translate, and I had to let go a bunch of things that were just so odd they couldn't be translated. I felt we should have had more French stories in that, but I was surprised by the quality of the stories, and I've often seen that the stories I chose or asked for changes on have been chosen by other editors for anthologies, and that gave me more of a thrill.

VAN BELKOM: You've continued editing, working as the poetry editor at *Transversions*. Whose idea was that?

GOTLIEB: Mine. I heard they were looking for an editor and it's been a nice thing to do. I don't know how long they'll be able to keep publishing the magazine, but I've enjoyed it.

VAN BELKOM: What was your motivation behind that?

GOTLIEB: I needed something more to do. It's volunteer work. I've always respected and envied people who worked at a job and got money every Friday or every month or whatever. Except for a couple of summers that I worked for the Board of Education checking final exam papers, I've never worked regularly.

VAN BELKOM: Are you happy with the way things have gone? Are you happy with your career path, or if you could go back and do something different would you?

GOTLIEB: The only thing I wish I had done different was become a librarian instead of taking that useless M.A., but I really went to university to get the experience of learning and writing.

But in the first years of my writing, I accumulated a whole book of ancient and yellow clippings about Phyllis Gotlieb the "housewife poet." It makes me laugh, because at that time in the 1950s everybody was a Martha Stewart and I wasn't. And neighbors who came snickered at the dust on my furniture, but then afterwards they said, "Phyllis you had the right idea!"

Terence M. Green –

Terence M(ichael). Green's career has been characterized by strange turns and an assortment of peaks and valleys. For example, although his finely crafted short stories eventually came to be published with regularity in the top US magazines, they took a rather circuitous route getting there. Green's first short story, "Japanese Tea," was published in the Australian anthology *Alien Worlds* in 1979, while his story "Of Children in the Foliage" appeared in *Aurora: New Canadian Writing 1979*. It wasn't until 1981 that Green saw publication in the United States: "Til Death Do Us Part" was published in the December issue of *The Magazine of Fantasy and Science Fiction*.

Green's first novel, *Barking Dogs*, was sold to Blue Jay Books, only to languish when the publisher went out of business. The novel was then sold to St. Martin's Press and published in 1988 on the heels of a 1987 short story collection, *The Woman Who Is the Midnight Wind*, published by Lesley Choyce at Pottersfield Press. Green's entry into the American SF novel market seemed to be on strong footing until St. Martin's dropped their SF line. Green was once again without a publisher. His next novel, *Children of the Rainbow*, eventually found a home at McClelland & Stewart in 1992. Publication by a major mainstream Canadian publisher should have heralded a new age of Canadian published SF, but McClelland & Stewart declined Green's next book and he was yet again forced to find a new publisher.

By 1996 he had found a home at Tor Books, one of the premier SF houses and publisher of many Canadian authors. Green's Tor hardcovers include World Fantasy Award nominee *Shadow of Ashland* in 1996 and *Blue Limbo* (a sequel to *Barking Dogs*) in 1997. It is interesting to note that *Barking Dogs* and *Shadow of Ashland* are both expansions of two finely crafted tales: "Barking Dogs," which appeared in *The Magazine of Fantasy and Science Fiction* in May 1984, and "Ashland, Kentucky," published in *Isaac Asimov's Science Fiction Magazine* in November 1985.

Born in 1947, Green grew up and still lives in Toronto, teaching English at East York Collegiate Institute since 1968. He has a B.A. and B.Ed. from the University of Toronto and a M.A. in Anglo-Irish Studies from University College, Dublin.

EDO VAN BELKOM: Your first novel, *Barking Dogs*, was set in Toronto. Did you have to think about that or did it seem natural for you to set it there?

TERENCE M. GREEN: I live in Toronto; it was a natural place to set it. I think we like to read about places we know — we like to experience them in print — and I'm no different from anybody else that way. I've had people say to me, "I like to read about a car going up and down the Danforth." Why do we like that? It's some kind of a touchstone of familiarity of our world. Somebody has created our world in a fictional environment and this is fascinating.

As well as setting *Barking Dogs* in Toronto, I set *Shadow of Ashland* in Toronto and in Ashland (Kentucky); and in Ashland they loved the fact that it was set there. I think it was Updike who said that putting a place in a work of fiction is an act of praise, even if you're criticizing the place, because you have taken the time to try and get it right. And I think there's something to that.

VAN BELKOM: Does the same reasoning apply to *Children of the Rainbow*, a novel that features Canadian characters?

GREEN: I think it's very much not having an inferiority complex as a Canadian and realizing that our world is as interesting to outsiders as it can be to insiders. Toronto is as interesting as any place on the globe or as dull as any place on the globe, depending on the treatment you give it.

VAN BELKOM: Both *Barking Dogs* and *Shadow of Ashland* were expanded from short stories. Why that way, rather than starting with an all-new novel?

GREEN: It had to do with good feedback I had on those particular stories. In the case of "Barking Dogs," it was published in *The Magazine of Fantasy and Science Fiction* in May 1984 and I got a couple of good letters from other writers about it. This astonished me. And then, I was at the point where I wanted to write a novel and thought this was the one. So, I expanded what I had a good response to.

And then I took another direction on my second novel and wrote it from scratch. Then, I went back and did something else for another one and by the time I got around to *Shadow of Ashland* I had gotten a tremendous response to the story, "Ashland, Kentucky," from editors who let me know I had something special again in a way I hadn't quite been prepared for. So, in both cases I expanded what had been responded to positively. I still felt there was a good long story to tell.

There might be still much longer stories to tell. For instance, the character in *Barking Dogs* that I wrote the short story about is this cop who is having trouble with his personal life and his job, and I thought, who doesn't have problems with his personal life and their job? And then, when I wrote the novel, I expanded it so that the crisis in his personal life and his job and his family and his friend who died, they all became a bigger issue — and people responded to that. Now I've written another novel about the same character, *Blue Limbo*, and it's taken the guy further.

VAN BELKOM: Some of your early stories were published in Australia. How did that come about?

GREEN: It probably came about by me not knowing how to market stories. I was fascinated by the fanzine print world, and I subscribed to everything in the 1970s and was fascinated by reading it all. And when I wrote my first two stories, I sent one to *F&SF* I think, but I sent it in so poorly because I was a novice.

You know when people come up to you and ask you how to get published and you say you have to go through all the steps and make all the mistakes, and you learn by doing — I learned by doing.

Then I saw this ad in one of these fanzines for a guy who was asking for stories in Australia. It sounded quite exotic, so I sent it down there and it got published that way, almost by accident. And the irony is that once this fellow Paul Collins starting to publish my stuff, I thought great I'll publish there, I don't really care, I'm not trying to make a living at it. So I wrote another story and sent it to him, and he didn't want it, and I turned around and sold it to *F&SF*.

So, I didn't know how to market. I ended up with one in Canada in *Aurora: New Canadian Writing 1979* at the same time, so I was publishing in Australia, Canada, and the US, not knowing what I was doing.

VAN BELKOM: You began your career writing some very fine short stories, which were well received and appeared in the top magazines, but your production seemed to have stopped in the 1980s. Why was that?

GREEN: I've become more interested in the novel. It's a more complex, challenging form for me right now. But I have the best of intentions and I firmly believe I will write short stories again.

VAN BELKOM: You need more ideas for your novels?

GREEN: I need more time, too. Every writer says that, but I mean it because I juggle a full-time job and I have this quasi-plan, quasi-illusion that after I retire I'll be able to do more of everything in terms of writing as a second career. Right now, when I have time there's only one project that I can work at. And I actually have a publisher that is interested in my novels, so I'd like to supply them while the getting is good.

VAN BELKOM: You tend to write a lot about family, and I feel that a lot of your personal life makes its way into your work. Is writing in some way a means of catharsis?

GREEN: I don't know if catharsis is the right word, but there is some cathartic value in putting into a work of fiction a shadowy form of an anecdote or a situation that may have happened to you personally, structuring it so that it gives shape to the situation or commemorates it in some way. I admit to doing that, and a part of me knows that whatever books I'll be leaving behind will be some kind of unofficial family history of things that may have happened to me and or members of the family. No one's ever sure of how much of it is true, but that's okay. I want to deal with things that happen in my family because the older I get the more interested and obsessed I get with family and the passage of time.

VAN BELKOM: Does it make the writing more real for you?

GREEN: I think it makes it more meaningful for me. The book then becomes not just a construct that I think I did cleverly and that I take some superficial pride in. It has to say something about my life and my family's, and it becomes something I'm proud of having created, and I want it to have a life longer than mine. So in many ways I guess I'm an archivist for my family.

VAN BELKOM: What was the thing that first starting you writing?

GREEN: That's a question I don't know if anybody can fully answer. It's not so much that you start it as you were always going to do it, and you don't know why you were going to do it. I was always going to write and I don't know why.

I was always interested in stories and books when I was a little kid. Whatever gift I got at Christmas, the book was the most interesting one, even as a child and as a teenager.

VAN BELKOM: What first turned you on to science fiction?

GREEN: It was something I discovered in the library, probably the adventure story in general. As a kid I was interested in the adventure story, the fantastic story, the fabulous story, the fable, if you will. By age twelve I stumbled on Arthur Clarke and then up through age sixteen I devoured just about everything there was in the field.

So my life consists of reading and absorbing and talking about books. I'm teaching them now, and writing became a natural outflow. I always thought I was going to try to write, but there came a point in my mid-twenties that I thought, now is the time to try, to give it a shot.

It's not so much when you decide to do it, as much as what you are. You wonder why some people play piano, and it's because they sat down and took to it immediately. Or why is one of my sons playing baseball? — he took to it instantly. Why am I writing? — I took to it instantly. I took to books instantly. There is something in us — we hope we can all discover what that is and pursue it.

VAN BELKOM: You've gotten a lot of great reviews for your books, *Shadow of Ashland* in particular, but you've also gotten your share of poor, and even nasty, reviews. What's your take on the whole reviewing process as it relates to you the writer?

GREEN: As a writer, you write a book or work and you want it to be read and judged by what you tried to achieve and how well you achieved it. Just as there are strong writers and strong filmmakers, there are strong reviewers and weak ones — there are people who shouldn't be reviewing.

One of the things that fascinates me, in Canada especially, is how few reviewers at major periodicals and journals have any real concept on how to read a work of the fantastic. All over the US there are people teaching courses in SF and fantasy; even in Quebec there's all kinds of people who know an awful lot about it. But if you publish a book of SF in English-speaking Canada or it comes into Canada they tend to hand the book off to somebody who once read a science fiction book or who's always been a comic book fan. I find this flabbergasting when there are people they should seek out who understand this field.

A major reviewer in Toronto said in print, in the last few months, that an historical novel has a better chance at being literature than a science fiction novel because one deals with things that have happened and the other deals with things that have happened only in that author's head. This is the take.

So, though I think reviewing is an interesting process, you have to understand who's writing the reviews. The danger is that, in a confined market like Canada, if you don't win over the Toronto market, this can kill a book. This is the danger because it's too small a market and this (Toronto) is too big a pond.

I like to think that if somebody is going to review a book, they should have some experience writing in that field, have some sympathy as to what's going on in the field, and have a track record, as opposed to just being handed a book. I would hate like hell to be handed an historical romance to review when I have no feel for it.

VAN BELKOM: Of all the writers I know, your career seems to be the one that's on the giant roller-coaster. Has it felt that way to you and how do you rebound from a publisher going out of business with your book still scheduled, or a publisher dropping one of your books?

GREEN: I hadn't really thought about it till you said it, but I think you might be right, and it may be the story of my life actually, as opposed to just my publishing.

VAN BELKOM: Well, when McClelland & Stewart published *Children of the Rainbow*, you'd think that there'd be no better place an SF writer in Canada could be than with one of Canada's largest publishers. It was the pinnacle, and then . . .

GREEN: They wanted no more.

VAN BELKOM: No more Terry Green books and we all wondered what happened. You were supposed to open up the door and we were all supposed to follow your lead.

GREEN: Well, I'm just as surprised as you are and just as flabbergasted by most of the things that have happened to me, and it's sort of colored my philosophy of life. But my personal life has been like that too sometimes. Things have happened to me that have just flabbergasted me, things that I had no control over. Sometimes I feel like a guy flying a plane that's going down, and I'm pulling on all the controls, but it's going to go down anyway.

What amazes me, as you say, is that I survive the crashes and

I get up, dust myself off and then I go again. I think it's the nature of the business. It's a very volatile, rollercoaster type business. I probably am a very unusual writer to have had this happen to me. Sometimes I can't believe it's happened to me so many times.

I think, hopefully, I've gotten onto a more level plane in the last few years, but I don't know. I got to the point where I started saying to myself, I'll believe it when I see it. Somebody says to me, "Your latest book is being made into a movie," I say, "I'll believe it when I see it." Although I'd like it to happen, I'm very cautious about celebrating what may or may not happen in this business.

VAN BELKOM: I always say I'll believe something's in print when I have the book in my hand.

GREEN: I think it's a good way to be in this business because you can become . . . I don't know if shattered is the word. But if I had done this for a living I probably would have gone and done something else by now after my personal experiences. And that's happened to a lot of people. There's probably a lot of reasonable writers who have drifted into something more sane because this business is too volatile.

VAN BELKOM: After a lot of ups and downs, and with a good and secure job to pay the bills, what is the thing that keeps you writing? You're in it for presumably the pleasure of it, yet it doesn't always come through, so what is the thing that keeps you going?

GREEN: Isn't that a mystery? That's why I believe some of us are born to write and some of us are born to play the piano. And if you can play the piano and you don't, then you're doing something wrong. Well, I can write, so if I don't do it I'm wasting myself.

It's almost freedom not to be confined to the success or the money tied into the book. I'll write a book and if it works great, if it doesn't work I'm still going to write the next book. Now I want my books published. If I wrote four or five books that didn't get published, I might stop. I'm not a guy who just wants to write because I love the actual mechanics of writing. I like getting published. I actually like my books. I like to see them, I like to have them, I like them out there. I like people reading them, I like the response I get to them. I like to have this kind of feedback. I like to think I've achieved something that is difficult to achieve.

VAN BELKOM: You say you like being published and you like your books. How satisfying is it to have a book given the type of packaging

— and one could almost say "Special Book" packaging — that *Shadow of Ashland* received in hardcover — and to have the publishers so enthusiastic about its publication. It must have been very gratifying.

GREEN: That's a good word for it. It was tremendously gratifying. It made me think that finally I have done something that has worked. I can't guarantee what its sales are going to be; I can't do anything other than what I've done. I will write it; I will help them promote it; I will do whatever I can. Whether it's read or not is out of my control, but I've done the best I can.

Now the packaging of the thing is, in my opinion, quite marvelous and quite, quite satisfying. Tremendously gratifying. I sometimes look at it and think that even if I don't write another book, then at least I got that one out.

VAN BELKOM: So now with your career path, you've got this tremendous high.

GREEN: Well, you know the irony of it is that you have to do it again or the high goes. You ask why you're writing. I don't know. It is a tremendous high and I want it again, and I want it again, and I want it again. So you strive for it. Certainly there's some ego involved in all this that is difficult to analyze. I don't pretend to have it all pinned down, but I'm not stupid enough to think there is no ego in this. There's lots of ego in this.

But I also have a strong ego and I have achievements in other areas of my life that are quite fulfilling, but what this whole thing does is tell me that creating a book is something that is a remarkable achievement for anyone. And to do it well so that people admire and enjoy it is tremendously gratifying.

VAN BELKOM: How much research did you have to do to go from "Ashland, Kentucky," to *Shadow of Ashland*?

GREEN: I did a good amount of research and I did the kind of research to tell the story properly. As soon as I decided to set a major part of the story in the 1930s, I realized I didn't know enough about the 1930s, so I went down to the public library.

I read all kinds of books and made notes, and I did this for quite a while. But such things as the Battle of Toledo in 1934 wasn't a common thing and I read about that in a history of labor. And it just dovetailed perfectly with my story because Jack Radey had gone through Toledo about that time, so I used it.

VAN BELKOM: There's no excuse not to do the research?

GREEN: That's absolutely right. This is background and milieu. I wasn't writing about the Battle of Toledo, I was writing about what happened to a character who would get caught in that and what it would do to a young man who got on the wrong side.

VAN BELKOM: Where is Terry Green today? Is he a literary writer, a Canadian writer, a science fiction writer?

GREEN: I like to think of myself as all three of those things, since you've given me the tags. I don't have a tag for myself, so when I heard them I thought, yeah I'd accept any one of those.

VAN BELKOM: Do you consider yourself a professional writer or an amateur or a hobbyist?

GREEN: I consider myself to be a professional. I just don't think I'm a very efficient professional in terms of accruing funds. Some people are professionals — they're bookkeepers in their minds. I'm not a bookkeeper in my mind, and if I was I would probably be much more "successful" in this business. But I am a professional in that each book that I write is an all-consuming professional effort.

VAN BELKOM: Was there a time you wanted to be a full-time writer?

GREEN: Yes, I think so. That is something that I honestly would have liked to have tried, but it wasn't in the cards and was probably unrealistic. I explained to you earlier how I didn't know what I was doing at the beginning of my career, and I think that when we want these things we usually don't know what's involved.

So probably when I wanted it, I wasn't capable of it. I will be a full-time professional writer within the next decade — I believe that firmly because my teaching tenure will run out in terms of retirement and at that point I'll be moving toward a second career.

VAN BELKOM: Despite only a small number of books published, you've achieved a lot in your career — a short story collection, hardcovers, Canadian mainstream publication. What's the next thing you'll be shooting for?

GREEN: I want to try and write another book that I want to write, that is very personal and important to me and that's going to be a novel of character and situation, as opposed to plot. I want to write a longer novel in which I write the best book that I can. That's my next ambition, my next level of intended achievement.

Ed Greenwood

Most fans of traditional fantasy might not be familiar with the name Ed Greenwood, despite the fact that he is likely one of the best-selling fantasy authors in Canada.

That's because Greenwood writes novels for TSR, the Seattle-based gaming company that introduced the world to role-playing games and their ever-popular Dungeons and Dragons.

But while some might discount gaming tie-in authors as hacks writing in other people's worlds, that stigma doesn't apply to Greenwood because the gaming universe he writes in is the very same one he created. Greenwood sold TSR his Forgotten Realms campaign in 1986 and since then has written countless gaming modules, supplements, adventures, novels, and short stories in the world of the Realms. In just over ten years, the Forgotten Realms has become TSR's best-selling product line, with copy sales in the tens of millions. In addition to gaming material, Greenwood also writes numerous articles and columns for such gaming magazines as *The Campaign Hack, Cryptych, Polyhedron,* and *Dragon.*

TSR published Greenwood's first Forgotten Realms novel, *Spellfire,* in 1987. It was followed by a sequel, *Crown of Fire,* in 1994. That year also saw the publication of Greenwood's first hardcover novel, *Elminster: The Making of a Mage,* which chronicled the life of his most popular character. In 1995 TSR published The Shadow of the Avatar trilogy, *Shadows of Doom, Cloak of Shadows,* and *All Shadows Fled. Stormlight* and the hardcover novel *Cormyr* (co-written with Jeff Grubb) appeared in 1996, followed in 1997 by another hardcover, *Elminster in Myth Drannor.*

Greenwood's novels make regular appearances on the bestseller lists of *The New York Times, Chicago Tribune, Wall Street Journal, USA Today,* and *Locus.* How well do Greenwood's books sell? Well, his first hardcover novel, *Elminster: The Making of a Mage,* was delivered to bookstores on Boxing Day in 1994, and sold out almost all of its 75,000 print run by the end of the year!

Born in 1959, Greenwood grew up in North York and now lives on a farm near Colborne, Ontario — with a collection of some 40,000 books — and still works full-time as a library clerk.

EDO VAN BELKOM: You're probably best known as the designer of the Forgotten Realms. How did you start designing game settings?

ED GREENWOOD: I was an avid fantasy reader in my youth and round about 1967 I started writing terribly bad sword and sorcery short stories along the lines of Fritz Leiber's "Fafhred and Grey Mouser" stories I'd read in *Fantastic* magazine. I liked the way they were episodes in the same world, so that although the author didn't stop the action to explain any geography, if you paid attention they each added little bits to the world, so the world built up in color while the action was flowing along. I liked that, and I started doing that for my own stories.

Dungeons and Dragons wasn't yet on the market — it came along in 1974 and I didn't see it until 1975. Now the first D&D was sort of like, "Let's make up a story as we go along and argue about what happens." It was a great idea, but the execution wasn't there. In 1978, the *Monster Manual* came out taking all the familiar monsters of literature, vampires and dragons and so on, and quantifying them so you knew which was more powerful and exactly what they did. I liked this because I always felt uneasy when a fantasy author would have a dragon with a power that you didn't know about until the climax of the story. And the *Players Handbook* was a magic system in the same way, telling you exactly what spells you could do, so a wizard couldn't just "Poof!" do whatever he wanted. There were limitations built into the system, and this immediately made magic-users human, as in having drawbacks.

So I switched all the things in my settings to match D&D and I went on writing stories. At the same time (1979), I was writing D&D articles for *Dragon Magazine* and TSR got to the point where they wanted a new fantasy world for the second edition of the Advanced Dungeons and Dragons game. I had already been sneaking background lore into all of my *Dragon* articles because it made them more colorful. So, that's how I started the fantasy setting.

Ed Greenwood

VAN BELKOM: How did this fantasy setting come to be purchased and taken over by TSR?

GREENWOOD: Well, when TSR wanted to revamp Advanced Dungeons and Dragons, they wanted to have a fantasy world setting for it. The original D&D world was the world of Greyhawk, and Greyhawk was large, sprawling and had one main difficulty — its creator was also the owner of TSR at the time. The difficulty was, as anyone who has tried to do too many things at once will tell you, you can't run a company, be a game designer, and be a novel writer all at the same time and do a good job. And as a result, Gary Gygax, the gentleman in question, was the bottleneck. Stuff about the world that fans were asking for wasn't getting published — literally for years. And when you're talking about game things, it's not the same as an avid reader waiting to find out what happens next. In gaming terms, you sometimes can't continue the game in a certain geographical area until some details are published about it.

So they wanted to come out with a complete world. They had designed the world of Dragonlance, but that had taken all their designers a couple of years and it was an epic tale in the way that *Lord of the Rings* is — Good vs. Evil, good wins and we save the world. What do you do for an encore?

They needed a world with more breadth than that, a world in which there were merchants and the caravan routes were all worked out and that explained why there were mountains here and why the dragons lived there . . . And they needed all that in a hurry, and it was easier to find one and buy it rather than start all over again. One of the people at TSR, Jeff Grubb, read *Dragon* regularly and he called me up and basically said, "Do you make this stuff up as you go along, or do you really have pages and pages of background lore of an incredibly detailed fantasy world?"

And I said, "Yes, and Yes. I do make it up as I go along and I do have all this stuff piled up."

He said, "Good, send it."

VAN BELKOM: Did you relinquish your world?

GREENWOOD: Yes. The way TSR, and in fact the way all gaming companies work, is that in order to control the game creatively and continue to bring out supplements and change its direction to be what the people playing it want it to be — and all games are dynamic things or they die — the company has to have creative control over it, so it was understood from the beginning that they would be buying the world, lock, stock and wizard, as they put it.

Now you can say, "That isn't fair." Well, maybe not, but I knew the deal going in so I'm happy because my fantasy world, known only to a few friends, would have stayed that way. This way it has become huge with lots of people writing in it, lots of Forgotten Realms products, known internationally; I get to go all over the world. It's great fun because I said, "Yes."

VAN BELKOM: My question was going to be, how much material did you contribute to the Forgotten Realms before you wrote your first novel set in it, but I guess the short answer is, all of it.

GREENWOOD: Pretty well all of it. The first novel I wrote in the Forgotten Realms was *Spellfire*. It was published in 1988, written in 1987. Throughout 1986 I was literally photocopying, typing or hand-writing things as fast as I could and sending it off to TSR. That went on for a year until they said, "Enough, enough!"

Since then, I've written tons of supplements, and so have lots of other people, basically responding to customer demand — what the fans wanted to find out more about. If there are characters they find very intriguing, we do stuff about them.

I was very clear in my original game that I wanted this to be adult — and I don't mean adult as in sex oriented, I mean adult as in complex — with intrigues going on and power groups, so there was enough depth to the campaign so it would in effect tell its own stories. So instead of me as the game master being like a fantasy author saying, "This happens and then this happens and then this happens and you're coming along for the ride," I'd say, "Okay, what do you want to do? Where do you want to go?"

Therefore, the world was there at a level of detail before I ever wrote a novel about it.

VAN BELKOM: Was *Spellfire* the first Realms novel?

GREENWOOD: No. The first Realms novel was *Darkwalker on Moonshae* by Douglas Niles. Doug Niles had been preparing a Celtic campaign of his own to sell to TSR and had done so. And what happened is they took my *Moonshae Isles* and set his campaign on those islands. As a result we got what became the second Forgotten Realms game supplement and the first three novels, all by Doug.

Which was fine by me because the whole idea of the Realms was that it would be broad and have different flavors to it. It would not be a one-note story, so to start right off with other people writing in it was okay.

VAN BELKOM: All your novels are set in the Forgotten Realms, as well as those by many other people. Is that part of the plan you started out with, that it was big enough so that everybody could contribute to it?

GREENWOOD: Well, it was TSR's plan in the beginning that it was supposed to be a shared world, and I had no problems with it.

As most North American males of my age, I grew up reading comics, and if you read comics, particularly the ones published by Marvel, the Universe hung together. There were times when things were very unbelievable — people you thought had died when they fell off cliffs suddenly reappeared alive again and there was some pretty fast explaining to do — but the point is they went to the trouble to explain it. In the same way, the Realms is supposed to dovetail so people don't die in one book and reappear without any explanation in the next. It's all supposed to be real life: I don't mean that we're all nuts and we think it's real, I mean we treat it with the respect that a reporter in the real world would, checking his facts before printing a news story. So yeah, there have always been lots of people at work. Last count there were over sixty people who have either adventures or short stories or novels published in the Realms, and to that you can add all the unofficial ones published in the magazines.

VAN BELKOM: You write as much or more non-fiction and gaming material as you do novels. How much of a difference is there to the two kinds of writing?

GREENWOOD: As a matter of fact, and I know most writers are going to laugh at this, but writing fiction is a lot easier. A fiction piece has to hang together as a story, it has to be self-consistent. If it's set in the Realms, it has to be consistent with the agreed upon facts. You do have to check those. But when you're doing game writing for AD&D, it is like writing a legal brief, everything has to be checked against the previously published sources, so it's a lot more work.

Now, it's more fun for me to write fiction. But I can take great pride at the end of the day when I sit back and take a look at *Volo's Guide to Everything Magical* and it's full of how these spells work, how you prepare for this, and the mighty artifacts that have been around the Realms for thousands of years. I can sit back and say, "Yeah, that's well done. That's useful. Other people can use this and they can tell more than one story." Regardless of how great, or bad, my latest novel is, it's one story. If I click with someone, they can read it over and over again and enjoy it, but it is the same story. You can say "What if?", but in D&D you can create that "What if?" for yourself. You can change the plot, you can add something, you can go beyond where the book ends.

So, game-specific writing has to be very carefully crafted. And like all writing, some are great, some are not-so-great. I try to keep mine in the good category.

VAN BELKOM: You seem to write very quickly. What's the quickest you've written one of your novels?

GREENWOOD: There is a novel sitting at my house right now called *The Mercenaries;* it will be part of a long series. I wrote the first draft of the novel in one day. That was 20,000 words so that was not a heavy-duty novel. And I will revise it in one day, because that will be all the time I will have.

The fastest big novel that I've written, *Elminster: The Making of a Mage*, was written in eight days, first draft. It was revised over a month, but the month is really another eight days — four weekends. So, in effect that's a sixteen-day book.

In terms of how quickly could I write a novel, I don't set out for it to be a race. It's usually because scheduling forces me into this and there are certain things you can't do when you're writing at top speed. I can't go into that much detail and intrigue. I have to keep moving. I don't do it to be in a race, it's just that this previous year, 1995, I wrote eleven books for TSR. I hoped to have a far more sedate pace this year, but we're up over seven already.

VAN BELKOM: If you're so busy writing, and obviously making what for most people would consider a good living at it, why do you continue on with your full-time job?

GREENWOOD: Well, the practical reason is that my wife works for the library as well and the same sort of time would be taken up by the commuting. If I were to give it up tomorrow I'd still be driving in and out of the city each day, since my wife and I each drive both ways; she drives in the morning and I drive home at night after dark.

But from my point of view, number one, things wouldn't settle down, and number two, I love working at the library. I've been working at the library for twenty-two years now and working there has two advantages. There's the cheap personal writer's advantage. If you want to look up something, it's there. The other thing is the human contact. Because I have to work as a clerk, checking in and out books and finding books for people, I meet both old friends on a repeated basis and new people — hundreds of people each day.

Now, yes that's wearing, but it's also like fresh air for the writer, new blood. You're never at a loss for what someone looks like because there's always someone new coming in the door.

VAN BELKOM: But certainly at some point it will all be too much.

GREENWOOD: Oh yeah, it is getting harder than when I was younger. Everybody always thinks of themselves as being the same age. The world flows past them and they're always themselves. But yeah, some things just aren't as much fun as they used to be because I just don't have the energy to do them.

I never was the kind of university student who pulled all-nighters. When I go to conventions, some of the people look upon them as a party because that's what they do at conventions. So at 11:30 in the evening they're just raring to go out drinking and do stuff while I'm looking for my bed.

I mean financially I don't have to keep working for the library, no. I'm sure Revenue Canada would like me to keep working for the library so they can take more. (laughs)

VAN BELKOM: Do you have a fear that it might all end, or be otherwise beyond your control?

GREENWOOD: There are no guarantees; it's built in, it's understood. In gaming, most things have a short life cycle. On the other hand, to keep a registered trademark, at least in America, you have to publish something every five years to defend the trademark to keep it yours. But the Realms has been unusual in this, its longevity has surprised the people in the industry.

So yes, each book could be the last, and that's another reason you don't give up the day job. But I would think that even if the Realms finished as something that is published, the fans would keep it alive forever; and now that we have the Internet, there's no way to stop them.

Ed Greenwood publishing Realms novels, stories, and supplements at a frenetic pace, yes, that will come to an end and probably not too far off now. I will miss it.

VAN BELKOM: How does it make you feel when someone like R.A. Salvatore is phenomenally successful writing in a world which you created?

GREENWOOD: That's fine. In fact, I read the manuscript for his first book, *The Crystal Shard*. The folks at TSR sent the novel my way and told me to read it and fix anything that was out of whack, because, guess what, there's only one living expert on the Realms, or there was then because TSR hadn't developed its own yet. So I read it and said, "Change this, change that, and it's fine. The guy's a storyteller. Publish it."

It doesn't bother me. I'm a good friend of Bob. And I think, arguably, Bob's novel *Homeland* is probably the best Forgotten Realms novel ever written. And even though the language is simpler than some fantasy classics, I don't think Forgotten Realms authors have to be ashamed or think this isn't real fantasy, because it's storytelling. It's phenomenally successful storytelling and hundreds of thousands of readers are into this who otherwise might not have picked up a fantasy book.

Am I jealous of someone else? No! It helps us all. Goodness knows, with this new generation of kids — and I hate to say that because I sound like an old fogey — the only thing they read is the instructions on how to make the CD-ROM work, or how to hook up their VCR to do something my VCR can't. And then they stop reading the instructions and start watching, or pushing buttons.

Anything that gets them reading is something I'm in favor of. So if somebody else is a great success, that's great, I want that!

The only thing that bothers me in the small sense, it annoys me when teachers and academics pooh-pooh fantasy and science fiction as not being real writing. Now, if they're going to hold up Robertson Davies as an example of great writing, I won't dispute it with them, but at the same time to say, "Who's Ed Greenwood, I've never heard of him?" To which, you can if you wish, reply, "Well, he outsells Robertson Davies."

To a literati, that doesn't mean anything to them, but to a publisher, it does mean something to them. And that's something I'm glad of — not because I want to outsell Robertson Davies; I don't care one way or another — but because it means that people are reading.

VAN BELKOM: You've done so well in the Realms universe, but you haven't made any attempt to move outside of it the way Margaret Weis and Tracy Hickman have. Is that something you'd like to do someday?

GREENWOOD: All sorts of people have come up to me at Gencon and other events and said, "Wouldn't it be nice . . ." or "We'd like you to do a novel for us . . ." and I say, "Sure, when I have time. Get in touch with me," but they never do. That's okay with me because, from my point of view, I'm just so busy.

I hear stories about writers who can't get a contract, and I know writers like that are going to be furious hearing me be glib about it, but I'd like to know how to you find some time between contracts. I've never had that problem; my problem has always been time.

Now, TSR doesn't own me. I could publish with anybody I wanted to, but nobody else has come calling and I haven't had the time. On the other hand, if I was going to change the way I do things now, if I was going to change the arrangement with TSR, I would want to have the artistic control that I can't have at TSR and I would want to have the time to do things. In other words, I would want to be treated like a big-name author. Now a publisher might say you don't have a track record outside the Realms and they might not want to do that. It might flop.

Well, yes, that's the risk. On the other hand, I am the Realms. The track record of the Realms is my track record. I wouldn't want to do it just to start off with a first novel contract and have them not bother promoting it.

The one time I approached people was the launch of the Viking Canada line. They published *Tigana* (by Guy Gavriel Kay) and announced they were going to publish stuff. So I called them up to see if they were interested since, after all, I'm a Canadian fantasy author. When I called and asked if they wanted me to do a novel, they said, "Well, who are you?" and I said, "My name's Ed Greenwood and I've published this, this, and this . . ." and they said, "Oh, I've never heard of that," which was not reassuring. The woman on the line knew little about fantasy literature and nothing about the publishers and classic fantasy novels and stock story elements I cited.

But I was so busy doing work for TSR I didn't go home crushed. I just thought, okay, I've got another four novels here I have to work on. And I went on with them, and it's basically gone on like that ever since.

If somebody comes up and says, "Mr. Greenwood, stop whatever you're doing. Here's $4.5 M, and we're paying the taxes on it for you. Go away and write the fantasy masterpiece." I would say, "Yes!" Believe it or not, you could twist my rubber arm.

Tanya Huff

Tanya Huff was born in Halifax, Nova Scotia, in 1957, and although she spent very few years in the port city, she says the experience left a lasting impression on her. "Although I haven't actually lived 'down east' since just before my fourth birthday, I still consider myself a Maritimer. I think it's something to do with being born in sight of the ocean. Or possibly with the fact that almost no one admits to being from Ontario . . ."

Huff grew up in Kingston, Ontario, and must have felt the ocean calling her as she spent three years in the Canadian Naval Reserve, an experience, she points out, that never got her out to sea but left her with no tattoos.

Like another northern dreamer, Robert J. Sawyer, her education consists of a degree in Radio and Television Arts from Ryerson Polytechnical Institute (now university), and like Sawyer and fantasy writer Michelle West, she also worked at Bakka Books in Toronto, the oldest surviving science fiction book store in North America. She spent eight years there, most as manager, and during that time she wrote many of her subsequent novels and short stories, several of which were published under the name T.S. Huff.

Her first novel, *Child of the Grove*, was published by DAW in 1988 and was followed by a sequel, *The Last Wizard*, and two standalone fantasy novels, *Gate of Darkness, Circle of Light* (set in and around the University of Toronto) and *The Fire's Stone*. Then followed the successful Blood series of fantastic mysteries set in Canada and featuring former policewoman Victoria Nelson and her sometimes partner, the 450-year-old vampire Henry Fitzroy. The series includes *Blood Price, Blood Trail, Blood Lines, Blood Pact,* and *Blood Debt*. After the contemporary fantasy of the Blood series, Huff returned to more heroic fantasy with the Quarter series, comprised of *Sing the Fourth Quarter, Fifth Quarter,* and *No Quarter*. Huff also did a single novel for TSR, set in their Ravenloft universe, entitled *Scholar of Decay*.

She currently lives in Prince Edward County, Ontario with four cats and fantasy writer Fiona Patton (*The Stone Prince*), in a house whose location she describes as being "just south of the middle of nowhere."

EDO VAN BELKOM: You've written many different kinds of fantasy, from high fantasy with your most recent series, to urban fantasy with *Gate of Darkness, Circle of Light* . . . and dark fantasy with the Blood series of books. What differences have you found between the three and how much more difficult, or easy, are they to write?

TANYA HUFF: To begin, I wouldn't say that I write high fantasy. High fantasy for me is much more archetypal than what I do — I see it as a broad canvas involving the continuing battle between good and evil, whereas my books are very tightly character focused. The only time I ever actually used the good/evil theme was in *Gate of Darkness, Circle of Light* and that was very definitely a contemporary fantasy. Unfortunately, I'm not sure what I would call the non-contemporary books. They're not heroic fantasy — too much talking, not enough hitting — nor are they, except in a broad sense, quest fantasy. I could cope with Romantic fantasy if we all understood that we were using "Romantic" in its historical sense. Since that's not likely to happen, lets just call them non-contemporary fantasy and leave it at that.

I enjoy writing both the contemporary and non-contemporary books and I couldn't actually say that I like one better than the other. Although, as I've said before, at least with the contemporary, you don't have to invent the expletives. It's important to remember that one "Damn it!" creates an entire theology.

In contemporary fantasy, you get to toss in one little thing, say the existence of magic or vampires, and watch the ripples of change spread. I love working out just how to make that extreme possibility real in the world-as-we-know-it. With non-contemporary fantasy, however, you have the joy of creating an entire world to support the story you want to tell. The biggest difference is that the infrastructure — physical and cultural — is already there with a contemporary plot so that the pre-writing research only concerns specifics, whereas with the other you're starting from scratch. But it's really two sides of the same coin because the important point is that both worlds, the not-quite-ours and the never-has-been, have to be completely believable if you're asking the reader to suspend disbelief over other things.

Adding the darker elements is definitely easier on a contemporary stage because the characters share cultural beliefs and terrors with the reader. *Gate of Darkness, Circle of Light* was in many ways as dark as the Blood books — some of the scenes in the shadow realm are as horrific as any I've written. The largest difference there was that the dark elements were not the elements advancing the plot.

VAN BELKOM: What writers had the most influence on you and your work in each of the three fantasy subgenres you work in — contemporary, non-contemporary, and dark fantasy?

HUFF: Funny you should ask that; I just gave a talk on "influences." The way that I've been influenced by other writers can't, however, really be broken into those kind of categories — it's been more an influence across the board. For short stories, I look to Robert Heinlein. While his longer works are, well, longer, his short stories are gems, beautifully self-contained. For mood, I look to Tanith Lee. I'm not always certain what she's saying, but she says it so well, it doesn't matter. There are times when her words seem to rise off the page like smoke. For humor, Terry Pratchett. If you can't laugh at Pratchett, you're probably dead. For pacing, Georgette Heyer. No one moves a plot along quite the way she does.

And then there's "A Thousand Deaths," a story by Orson Scott Card. I read it when it first came out in *Omni* in December of 1978. It's about a man tried by a conquering evil empire for treason and made to say, in front of a media audience that he was wrong and the empire wasn't evil after all. The audience doesn't believe him, so he's put to death, his soul moved into a clone body, and he goes through it again and again. For years, although I'd forgotten the title and about ninety percent of the plot, I remembered the climax. This poor guy's been killed so many times, he just doesn't care any more — there's a wonderful line about him hastening death, thrashing around to attract the sharks — and the next time he has to give his speech in front of the cameras, he tells them what he actually believes. And corrupts all but three members of the audience. When you tell the truth, people know it.

Now I read a lot of other authors — I'm a huge fan of Charles de Lint — but those are the people who've actually influenced my writing. I don't, by the way, read in the sub-genre I'm writing in from the time I sell the book until I finish it. It's just too easy to be, shall we say, "influenced."

VAN BELKOM: Your third novel, *Gate of Darkness, Circle of Light*, was set in Toronto, as were all four of the Blood series of books. Although it's a fantastic city, Toronto is not exactly familiar territory for fantasy novels. Was the decision to set the books in Toronto a hard one to make, or was it even a question in your mind?

HUFF: It was never a question in my mind. The idea for the book came from two things: the first was the old belief that "simple" people are aware of things that others are not, and the second was geography. Everything I needed in order to tell the story in *Gate* was in Toronto — why should I go anywhere else? Now for the Blood books, I moved around a bit more. *Price* and *Lines* were in Toronto, but *Trail* was set just outside London (the working title for *Blood Trail* was *A Canadian Werewolf in London, Ontario*) and *Pact* is set in and around Queen's University in Kingston. The new book that I've just handed in, *Blood Debt*, is set in Vancouver. For the record, my publisher, DAW Books Inc., based in New York City, never once suggested or even hinted that I should use an American city. In fact, my editor commented (although it may not have been in reference to one of the Blood books) that American readers find Canadian locations exotic.

VAN BELKOM: When you lived in Toronto, you were manager at Bakka, the oldest continuously operating science fiction specialty book store in North America. Did that experience, especially getting to know the people who actually read SF, help you at all in terms of your writing?

HUFF: Yes, it did. Although it wasn't getting to know the people so much — I had, after all hung around with SF readers most of my life — as seeing just what exactly they (as a demographic entity) were reading. I saw what books sold well and why, I saw what plots had been done three thousand times and when you could get away with doing them again, and I saw just how loyal SF readers are to writers they believe in. Also, working at Bakka helped in one other very important way — I read all the time. When I was being interviewed for the job, John Rose, the owner, said employees were expected to read at least one new title a week. Well, my response to that was, "Only one?" Given access, I can easily be a book a day reader — and reading is a crucial part of writing.

I've always really liked Asimov's three rules of writing. "Read. Read more. Don't give up your day job."

VAN BELKOM: In addition to working as a bookstore manager, you also did three years of military service in the Canadian Naval Reserve. How did that experience prepare you for your later career as a writer?

HUFF: I come from a military family — both parents, both grand-fathers, one great-grandfather — so my time in the reserve managed to be both a unique time and a traditional experience. I loved almost every minute of it, but as far as preparing me for a career as a writer, I'd say it had no more effect than any other time of my life. Everything is grist for the mill. Every experience gets filed away to be used later — I'm guessing that's the biggest reason for divorce among writers. There you are in the middle of an intense personal situation and this little voice in the back of your head is muttering, "Man, this is great stuff, I've got to remember it."

VAN BELKOM: One final question about your formulative years. You spent time as a member of a Toronto writers workshop called "The Bunch of Seven," a group which included the likes of S.M. Stirling, Karen Wehrstein, Shirley Meier, and Marian Hughes. Writers usually have two views about workshops — they're either highly beneficial, or simply a case of the blind leading the blind. On which side of the fence do you fall on?

HUFF: The Bunch of Seven was an interesting experience. It was, in many ways, more an emotional support group than a a writer's workshop. At the risk of being cliché, writing is a lonely business and at some point in the process before the checks start coming in, we all need some positive reinforcement.

More important that positive reinforcement, however, is having a first reader who can tell you when what you've just done is crap. Now, eventually most writers learn to look at their work objectively, but, in the beginning, it's hard to accept that every word you put on paper isn't holy writ. Unfortunately, the Bunch was never very good at that kind of criticism.

I did find it useful, however, to have an externally applied discipline, in that something had to be finished and read every month; but it didn't actually affect the quality or style of my writing. So, I guess you could say, they can be a highly beneficial case of the blind leading the blind.

One would assume that living with another writer, Fiona Patton (*The Stone Prince*, DAW, 1997), I'd have a built-in first reader and so, for that matter, would she. Unfortunately, it doesn't work that way. We're both so busy that, although we manage to read specific scenes when asked, we just don't have the time to follow each other's work.

VAN BELKOM: You mentioned your publisher before, DAW Books. With the exception of a commissioned novel for TSR, DAW has published all of your book-length work to date. Since it's uncommon these days for a writer to stay with one house through a career, I'm wondering why you haven't tested the publishing waters with some of your more recent books?

HUFF: There's no reason why I should. I'm very happy with DAW. I like and respect the people, I like and respect their policies, I like and respect the way Sheila Gilbert, my editor, handles my work. They're continually willing to take a chance on new authors, stick with them, support them, and keep publishing them until they gain a readership. They're one of the few companies who keep an author's backlist in print and they have never, that I know of, turned down a request for help. While I'm willing to publish with other companies — and I certainly had fun writing *Scholars of Decay* for TSR — any gain I might make by actually going to another company for the bulk of my work would be completely offset by what I'd lose in leaving DAW.

VAN BELKOM: What was it like writing a work-for-hire novel — working within someone else's established universe — after publishing eight or nine of your own books.

HUFF: As I said, I had a lot of fun writing *Scholar of Decay*. I've been a gamer since the old D&D days — yes, before AD&D — and writing the book was a little like running a campaign and playing all the parts. I was the GM, I was both the player characters and the non-player characters, and I was the impartial observer who didn't know what was going on. Although I never actually rolled dice, I used all my old handbooks and, because I never played wizards, had to call a friend at one point and ask his advice on an appropriate spell.

VAN BELKOM: Will there be more commissioned novels in the future, say in the *Star Trek* or other similarly licensed universes?

HUFF: All right, I admit it, I'm a media fan. I've pitched two *STNG* books and an *X-Files* book — none of which were accepted, needless to say. But as soon as I get another idea, I'll be out of the bullpen and back in there pitching.

VAN BELKOM: You seem to have quite a large and loyal following of fans. In fact, I noticed an ad in the back of your latest book, *No Quarter*, for a bimonthly newsletter devoted entirely to your work. Did that kind of response to your novels take some getting used to?

HUFF: Yes and no. When I started being published back in 1988, I was working at Bakka Books, so right from the very beginning, I received a lot more fan attention than most writers. Readers were never slow at expressing an opinion, good or bad, and, behind the cash register, I was a captive audience. As I continued working the store's dealer's table at Ad Astra for a couple of years after that first book, I was at conventions doing panels and readings and auto-graphings long before many writers get that kind of attention. In 1993, a student from SUNY Brockport in Rochester, New York, did a thesis on my work. I've done readings from Edmonton to Charlottetown and been Guest of Honor at a number of conventions. That said, I still sometimes wonder why. In fact, my response to my very first invitation to be GOH was, "Me? Are you sure?"

I find the whole concept of a newsletter engendered by, if not devoted to, my work to be both incredibly flattering and a little frightening. The responsibility every writer has towards her readers has become a lot more personal because I know who at least some of mine are and I consciously work to make sure this admiration hasn't been misplaced.

Reviews have something of the same effect. In a *Locus* review for *Blood Price*, Ed Bryant said, among other things, that it was "genuinely witty." Every time I wrote something even remotely amusing after that, I worried about whether I was being genuinely witty. Mind you, there are those who say I worry too much . . .

VAN BELKOM: At last count you've published twelve novels in

eight years, but in that same time there have only been a few short stories. Why is that?

HUFF: Well, the easy answer is that twelve novels in eight years doesn't leave a lot of time for short stories, but actually I've done twenty short pieces and have another three that need to be written in the next eight months. While certainly less than some, that's not exactly only a few.

VAN BELKOM: So you are basically a full-time novelist, something that only a handful of people in this country can make claim to. But while people often equate publishing success with financial success, what can you say about the financial realities of making a living writing genre novels?

HUFF: I think that kind of depends on how you define financial success. To me, financial success is being able to afford to do something you love, and since I can, I'd say I was financially successful. Now, if I lived in an expensive city instead of in the much-preferred middle of nowhere, or if I had children, things would be different.

I don't know how other people manage — and to be honest, it's one of the few things I *don't* worry about — but I have a feeling that too many writers look at the kind of money Stephen King or David Eddings are getting and measure their success against those incredible numbers — and that's a big mistake.

If writing genre novels could get me twenty-eight hours in a day, now that would be something!

VAN BELKOM: You used to live in Toronto — a very expensive city — but moved to Milford, Ontario — a very rural area. Was there financial concerns at work, or was it always a dream of yours to live out in the country and write books?

HUFF: Prince Edward County, where I live (Milford is just the rural route, I'm almost eight kilometers from the village), is south-east of Toronto. While it was always a dream of mine of live in the country and write, I can't deny it's one heck of a lot cheaper to live here than in the city. Also quieter, cleaner, and safer. We have a great bookstore, a helpful (and forgiving) librarian, and more-or-less full Internet access. I can write all day and not be disturbed by anything louder than a pair of blue jays fighting over sunflower seeds.

VAN BELKOM: With the clarity of hindsight, is there anything about your writing career that you might have done differently?

HUFF: I wish I'd been more articulate when I met C.J. Cherryh at the last Boston Worldcon, but other than that, no. Although I've said on a number of occasions that worrying is kind of a hobby of mine, I tend to worry about what might possibly happen say if a wheel pops off the car while passing farm machinery on the drive into town for groceries thereby throwing us into the path of a milk truck which bursts into flame and we're poached under a cascade of boiling milk. I don't bother worrying about what I've already done — there are too many potential disasters out there claiming my attention.

Monica Hughes

Monica Hughes struggled for years trying to find something that suited her writing talents. She found the perfect match in 1971 when a book on writing for children got her started down a path that would eventually lead to the publication of thirty books for young-adults and the honor of winning numerous awards, including the Vicky Metcalf Award and the Canada Council Prize for Children's Literature in 1982 and 1983.

Hughes's first book was *Gold-Fever Trail*, a novella commissioned for grade school use published in 1974. Her first novel was *Crisis on Conshelf Ten* in 1977. Soon after came the SF titles *Earthdark* and *The Tomorrow City*.

In the 1980s Hughes published seventeen novels, ten of them science fiction, including the Isis trilogy — *The Keeper of the Isis Light*, *The Guardian of Isis*, and *The Isis Pedlar*; the Arc One novels — *Devil on My Back*, *The Dream Catcher*, *Sandwriter*, and *The Promise*: and four stand-alone SF books — *Beyond the Dark River*, *Ring-Rise, Ring-Set*, *The Beckoning Lights*, and *Space Trap*. Mainstream titles of the 1980s include *Hunter in the Dark*, *My Name is Paula Popowich!*, *Blaine's Way*, and *Log Jam*.

In the 1990s, Hughes has continued writing SF, but her output has been evenly matched by more mainstream works. *Invitation to the Game*, *The Crystal Drop*, and *The Golden Aquarians* are all SF, while her three most recent books are *Castle Tourmandyne*, *Where Have You Been, Billy Boy?* and *The Seven Magpies*.

Hughes has published roughly a dozen juvenile SF short stories, most notably in the magazine *On Spec* and in the anthologies *Dragons and Dreams* (edited by Jane Yolen) and *Canadian Children's Annual* (edited by Brian Cross). She has published just one adult SF story, "The Price of Land," in Lesley Choyce's landmark *Ark of Ice* anthology.

Born in Liverpool in 1925, Hughes attended Edinburgh University in 1942–43 before serving in the Women's Royal Naval Service from 1943 to 1946. Following the war she lived in London and Rhodesia before coming to Canada in 1952. She was married in 1957, the same year she became a Canadian citizen. She lived in Ontario seven years before settling in Edmonton in 1964.

EDO VAN BELKOM: Two of your novels, *Beyond the Dark River* and *Ring-Rise Ring-Set*, are set in Canada. How did you find writing stories set where you live — albeit in the future — after writing stories set in such places as under the sea and on the moon?

MONICA HUGHES: Actually, I quite enjoyed them because I didn't have to do quite as much research. For *Beyond the Dark River* I just got out the good old Shell map of Alberta. I knew the center was going to be Edmonton, and I needed a Hutterite colony, so I found out where they were south of Edmonton and put my native people not quite as close to the mountains as they are in real life. So I had this dynamic, imaginary triangle and all I had to do was have events move within it. It was wonderful.

VAN BELKOM: So did it take more research or less?

HUGHES: Oh, less research. But it doesn't always work out that way. For *Crystal Drop* I did a huge amounts of research because I could. I hauled my husband down to Fort MacLeod and we covered the whole of the area the kids trek along by car, which means back roads with no telephone or hydro lines, nothing. It's just empty. The map of the area is almost entirely white with a little dot in the middle that says "abandoned poultry farm." It just gives you an idea of the landscape — even nowadays the landscape is pretty sparse.

VAN BELKOM: You began writing in earnest in 1971. How serious were you at the time about making a career of it?

HUGHES: Oh, I had been serious about making a career of it since I got out of the WRNS, which was in 1946. I merely failed all those years in between. I thought I'd become a short story writer or I would write magazine non-fiction. And I tried all these things and failed, failed, failed all the way down the line.

VAN BELKOM: You hadn't published a story or piece of fiction in all that time?

HUGHES: Not a piece of fiction or non-fiction, except for a story in a school magazine way back before those days. Not a thing. And then I found a book on writing for young people. It wasn't particularly useful in itself; it was a very formulistic book. But the author had a good bibliography in it and that took me down to the library to look at literary criticism of children's works. I was absolutely bowled over to realize that there were three or four shelves of literary criticism of children's writing.

That sort of piqued my curiosity, so I went down to the children's stacks and, armed with a list of the best books they'd been writing about, read all of them. It just blew me away. And then I knew exactly what I wanted to do with the rest of my life.

VAN BELKOM: You said you were writing since 1946. What made you finally decide to do it seriously in 1971? I mean, that's a long time to think about writing.

HUGHES: I was writing all that time. I wrote three or four novels and a lot of short stories, some non-fiction. I took two year-courses from the University of Chicago Home Study Department. I mean, I was in the process, even when the kids were really small I was still writing. It's just that I wasn't succeeding.

VAN BELKOM: Perhaps I was misled by some of the biographical information which summarizes your life rather succinctly and says, in effect, that in 1971 you decided to write in earnest.

HUGHES: Yes, there were two events that happened in that year.

First, getting that book on writing for children and deciding that this is what I wanted to do for the rest of my life. I always knew I wanted to write, but I never did bring to it the enthusiasm that I suddenly felt.

The second thing was that I read an article in a magazine on diurnal rhythms. And it said, look to your own life and look at the time when you are the most intellectually productive, when you feel most physical and so on, during the day. Up until then I had always been giving to my writing whatever was left over from my family — nine to eleven at night, exhausted. And I'm a morning person, I realized. So I made a pledge to myself that I would write for a year, write a book for children. And I would write every morning — and this was putting a discipline to it that I had been lacking — and if I failed at the end of that time then I would give up on the idea. So it was indeed a serious commitment.

VAN BELKOM: How much influence did your parents have on your development as a writer?

HUGHES: Indirectly, a certain amount. When we were living in

Egypt and there were servants and life was easy, my mother played with writing stories for women's magazines in Britain and sold a couple. I knew about that and it just meant in my mind that there was nothing extraordinary about writing and selling. Ordinary people do it, whereas many of us grow up thinking it's done by all the strange people out there.

So that was one thing. The other was that my father had published books, even though they were of absolutely no use to a writer — he was a theoretical mathametician. So he wrote in this very esoteric field where if it isn't using Greek letter it's using Arabic. But again, I knew that books got published.

But the main thing I think was that he read aloud to us when we were young. There was a huge influence of books in our lives. The house was full of books, always had been. We didn't have too many of our own, we weren't given many things in those days. The only gifts you ever acquired as children back in those days were on your birthdays and at Christmas. So you thought very seriously when people asked you, "What would you like?" So, I acquired every E. Nesbit book, all fourteen or fifteen, painfully year-by-year by asking the aunts and uncles.

VAN BELKOM: And each one was another notch in your belt.

HUGHES: Oh, a miracle . . . I own this book now. The best thing in the world that ever came in the mail were these oblong packages in brown paper.

VAN BELKOM: You still have those books?

HUGHES: Yes.

VAN BELKOM: The whole set?

HUGHES: Yes. And I still occasionally go back to them. Certainly *The Enchanted Castle*, which has the most incredible paragraph that gives one permission to believe in magic.

VAN BELKOM: In school during World War II you won a chocolate bar as first prize in a writing contest. Was the story SF or have elements of fantasy in it?

HUGHES: I have no idea; I don't remember it. I remember the chocolate bar only because we never got candy in those days because of rations. I don't remember the story at all, but I don't think it was science fiction or fantasy. At that time — school during the war — I had already discovered the Carnegie Library in Edinburgh and I'd already met the works of Jules Verne. I used to read his stuff in French, and I'm not talking about modern editions; I'm talking about those 19th-century books with etchings. And I'd fight my way through each just to get the plot out of it.

It was worth it. Back then plot was the important thing. The rest of the stuff I read at that time was basically 19th-century adventure stories.

VAN BELKOM: There's certainly a lot of adventure in your work.

HUGHES: But you realize they were all male protagonists, every last one. They weren't writing for girls back then.

VAN BELKOM: I guess the girl stories were all romances about nurses . . .

HUGHES: Yeah, and it didn't appeal to me. I just got on my horse and rode off across France with the real heroes.

VAN BELKOM: At the end of the war you served in the Women's Royal Naval Service. How did that experience affect your life?

HUGHES: It was the most incredibly boring job in the whole world. I was working on the Enigma project, which now is public knowledge, but it was so secret that I'm still afraid to say the word. But after that there was a very small interlude in meteorology. And I do recall particularly being on nightwatch in Belfast — I was on a Fleet Air Arm base — and the incredible peace, and the night sky. Because apart from the searchlights and the floodlights over the harbor, there was no illumination, and the night sky was so beautiful. One of the books that influenced me at the time was Sir James Jeans's *Mysterious Universe*. I read it recently and it was old fashioned and pompously written, but to me at that time the whole idea of space was exciting.

VAN BELKOM: You traveled the world extensively. What made you eventually choose Canada as your home?

HUGHES: I didn't. I was on my way to Australia. I wanted to live in a warm country. I had really loved Rhodesia, as it was then known (Zimbabwe now), but I felt that the attitude of the white to the black was quite indefensible and I really didn't want to marry and have children there. I remember a particular scene walking by a house and seeing a little boy sitting on the stoop of his house and his black nanny was bouncing a ball in front of him and I thought, "The nanny is playing the game and he is watching . . . This is a weird world." And so I left, but I still wanted to go to a warm place.

At that time there was a two to three year waiting period to go to Australia because they had a fairly open immigration policy and in fact they paid your way almost entirely. So I sneakily thought that I could get to Canada quite quickly since getting there wasn't too expensive. Then I'll work my way across Canada and get a ship from the Pacific side, only I kind of got stuck.

It was weird really, because there I was in Ottawa, enduring snowfalls and all that, and I worked at the Research Council and I enjoyed the work so much. But when winter came again I'd think of Australia. My boss would wheedle me and say, "You're not really going to leave." And I'd say, "Yeah, I can't stand the thought of another winter." And he'd say, "We'll get you a pay raise." So I'd stay another winter.

VAN BELKOM: You have no regrets about settling in Canada?

HUGHES: Not when I think of the sort of conjunction of unrelated circumstances which led to my being where I was and writing what I wrote. Maybe I wouldn't have done any of that had I been somewhere else.

VAN BELKOM: In many of your books the classic Canadian theme of survival is often at work. Do you consciously inject that into your work or do you think it's just a product of being a Canadian writer?

HUGHES: Ah, you're bringing in Margaret Atwood at this point, I dare say. I don't think it's the Margaret Atwood bit, not directly anyway, although I'm sure country has something to do with it; I mean Alberta is pretty close to the edge.

Basically, the ideas I get come in the form of questions, and the questions usually ask something to do with survival — what would it be like to grow up in a city underground on the very edge of the ice and then be thrown out of the city?

VAN BELKOM: So it's just a product of what you write?

HUGHES: Yeah, I think so. I could make all sorts of speeches . . . This is the problem, you can rationalize almost everything you think about. I think it just happens I'm looking for good stories and they turn out that way.

VAN BELKOM: Another of your themes is that of isolation and the search for identity? Would you say these are Canadian themes or themes that run through many works of young-adult fiction?

HUGHES: I think they're universal. Well, not universal, that's not fair, because I imagine in countries that have a very tightly knit social system they may not be as important as in ones that are basically isolated, with a nuclear family and so forth. But I think it goes back to my own childhood and feeling isolated and rather lonely. Even traveling around the world . . . I suppose when you are a traveler you are in a sense apart from that culture and looking at it with alien eyes. And you tend, if you don't stay forever in that place, to keep the memory of being the stranger walking through. I think that's probably part of it.

It certainly was intensified when we came out to Alberta. We came out in 1964, and I took one look at the landscape and I thought it was so meager compared with Ontario. And I started to think, I can't live like this, so I started looking at it and discovering beauty in all the delicate colors in dead weeds and grass. And I got into a huge creative bout of design, embroidering, weaving and so on. And then eventually gave those up in favor of writing.

VAN BELKOM: Do you consider yourself Canadian now, or do you still feel ties to England?

HUGHES: Mythically, I'm still English. Can't get away from that. The stories you first read and hear, the Arthurs and Robin Hoods, they become part of one's identity. In fact, I'm sometimes astonished how much of my life has been spent in Canada — since 1952 — it's incredible.

VAN BELKOM: If you look at your life a very small proportion of it was spent in England, although a very important time developmentally, but the greater majority has been spent in Canada.

HUGHES: Yes, indeed. The only thing I put against that in terms of proportion is how slowly one lives one's childhood. When you're young there is an enormous time between November and Christmas. It takes forever and everything is stretched out, while nowadays I go from week to week and I think what happened to the last week? It vanished. The last year, it vanished.

VAN BELKOM: Many critics have said that you have an ability to get a moral message into your work without being too preachy or didactic? How hard is that to do when writing for children?

HUGHES: Don't do it. And I don't.

VAN BELKOM: Don't try to put a message in?

HUGHES: Yeah. The worst thing in the world you could do is sit down and say, "Now I'm going to write a book that illustrates prejudice." I don't always have a theme at the beginning of the book, sometimes I don't even discover it until it's finished, but sometimes I do and I have to be careful. *Crystal Drop* was definitely motivated by the terrible drought years in Southern Alberta — which has now changed totally (not nearly so dry), but there you are. The drought seemed to be a condition that was going to turn into a permanent trend — and illustrated the dangers of not paying attention to global warming and the ozone thinning. I knew I wanted to write a book about it, but I held back — because I knew it would be didactic — until an idea came and kick-started it into a story.

VAN BELKOM: You're also very prolific. Do you have to push yourself to produce, or are you always more than motivated to write?

HUGHES: Oh, more than motivated. I can't imagine . . . Well, I can actually remember a time a few years back when my husband was unemployed and I wasn't doing a lot of good work because I was really nervous about our future. It's not a good idea to write with the fear of not earning enough in mind, you know, to push oneself. But when I'm left to myself, I'm never without an idea for the next book.

VAN BELKOM: In a day, how much would you write?

HUGHES: About 2,000 words.

VAN BELKOM: And how many drafts do you go through?

HUGHES: Four. I write by hand and do the first one as fast as I possibly can, just to get the excitement that's in me out. Then I put it in the word processor carefully, doing quite a lot of editing at that stage. Then I print up a copy — I never work off the screen — and tear it apart with my red pencil, then put it in again. And the next one I'll leave for a while, a couple of months if I can find other things to do and if I can bear it; and then I do it again. So it's about the fourth draft that goes to the publisher.

VAN BELKOM: Your science fiction novels are very well researched; in fact you seem to take great pride in mentioning at the beginning of *Crisis on Conshelf Ten* that everything in the book is either an established fact or an extrapolation of a scientific theory. Do you enjoy the research, or is it a necessary fact of life when writing science fiction?

HUGHES: I used to enjoy it a great deal. I'd go down to the main library in Edmonton and I'd get out the appropriate card catalogs and I'd sit there and browse through. Titles would catch your eye on the subject, and they always had a precis of what they were about. I loathe the new computerized catalogue. It leads you into areas where you can't specify sufficiently. It nearly drives me crazy.

VAN BELKOM: Don't you find yourself just browsing shelves?

HUGHES: Oh yes, certainly I do. What I often do nowadays is look in the ComCat, find an appropriate call number, then go there and start looking. But of course, the shelf doesn't tell you what's out.

I can see why they got away from the old card catalog. If I'm sitting there with E-F, nobody else is going to have a chance for half an hour and that's not sensible. But they did have this huge advantage; I just wished they'd kept them *as well as* . . .

Another thing, if I was between books or just thinking about life in general, I'd sometimes go down to that library and literally fish "Space" for instance. And a title would intrigue me and I'd go off and start reading about this subject.

VAN BELKOM: You began writing and publishing SF in 1977 and since then have watched the Canadian SF community grow up around you. What can you say about being an SF writer in Canada now as opposed to 1977?

HUGHES: Of course, there's much more good company. I don't think it's made much of a difference for me because the fields are so far apart. There's grown-ups and there's juveniles, and there's this rift between them — a conceptual rift, not one between writers — which is a stronger rift than there is between the writers of mainstream fiction and science fiction.

VAN BELKOM: Have you noticed this rift in terms of the mainstream because you do mainstream juveniles as well?

HUGHES: Oh yeah, oh yeah. The chasm is between juvenile and adult work.

VAN BELKOM: I remember reading about Joan Clark, who had written many well-received juvenile novels, then wrote a novel for adults, and that book was considered to be a first-novel and she was very upset by that.

HUGHES: Yes, and she had every right to be because she wrote some very beautiful works for children, and very serious works.

VAN BELKOM: I guess the implication is that it takes less ability to write for children than it does for adults.

HUGHES: That is certainly the implication. Until people try to do it. And you find quite a few adult writers who decide they'll knock off a children's book, or perhaps their publisher suggests it to them, and they are by no means always successful.

It is a different mindset. But it requires all of the plotting, all of the character development, just as much setting, and so on. The only real difference, and I do admit this is an important one to me because I'm not good at juggling sub-plots, is you tend not to have secondary plots in a juvenile novel.

Even flashback can be a problem. *Hunter in the Dark* has a lot of flashback in it and I thought kids nowadays could handle that because they watch a lot of television and many scenarios are not linear, but when it comes to the written word they have problems.

VAN BELKOM: Do you feel you're always competing with the other media like television and video and computer games?

HUGHES: No. One always hears these woes about what the future will be like, but I think the book is always with us. You can't take a CD-ROM to bed, you can't turn down the corner of the page, you can't read it in the bath. Books are books.

I think one of the real problems is the conceptual attitude children have developed, the short attention span and the need for instant gratification in terms of plot heights and so on.

VAN BELKOM: Have you read any R.L. Stine to see what all the fuss is about?

HUGHES: No I haven't actually. I see them in the store — where they get you to sign books, you're usually next to about 500 Stines and Pikes.

VAN BELKOM: He must be doing something well to have such a following.

HUGHES: Not necessarily well, but *right*. I'm sure he does a good job, but I gather that they are very one-dimensional, not a lot of character development and so on. What I hope is that kids will read them until they are saturated and bored, and then they'll go and read something else.

VAN BELKOM: Anything that gets children reading can't be all bad.

HUGHES: But of course reading needs a mediator, and I don't think the bookseller is the same kind of mediator as the librarian or teacher.

VAN BELKOM: You've written one SF story for adults, "The Price of Land" in *Ark of Ice*. How much different is it for you to write for adults rather than for children?

HUGHES: I've never felt myself capable of writing adult science fiction. You know, ideas come into my head for novels for young people, 40,000 to 50,000 words, there they are just pouring in. I try and think of an adult science fiction short story and I draw a blank. I don't know, maybe that story was a fluke. Or maybe another idea will fly into my mind. But most of the adult short stories are not in the science fiction genre.

VAN BELKOM: What is it like being published in Canada? Has it been any different from being published in the US or the UK?

HUGHES: I was extremely fortunate with my editors in Britain. There is a very strong tradition of excellent editing there. They know how to edit. The Americans tend to want to rewrite your book. In England it's hands-off and very gentle suggestions. Canada lies somewhere in the middle, closer to the British ideal, but they're not as many great editors around — but that's because we're a smaller country.

VAN BELKOM: After writing for more than twenty years, is there something you'd like to have achieved, but haven't yet?

HUGHES: No, I'd just like to have done it all twenty years earlier. I think I wasted — now some people will philosophically say that nothing is ever wasted — those twenty or thirty years when I wasn't succeeding as a writer, but I think it would have been lovely to have found my voice a lot earlier and then had a lot of fun writing these novels.

That's about it.

VAN BELKOM: But you've had fun.

HUGHES: Oh, I have. But I'm being greedy. I looked forward to twenty more years back then. I look forward to some in the future, too, God knows how long, but we'll see what happens.

Guy Gavriel Kay

Guy Gavriel Kay began his writing career in 1981 when shortly after being called to the Bar, he was invited to be a part of a new CBC Radio Drama Series called *The Scales of Justice*. His initial scriptwriting effort was successful and he stayed with the show for the next nine years as both associate producer and principal writer. When the show moved to CBC television in 1990, Kay went with it, working as scriptwriter and as script and legal consultant until 1994.

It was while working on the radio version of *The Scales of Justice* that Kay began writing what was to become The Fionavar Tapestry trilogy. The first book in the trilogy, *The Summer Tree*, appeared in 1984 and was followed in the next two years by *The Wandering Fire* and *The Darkest Road*. The series was a huge international success and garnered Kay a nomination for the John W. Campbell Award for best new author in 1986. The trilogy was first published by McClelland & Stewart and then by Harper & Collins in Canada, in hardcover in the United States by William Morrow and in paperback by Berkley, and in the United Kingdom by Unwin Hyman. It has since been reprinted in the US by Roc, with a 10th anniversary edition in Canada, and most recently was reprinted in a single omnibus edition. Translation rights were sold in fourteen languages, and the middle book, *The Wandering Fire*, won the 1987 CASPER (now Aurora) Award.

Kay followed The Fionavar Tapestry with three standalone novels. *Tigana*, published in 1990, was a national bestseller and won the Aurora Award in the Best Long-Form Work in English category. It was a World Fantasy Award nominee with translation rights sold in twelve countries. *A Song for Arbonne* was published in 1992, was a national number one bestseller in Canada, an alternate selection of the Book of the Month Club, and translated into ten languages. *The Lions of Al-Rassan*, a 1995 release, was a national bestseller and was translated into many languages.

In addition to being a novelist, Kay has published poetry in a number of Canadian magazines and has been a guest lecturer at the University of Waterloo and University of Toronto. Kay has worked with Christopher Tolkien, son of J.R.R. Tolkien, on *The Silmarillion* project. He was Toastmaster of the World Science Fiction Convention in 1993. A recent project is a television adaptation of the Robertson Davies novel *What's Bred in the Bone*, co-written with George Jonas.

Born in 1954 in Weyburn, Saskatchewan, Kay was raised in Winnipeg and now lives in Toronto with his wife and children.

EDO VAN BELKOM: You worked with Christopher Tolkien, the son of J.R.R. Tolkien, as an editorial consultant in the preparation of his father's *The Silmarillion* for publication. How did he come to contact you for the project?

GUY GAVRIEL KAY: My connection to the Tolkiens is fairly well-known by now: I grew up in Winnipeg, Christopher Tolkien's second wife was a Winnipegger, and our families knew each other. I met him a few times when they visited his in-laws, and after his father died in the winter of 1973, he invited me to come over to Oxford to assist in the work on *The Silmarillion*.

VAN BELKOM: It must have been a daunting task, piecing together and completing the work of someone you've admired for years.

KAY: Undeniably so, for a myriad of reasons. Certainly the sheer scale of the project, working with material that had been begun in 1917 and was still undergoing revisions fifty-five years later was intimidating, in and of itself. On the encouraging side, seeing the false starts, dead ends, "errors" in the drafts and manuscripts was reassuring in an odd way. It gave me a core awareness of something I'd only been able to appreciate on a cerebral level before: that major works of fiction emerge from struggle and confusion and that even the most gifted writers go through this.

VAN BELKOM: How much did the experience of working on that project help you in the later writing of your own fantasies?

KAY: That's a complex question (and answer). On the most basic level, the year in Oxford crystallized my own sense that I wanted to write fiction. I never *expected* to be able to do so for a living, which is one reason I took a law degree on my return to Canada, but the desire coalesced in that year. The year with the Tolkien papers also helped de-mythologize (if I can put it that way) the writing process. Seeing and working with early drafts, false starts, outright errors, obvious roadblocks in the work of a master aided me greatly years later when I ran into these in my own work.

In another way, being that close to the "source" of a major text also helped reduce the awe and intimidation that might have otherwise been present at the thought of attempting a very large high fantasy. My own sense is that at that time, with the exception of Stephen Donaldson and one or two others, most serious writers of fantasy had chosen to work *away* from Tolkien (minimalist work, urban fantasy) leaving the big high fantasies to more consciously commercial projects.

VAN BELKOM: After spending a year in England working on *The Silmarillion*, you finished your law degree and became a lawyer. But despite that, you became television writer and producer. How did that come about?

KAY: The answer's partly implied in the previous response. I always hoped to find a way to write, and in the year of my call to the Bar I was offered a modest opportunity with *The Scales of Justice*, a CBC Radio Drama series being gestated by George Jonas and criminal lawyer Ed Greenspan (for whom I had articled). I was named legal consultant and offered a single "test" script. At the time I was young, had no dependents, no debts, and saw this as a chance to find more free time for my own work than the law would ever have offered. The test script turned into several that first year, and by the second season I was principal writer and associate producer for the series, which ran for many years and ended up being transferred to television. *Scales* was both a highly enjoyable project for all those years and a perfect balance for my first books, leaving me time to write and paying the rent while Fionavar appeared and began finding a market.

VAN BELKOM: Have you ever practiced law?

KAY: As I mentioned earlier, in the year I finished my articles of clerkship I received an offer to associate myself with *The Scales of Justice*. I accepted this and, so, never engaged in the formal practice of law. I did finish the Bar Admission Course, took my call to the Bar and was a member in good standing of the Law Society for about fifteen years.

VAN BELKOM: With your background in law and your experience with *The Scales of Justice*, you would think that crime and mystery would be the natural genre for you. What made you want to write high fantasy?

KAY: Well, fairly obviously, crime and mystery *were* a genre I worked with — in radio and television. The simplest and most accurate answer to the question is to suggest that a writer (or this writer) might easily have more than one area of particular interest, both creative and intellectual. I've always had a passion for myth and legend and for the study of history . . . both of these dovetail quite smoothly into the writing of fantasy.

VAN BELKOM: The first book in The Fionavar Tapestry, *The Summer Tree*, starts out at the University of Toronto and features UofT students as central characters. Was it a conscious decision to use a Canadian setting as a starting point, or was it something you didn't give a second thought?

KAY: In the inception, the latter is closer to the truth. I simply chose settings I knew and thought I could describe well. I also remember attending a conference at UofT's Convocation Hall where, among other people, Joseph Campbell spoke, and finding the setting wonderfully evocative, especially when I looked up at the high windows. "Philosopher's Walk" at UofT used to be even more mysterious (and dangerous) before it was re-landscaped and better-lit. After the opening scenes were drafted and some people read them, I was made aware that it might be more "politic" to transplant the opening to somewhere American . . . and at this point I just laughed.

Certain things feel right to me, and the setting stayed just as it was. In the same way, it was a "given" for me that Canadian rights to my work would be separated from American (or British) rights and sold to a Canadian publishing house.

VAN BELKOM: Did The Fionavar Tapestry start out as a single book, or was it conceived to be a trilogy?

KAY: I would think it is pretty obvious it was always a trilogy from the structure. I was embracing as many of the tropes of the genre as I could . . . as part of an attempt to show (quixotically or otherwise) that there was considerable vitality in high fantasy, that it need not be consigned to purely commercial post-Tolkien efforts. The trilogy format was a part of that. What this meant, among other things, was a lot of thought given to the "middle book problem." The volume that lacks the energy of a beginning and the energy of a resolution. If you look at the "shape" of *The Wandering Fire* . . . how it begins and how it ends . . . you'll see my attempt at "solving" that problem. The formal introduction of the Arthurian "thread" is deferred to the opening of that volume, and the introduction and the resolution of the winter crisis frame it.

VAN BELKOM: Your books following The Fionavar Tapestry are all set in a specific local and time period. For example, *Tigana* had a definite Italian-Renaissance feel to it, and *A Song For Arbonne* follows the history of Provence quite closely. Is this sort of writing more or less challenging than creating secondary worlds like Fionavar?

KAY: In a way this is an "apples and oranges" issue, in another way I'd say the more recent worlds have been harder to create because the historical parallels operate much the way, say, a sonnet does in poetry . . . they compel a structure for your creativity. If it works, the structure *adds* to the created achievement; if it doesn't, the invention lies uneasily and awkwardly within that structure. I'm still creating "secondary worlds" in the last three books, though, shaping religions, myths, histories . . . the added element is that *some* of these elements cut close to the bone of actual history. I'm challenged and energized by the interplay this offers between the invented and the "real." For example, in *The Lions of Al Rassan*, the "Day of the Moat" which some found a too-violent or over-the-top exercise in Grand Guignol was *very* closely modeled on a real incident in the history of Toledo, that happens to be known to us as "The Day of the Ditch."

VAN BELKOM: Over the course of your career, you seemed to have made the shift from writing high fantasy to historical fantasy? Will there come a time when you will be writing straight historical novels?

KAY: I honestly can't answer this one. I never know what my *next* book will be, so it would be purest speculation to try to sort out what I'll be doing in the future. I can say that there is no deliberate "through line" to my work. In other words, I haven't been consciously eroding the fantastical elements as a "weaning" process or some such. The use of the fantastic, for me, is an authorial tool as much as any other, and in each book the tools I use are the ones that seem suited to the subject and themes of that book. The newest one, for example, will have more of the "magical" than *The Lions of Al Rassan* did. The setting and motifs suggested that this was appropriate.

VAN BELKOM: How much time do you spend researching your novels as compared to writing them?

KAY: It has varied, but for the last four (including the in-progress work) there's been about a year of reading and note-taking, and some travel before I begin writing. The research reading continues while I'm writing, but there comes a point where I fear "graduate student syndrome" — the tendency to keep researching because there's always one more article to chase down — and I just begin the writing. The drafting of a book takes me about twelve to eighteen months, usually, though the most recent one has been slower because a number of projects intervened.

VAN BELKOM: How much did your novel-writing routine change from The Fionavar Tapestry — a time when you were also writing for *The Scales of Justice* — to *The Lions of Al Rassan*?

KAY: A fair bit, actually, though for largely domestic reasons. I began Fionavar as a single man and am now married with small children . . . the nighthawk lifestyle I used to enjoy is an obvious casualty of parenthood. I'm very much on a five days a week, normal working day schedule now than I ever was. By contrast, I wrote *The Wandering Fire* in New Zealand, working seven days a week for about three months to draft it, often writing into the evening. Over time I've also learned to treat my writing as a marathon, not a sprint . . . if I settle into a steady pace it is ultimately more productive than having days of furious output, followed by three or four days where I digest and process what emerged in the frenzied day. I'll actually stop now, some days, and make notes for what is to come, rather than push on to have a 3000-4000 word day. I pay a price for such a day, I've learned. There's always a slowdown after.

VAN BELKOM: All of your novels have been long, and they continue to get longer and more complex. Was there ever a time when you wanted to write shorter pieces, short stories perhaps, or a novella?

KAY: Often when I am in the middle of a book, I realize that many writers I know would be *done* at that point — and celebrating the fact! But the truth is, I am drawn (as a reader, not just a writer) to complexity and nuance and this results in subplots and secondary characters who demand time and room to incarnate themselves. This will, of necessity, produce longer books.

VAN BELKOM: You've lived in places like Provence, New Zealand,

and Greece, and you spend much of your time outside of Canada. Do you ever consider yourself to be a "citizen of the world" rather than Canadian?

KAY: I don't actually acknowledge the dichotomy suggested. We are all citizens of the world. Indeed, I've argued that one odd virtue of Canada's relatively mild form of nationalism is that it allows us to more readily see ourselves as part of a larger whole, rather than *purely* as members of the tribe of "Canadians." I'm proudly Canadian, am deeply unsettled by threats to our national existence, but am also engaged both intellectually and emotionally by the histories and cultures I find elsewhere, in my travels and my research. I'm also keenly interested in the success (or lack of it, sometimes) of translation editions of my books. I like to be in touch with my translators and foreign editors myself, and try to take a "global" view of my writing career. My German editions are as important to me as my British ones.

VAN BELKOM: Your books have certainly been translated into many languages, but they are more popular in some than in others. Do you ever wonder at the popularity specific books enjoy in certain cultures?

KAY: Frequently, in fact, with no ready answers emerging. There is often a wide and inexplicable variance between sales in one country and sales in another and this happens to writer friends of mine who work in entirely different genres, as well. One can say, in a banal fashion, that the Germans and Scandinavians have a mythic and cultural receptivity to heroic fantasy, whereas the French (say) prefer Cartesian seriousness and the genre does less well there. This seems more or less true, based on thresholds of genre sales in these countries, but I do suspect the reasons are far more complex. In some instances, with regard to my own work, I have been pleased by successes that reflect a response to the *subtext* of the books. As an example, *Tigana* was the first of my books to be translated into Croatian, and it was chosen specifically because the editors there were sharply aware of the thematic links to the re-emergence of eastern Europe from totalitarian control. (The relationship between history, language, and identity is central to the novel, and to the means with which *many* oppressive regimes have suppressed conquered or subjugated peoples.)

VAN BELKOM: Considering your experience with *The Scales of Justice* and your success as a novelist, one would imagine that you've had offers to write television and movie scripts? Has that been the case, or have you been more than satisfied concentrating on the novels?

KAY: Script offers surface at fairly regular intervals, and I've accepted a few. The first ones were associated with *The Scales of Justice*; they were invariably an enjoyable and even a relaxing (dare one admit that?) exercise compared to the very long, draining process of writing novels. As the question's phrased, I'll have to do an end-run around it, though: I find the novels far more consuming and demanding, and the creative rewards flow, of course, from those things. At the same time, when I am "in between" books, it is challenging and engaging to take on certain projects for television and film. I think I benefit from being in a position to choose my projects with some flexibility, given that I define myself as a novelist and do not pursue media work.

Nancy Kilpatrick

Nancy Kilpatrick came to Canada one weekend in 1970 and never left. And although still a landed immigrant, she's seen and experienced more of this country than most Canadians ever will. "I've lived in different parts of the country," says the Philadelphia native, born in 1946, "traveled to both coasts many times, and lived on a farm for a year."

Kilpatrick's first novel, *Near Death*, was published by Pocket Books in 1994. She followed it with a collaboration with Don Bassingthwaite, *As One Dead*, set in the world of White Wolf's role-playing game Vampire: The Masquerade. A third vampire novel, *Child of the Night* (set in the same world as *Near Death*), was published in the UK by Raven Books. She has co-edited an anthology with Thomas Roche, tentatively entitled *Gargoyles*.

Her short fiction has appeared in countless magazines and anthologies with some of the best being gathered into three collections: *Sex and the Single Vampire*; *Endorphins* and *The Vampire Stories of Nancy Kilpatrick*, forthcoming from Canadian specialty publisher Transylvania Press Inc.

As Amarantha Knight, Kilpatrick has been even busier and more prolific, editing erotic horror anthologies and writing *The Darker Passions* series, retellings of classic horror tales with a new and erotic twist. Her first Knight novel was *Dracula* in 1993, followed by *Dr. Jekyll and Mr. Hyde*; *Frankenstein*; *The Fall of the House of Usher*; *The Picture of Dorian Gray*; *Carmilla*; *The Pit and the Pendulum*; and *The Curse of the Mummy*: *Pharos the Egyptian*. There has also been a series sampler, *The Amarantha Knight Reader*, with excerpts from four novels. The anthologies, erotic in content, have all been based on some supernatural or horrific theme: *Love Bites* (vampire), *Flesh Fantastic* (Frankenstein), *Sex Macabre* (supernatural), *Seductive Spectres* (ghosts), and *Demon Sex* (demons).

Kilpatrick has scripted comics for *VampErotica* and co-wrote a bilingual play with Benoit Bisson, *Ghost Rails/Les Fantomes Deraillent*, which was performed at Toronto's Fringe Festival in 1996. She has twice been both a Bram Stoker and Aurora Award finalist, and in 1993, won the Arthur Ellis Award, presented by the Crime Writers of Canada, for her short story "Mantrap".

EDO VAN BELKOM: Your first novel, *Near Death*, came out in 1994, but hadn't you been writing for a long time before that?

NANCY KILPATRICK: I did a lot of short stories, and interviews, and non-fiction articles, things like that.

VAN BELKOM: But nothing relating to the horror field?

KILPATRICK: Oh yes, all of the short stories were pretty much horror. When I first started I wrote and published literary stories, but I realized my bent was toward darker material. One story in particular that I wrote called "Root Cellar" I did both a literary and horror version of because the story lent itself to both. The literary version was one of the runners-up in The Toronto Star short story contest and the horror version sold to *The Standing Stone*, which was a Toronto publication. I resold the horror version a couple of times, and it ended up in *Year's Best Horror*, edited by the late Karl Wagner.

VAN BELKOM: Why did it take you so long to find your niche in the horror genre?

KILPATRICK: Who knows . . . The first novel I wrote was a horror novel in the *Near Death* world, in 1975. I worked on a typewriter — retyping and retyping — and it took me about nine months. I sent out thirty-five letters to publishers — going through the route that new writers go through. This was in 1976, the year that Anne Rice published *Interview with the Vampire*, and I thought, "This is great, her book is out. It's really a wonderful book and everyone is excited about it, so maybe people will be interested in reading another vampire novel." Foolish me. I got thirty-four rejections of my letter, and I'd worked in business so I thought I could write a decent letter. Many of them were form letters; nobody even wanted to look at sample chapters. I just did not realize it was such a closed shop.

The thirty-fifth publisher was a publisher in the States called Manor Books and they said they'd like to see some samples, which I sent. Then they wanted to see the whole manuscript, which I sent. And then I didn't hear from them for two years, and over that two years I wrote letters, I called trying to get some kind of response. And finally, I received a form letter from them that basically said they had returned the manuscript, but I was still at the same address so I'm sure it just got lost en route.

But all that left me crushed in a funny way. I didn't send anything out for several years after that; I was pretty devastated. And then I turned toward short fiction because the investment of time and energy was a lot less, and the market seemed more open. But I was so stunned that it took me another couple of years to start working on another novel. I just didn't realize the way things were. I was naive.

VAN BELKOM: *Near Death* seemed to establish you as a "vampire writer" but how much of what you had written previously had been vampire fiction?

KILPATRICK: Probably one-quarter of the stories I've published have been about vampires. But vampires are not all that I've written in the way of novels. In The Darker Passions series, for example, I have eight novels, six of which are not about vampires. But I have done a lot of vampire writing, partly because I'm interested in vampires and am a collector — as you can see around you — I have quite a library of vampire books. It's just been a subject that has intrigued me and my writing evolved naturally out of my interest.

VAN BELKOM: Why do you think vampire fiction is so popular?

KILPATRICK: There are a lot of reasons. On the surface: power, sex, blood, death, immortality, all those things. People have gotten into AIDS and the millennium, feminist empowerment and incest, and more. I hate to beat a horse that's been tortured enough, but to me the vampire is an archetypal energy. It sifts through time and space, through all cultures. It's just there, like many other energies that exist. We are drawn toward predators of the human race, just as we are drawn toward God. We're drawn to many, many archetypes and this one seems to generate universal appeal.

VAN BELKOM: Did the publication of the books bring you into the goth community, or were you a part of it before that?

KILPATRICK: I wasn't a part of it before because I don't think there really was a goth community. There were isolated — what you would call them? — people of gothic sensibilities here and there and the community — if goths can be communal — kind of evolved. I've dressed in black most of my life, so that's nothing new to me. But the movement, if there is a movement, is just people of a Gothic persuasion. Some of them are more organized than others, like the Gothic Society of Canada, and The SIN Society of Montreal — I'm a member of both. So, if there is a movement it evolved slowly and I just evolved into it.

VAN BELKOM: You did a collaborative novel with Don Bassingthwaite called *As One Dead* which is set in the universe of the White Wolf role-playing-game Vampire: The Masquerade. What was that experience like?

KILPATRICK: Working with Don was fantastic. He's very professional. And he is such a funny guy; we had a lot of humorous moments together. White Wolf came to me and asked me to do this novel. That was great, but I hadn't played the game, didn't know the world. And they also wanted the novel in a very short time frame. I thought about it and I was going to ask a US writer to collaborate, but I thought that was long distance and would be difficult. And then I remembered that Don had done some books for White Wolf, so I called him up and he was eager to do it. We took a tiny segment of one of his novels and basically expanded on it. White Wolf was really good to work for, doubling the advance, and giving us an extension, which it turned out we didn't need.

VAN BELKOM: Don has called it an "instant book." How long did it take to write?

KILPATRICK: I think it was thirty days, and for ten of those I was in San Francisco. We alternated chapters and did the last one together. There are fifteen chapters, so we did seven each, all via e-mail. It was wild. I would call him at work, and he said his co-workers would all turn to him when he said things like, "So, the room's filled with blood and everyone is dead . . ."

VAN BELKOM: You've published eight erotic horror novels in The Darker Passions series under the pseudonym Amarantha Knight. First of all, why the pen name?

KILPATRICK: I had a contract with Pocket Books for *Near Death* and there was a clause that said I couldn't use my name with any other publisher while they had an option on another book. When I got the contract from Masquerade, I thought I could do a variation on my name, like, N. Kilpatrick or Nancy Somethingelse. But it occurred to me that this was such a weird, outrageous series that I should have an exotic name to go with it. I looked through the baby-name books, and found the name Amaranth, which is the plant. And I thought, Amarantha would be a pretty name. I needed a last name that would complement it, so I came up with Knight as in "day and night," as in "Nick Knight" the vampire (from the shot-in-Toronto television series *Forever Knight*) and Knight as in "knight, a crusader with a lance." I thought that Amarantha Knight sounded très cool, not quite like a Harlequin romance writer, and not quite like a pornography writer, and a bit at the edge of a horror writer. Hopefully it's something in-between all that, which is generally what these books are.

VAN BELKOM: Did you enjoy writing those novels?

KILPATRICK: Very much.

VAN BELKOM: The early ones more so than the later?

KILPATRICK: Well, the first one was special because it was *Dracula*, right up my alley. They are easy to write because I try to keep them very true to the plot. That isn't always possible because when you take something like *Doctor Jekyll and Mr. Hyde*, which is a novella, and "The Fall of the House of Usher," which is a long short story, and try to turn them into novel length, you've got to introduce a few new characters and embellish. In *Jekyll and Hyde* there are no females, just three who are alluded to, each in something like one line, so I had to invent some women. I try to stick to the plot and I try to use excerpts from the original work and let some of the dialogue come through. I had a lot of fun in *The Picture of Dorian Grey* because I adore Oscar Wilde. There are many direct Wilde quotes in that book, and I also invented my own "Wilde-isms"; I'm hoping readers have a hard time telling which is which.

VAN BELKOM: You've also edited several erotic horror anthologies as Amarantha Knight for Masquerade Books, and the stories for each one have been solicited in a different way. How much of a learning experience has it been for you in terms of writers and publishers and the way anthologies are put together?

KILPATRICK: Initially I was dealing with a publisher who had not done anything like these anthologies. They'd done one or two, but they really didn't even know what an anthology was — it was not in their milieu. Convincing them to do something that embraced both horror and erotica was difficult. They had more control over the first book and then gradually I was able to wrestle control out of their hands because they saw that the books sell.

The books actually have two audiences: readers of horror and readers of erotica. Finally with the last book, I didn't have to have the names I had in the other ones to sell the idea, because the anthos have taken on a life of their own. The last was an open antho, not invitation-only, as the previous four had been.

VAN BELKOM: Which do you enjoy doing more, the novels or the anthologies?

KILPATRICK: I guess at this point I'm enjoying the anthologies more. But that always shifts around.

VAN BELKOM: You've also edited a horror anthology for Berkeley, tentatively titled *Gargoyles*. Has the experience with Masquerade helped you with that at all?

KILPATRICK: Oh yes. I've learned as an editor. I co-edited *Gargoyles* with Thomas Roche, a friend of mine. We were sitting around chatting on the phone one day, discussing the possibility of editing an anthology together, and I mentioned how I thought gargoyles were going to be a big thing soon. He got excited, so I called Ginjer Buchanan at Berkley and low and behold she's a gargoyle enthusiast; it came out of that.

We solicited "name" writers. It's a major book with major money and Ginjer needed big names to sell the idea in-house. We have some dynamite stories, at least three that I think are of award-winning calibre. It was a delight to edit.

VAN BELKOM: Your most recent novel, *Child of the Night*, was published in England by Raven. What can you say about British publishers' attitude toward writers, as opposed to those of American publishers?

KILPATRICK: It's harder with a British publisher because England is *long* distance. That book was bought by Stephen Jones who was the person who put together the Raven imprint for Robinson Publishing. The imprint was his, 100 percent, but that altered. He told me he had wanted to buy three of my novels, with an option for a fourth, first doing them individually and then in omnibus editions of two and two. But he'd been having problems with Robinson, and around the time he proposed this, they wouldn't let him buy all three books. So, he left. And he felt and still feels very badly about it, regarding me. But he'd bought one book from me, *Child of the Night*, and graciously agreed to edit that book even though he was gone. I didn't have a whole lot of contact with anyone else there. They kept saying they were interested in buying another book from me, pushing me to get back the rights for *Near Death* so they could reprint it, and I worked hard to get those rights back from Pocket, and then Robinson decided they weren't going to do any more horror books. *Child of the Night* was their best-selling horror title ever, and sold out within a few months, but that didn't change their perspective. This is, of course, the madness of the book business, in Britain, in the US, and probably in Canada as well. It makes no sense at all.

VAN BELKOM: You've written scripts for the comic *VampErotica*. How much different is comic book scripting to writing prose fiction?

KILPATRICK: My god. Day and night. First of all, it's a lot less work. I was adapting stories out of my collection *Sex and the Single Vampire* so I didn't have to write the stories from scratch. I just went through what already existed and snatched out the hot lines. I think each script took me about an hour, an hour and a half. It was really fun work, and an incredible experience, seeing how someone else — the artist — envisioned characters I had created.

VAN BELKOM: You're pretty well known as a "Vampire Writer" now. Is it a label that you're comfortable with?

KILPATRICK: I'm not uncomfortable with it. I have other novels that are not vampire novels that my last agent was trying to sell. Those books are still there, and I'd like to sell them.

VAN BELKOM: A short story of yours won the Arthur Ellis Award for Best Mystery Story of the Year. Have you considered branching out into other genres like mystery, or is horror writing in your blood?

KILPATRICK: I've got a mystery novel in the outline, three chapters stage, and I'm hoping to have the time to work more on it soon.

For me, winning the Arthur Ellis Award didn't manifest into anyone asking me to write a mystery novel, as has happened with other writers I know. I've set the novel in the US which means it may not find a Canadian publisher. I'm not opposed to Canadian publishers at all. I would love to publish a novel with a Canadian publisher. But I'm kind of resigned. You can't sell horror in Canada. There has been the occasional book over the last twenty-five years, like Nancy Baker's books, and Garfield Reeves-Stevens', and a few others, but that is an odd situation, not the norm. There are some mystery novels published here. But outside of literary, the publishing slots open to genre fiction are few. Publishers here just don't seem to want commercial books that will make them money. Which is a shame, since commercial absolutely does not mean poorly written. The Americans and the Brits are way ahead of Canada in their thinking regarding commercial fiction.

VAN BELKOM: You seemed to be either nomadic or restless, having originally come from Philadelphia, lived in Montreal, Vancouver, Chicago, San Francisco, Toronto for a long time, and now you've moved back to Montreal. How did you end up in Canada and why Montreal when the rest of the English speaking population there is going the other way?

KILPATRICK: Well, first of all, I don't think the rest of the English-speaking population is going the other way. I know quite a few people who are actually moving here. I don't think it's the massive exodus the media is pumped up about.

I came to this country because I had a boyfriend who wanted to come to Canada, theoretically for the weekend. We came for the weekend. He left. I stayed.

I was in Toronto for a year, then I went to Montreal for a year, then I came back to Toronto, then to Vancouver for a year, then back to Toronto. It was long past time for me to move. I don't know if I'm nomadic or adventurous or insane. Maybe all three.

Montreal is a really delightful city. It's esthetically beautiful, unlike Toronto, which can be extremely depressing to live in because everything is square and brown and uninspired. Montreal has gorgeous architecture, the lifestyle is very laid back, people enjoy life. I don't know if it's the French *joie de vivre* or what, but there's something here that lets people delight in the little things. Torontonians are grumpy a lot of the time. You run for a bus and the driver slams the door in your face then pulls away. Everyone seems so dissatisfied. I don't know if it's expectations that haven't been met or what. All I know for sure is that the Toronto I arrived in back in 1970 is gone. Toronto is a tough city now.

VAN BELKOM: What made you want to stay in Canada, for the weekend, and then for the rest of your life?

KILPATRICK: I adore Canada. People from this country who go to the States for a visit love the US. And the US has a lot going for it. If you have innovative ideas, the US opens its arms. But to actually live there is a whole different story. When you visit, people recognize you're different and there is a tendency to be hospitable and treat you well. As a person who lived there, in various cities, I found that overall the mentality in the US is the same pretty well everywhere. My paranoia level soared. When I moved here, it plummeted.

Canada is a kinder, gentler society overall. Even in Toronto with all its haste and tension, there's nothing in the way of the dark ugliness that embeds itself in the American culture. Just look at the murder rate alone — seventy murders a year average in Toronto. There isn't a similar sized city in the US that has anything under 300 murders a year. There are more murders a year in Philadelphia, the city where I was born, than in the entire country of Canada.

VAN BELKOM: How did the move to Canada affect your writing?

KILPATRICK: It gave me a chance to relax so that I could write.

W.P. Kinsella

When you think of Canadian fantasy writers, the name W(illiam). P(atrick). Kinsella doesn't immediately spring to mind. That's because even though much of his work contains fantastic elements, he has avoided being labeled a "fantasy writer" and is instead referred to as an author of "imaginative fiction" and "magic realism."

Kinsella was born in 1935 in Edmonton and began teaching creative writing at the University of Calgary in 1978. He left in 1983, shortly after the publication of his first novel, *Shoeless Joe*, to pursue a career as a full-time writer. Such a career couldn't have had a better start than *Shoeless Joe*, which won a Houghton Mifflin Literary Fellowship Award and the *Books in Canada* First Novel Award. It was also the basis for the hugely successful 1989 film *Field of Dreams*. Other film adaptations of Kinsella's work include the Canadian made *Dance Me Outside* and *Lieberman in Love*, winner of the Academy Award for Best Live Action Short in 1996.

But even before *Shoeless Joe* was published, Kinsella had garnered attention for his well-crafted and entertaining short stories published in dozens of literary magazines and anthologies (including *Best Canadian Stories* and *Best American Short Stories*) and four collections: *Dance Me Outside, Scars, Shoeless Joe Jackson Comes to Iowa*, and *Born Indian*. Always a hard-working and prolific writer, Kinsella continued writing and publishing stories following the release of *Shoeless Joe* and produced six more collections in the 1980s: *The Moccasin Telegraph, The Thrill of the Grass, The Alligator Report, The Fencepost Chronicles, Red Wolf, Red Wolf*, and *The Further Adventures of Slugger McBatt*. More recent collections include *The Miss Hobbema Pageant, Brother Frank's Gospel Hour*, and *The Dixon Cornbelt League*.

The 1980s also saw the publication of Kinsella's second novel, *The Iowa Baseball Confederacy*, another baseball tale, this time featuring such fantastic elements as time travel and a baseball game that lasts over 2,600 innings. Other novels include *Box Socials, The Winter Helen Dropped By*, and *If Wishes Were Horses*.

EDO VAN BELKOM: When you began writing, did you sometimes imagine yourself as successful as you've become, or were you just trying to write your stories as best you could?

W.P. KINSELLA: I think you have to have a certain ego as a writer. I always imagined myself successful and was never particularly surprised when it happened.

VAN BELKOM: So everything you did was always done in order to achieve that goal?

KINSELLA: Yes. It's always writing to be successful, writing to make a living at what I do, and I had to beat my head against the walls of North American literature for many years because of it.

VAN BELKOM: Your novel *Shoeless Joe* started out as a short story first published in *Aurora: New Canadian Writing 1979* as "Shoeless Joe Jackson Comes to Iowa." Did you intend the story to become a novel, or were there other forces at work?

KINSELLA: An editor at Houghton Mifflin in Boston read a review of *Aurora* and a two-line mention of my story. He wrote asking if it was a novel. I said, "No, but I'd like to write a novel and would need an editor to work with me." I immediately began thinking *novel*. The editor agreed to work with me, but not a lot of work was needed. I wrote the book straight through in nine months — just like a baby — while I was teaching.

VAN BELKOM: Would you have preferred *Shoeless Joe* to have been your fourth or fifth novel instead of first, and as a result, the book that all your subsequent novels are compared to?

KINSELLA: It would have been nice if I could have published *The Iowa Baseball Confederacy* first, because it would have gotten good reviews and then sort of set things up for *Shoeless Joe* to be a massive bestseller. I mean, it's been a good-selling book for fifteen years, but I never get up there to play with Stephen King or Danielle Steele or John Grisham. I think it would have been better for my career had the books been published in that order because *The*

Iowa Baseball Confederacy is actually a better book, although it's a darker book which readers are not as likely to get wildly enthusiastic about.

But no, you take what you can get. I was happy to get *Shoeless Joe* as my first novel made into a movie, and then the book and the movie opened a lot of international doors to me.

VAN BELKOM: Were you happy with the job they did turning *Shoeless Joe* into *Field of Dreams*?

KINSELLA: I loved it, and I don't see how they could have done a better job. Credit goes to Phil Alden Robinson who wrote the screenplay and directed. Most writers are not happy with what Hollywood does with their work and with good reason. *Field of Dreams* was the exception. *Dance Me Outside* was a disaster. And even *Lieberman in Love*, though it won the award, wasn't that well done.

VAN BELKOM: Do you have a preference between writing short stories and novels, or is it just the idea that comes to mind that gets written first?

KINSELLA: I prefer to write short stories. For a short story you're only going to give up a week or ten days, or two weeks at the most, and if it fails you can put it in the drawer. But with a novel you have to be very careful because a novel has to succeed. I can't devote eighteen months or two years to writing a novel and have it turn out not to be publishable.

So I want a good premise before I start, and then I look at the first thirty pages very carefully because if I don't think it will go the distance, I will junk it. You can't afford to waste time on unsuccessful novels.

VAN BELKOM: In the press release for *If Wishes Were Horses*, you're quoted as saying, "I write love stories that are peripherally about baseball." Do you feel that you have to include baseball in your stories because that's what people expect from you or is it just natural for you to write stories that relate in some way to baseball?

KINSELLA: Since *Shoeless Joe* was successful, I've discovered that there is a market out there for baseball fiction, so when I get an idea for a story I say, "All right now, is there some way that my main character can be a baseball player or should it go to Silas and Frank?" the books in my other line.

VAN BELKOM: So there's always a conscious decision to include baseball?

KINSELLA: Oh, definitely.

VAN BELKOM: What do you think it is about baseball that lends itself so readily to works of magic realism, that the sport of hockey doesn't have?

KINSELLA: It's the open-endedness of the game. The other sports are all twice enclosed, first by time and then by rigid playing boundaries. Of course, there's no time limit on a baseball game and on a true baseball field the foul lines diverge forever, eventually taking in a good part of the universe, and that makes for myth and that makes for larger than life characters, which is what writers are looking for and which is very conducive to magic realism.

It doesn't matter how wonderful Wayne Gretzky or Michael Jordan are, they are trapped on these tiny playing surfaces and there's very little prospect for anything magical.

VAN BELKOM: You said in an interview earlier today that you're a big fan of Sumo wrestling. Have you ever considered writing a story centered around or having to do with Sumo wrestling?

KINSELLA: I would have to get a Sumo fan to check the story because it would be the equivalent of an Englishman coming over her for five years and then trying to write about baseball. He would make idiotic mistakes. And while I understand much about Sumo wrestling, I do not understand some of the nuances and would need to work closely with someone who does understand, someone who could say, "You idiot, the word you want here is 'Sumotori' not 'Rikishi,'" which as near as I can tell mean the same thing.

I would like to write about Sumo sometime, but I'd have to have a collaborator who really understood the nuances of the sport.

VAN BELKOM: Are you much of a hockey fan?

KINSELLA: No.

VAN BELKOM: Reading your work I get the impression that for you there's a real sense of beauty and wonder about minor league or amateur baseball, and even baseball from the past, that isn't there when you write about modern professional baseball.

KINSELLA: I think quite a few of my stories are set in contemporary settings. It's the old thing — "You don't have to commit suicide to write about it."

I am not a minor league baseball fan. I find minor league baseball too slow, too many walks, too much time, too many high-scoring games. I really only go to see major league games, but I do write a lot about minor leagues.

Of course, I'm extremely pissed off at Major League Baseball at the moment — I haven't forgiven them for the baseball strike. I mean two groups of arrogant millionaires who have no concern for the people who put that money in their pockets. I haven't paid for a game since the strike and I don't plan to for another two or three years. I figure in that time most of the striking players will be out of the game and many of the owners will have found some new toy to play with.

The game of baseball will survive the nasty and arrogant people associated with it at the moment, but they can't ever have another strike. That would kill the game completely.

VAN BELKOM: Are you still a card-carrying scout?

KINSELLA: I'm a scout for the Atlanta Braves, but as I said, I don't see the kind of games where it would be necessary to find prospects. But it doesn't do the Braves any harm to have a famous writer on their scouting staff, and it doesn't do me any harm for me to be able to say that I'm on the Braves' scouting staff.

VAN BELKOM: Whose idea was it, yours or the Braves?

KINSELLA: The Braves. Bill Clark, the head international scout, is a close friend of mine.

VAN BELKOM: Is there something special about the combination of Iowa and baseball that you haven't found anywhere else?

KINSELLA: It's hard to say. I went there and really fell in love with Iowa City and the area around it. It's a place where I feel comfortable and there aren't many places where I've lived that I feel comfortable and that I actually enjoy. I feel the same about the Coachella Valley east of Los Angeles, but I haven't set any of my stories there and don't know that I will. But I do find there's a certain wonder in the warm Iowa nights full of fireflies and baseball games and things.

There's a line in one of my stories that goes, "Once you fall in love with the land, the wind never blows so cold again." And that's certainly the way I feel about Iowa City and the area around there.

VAN BELKOM: Do you go back there from time to time?

KINSELLA: I graduated there in 1978. I've been back there every year . . . I got to Dyersville this year but I didn't get to Iowa City so it's the first year I haven't been back to Iowa City in some eighteen years.

VAN BELKOM: You've never been tempted to move there or live there for part of the year.

KINSELLA: I would like to live there in the fall. It's a wonderful place when the humidity dies down from about the middle of September to about the first of December, but the occasion has never arisen when I can have the time to do that.

VAN BELKOM: You pride yourself on being a storyteller. Do you sometimes find yourself at odds with literary writers who think of themselves as creating "art" rather than "telling stories."

KINSELLA: Well, you know . . . I'd leave them alone if they'd leave me alone, but there are so many of these petty jealous little academic drones who have no idea what the writing world is about and who are incredibly jealous of anyone who should actually sell some books.

I think it was Margaret Atwood who said, "As soon as you get your head above water somebody starts shooting at you." She's had more criticism than the rest of us put together and for no good reason — she's an incredibly good writer — but because she is successful, all the academic critics take great glee in trashing her work. The same happens to me on occasion. I don't suffer fools gladly and there are a lot of fools in the academic community, not all, but many, and I don't put up with much from them.

VAN BELKOM: Do you still teach writing?

KINSELLA: Very seldom. I did a month at the Atlantic Center for the Arts in Florida because they paid me well to do it, but I generally don't teach. I don't like looking at manuscripts. It's very time consuming and I find I don't get much in the way of writing done while I'm teaching.

VAN BELKOM: Did you ever find it a source of frustration when you had students who were convinced that they were going to create "art" and gave no concessions to storytelling?

KINSELLA: I always told them what I thought, I tried to tolerate the ones doing artsy craftsy type stuff if they did good work, but if they were writing drivel they were told it was drivel.

VAN BELKOM: You were teaching out of necessity, not out of any desire to be a teacher.

KINSELLA: That's true.

VAN BELKOM: Did any of your students have any success?

KINSELLA: A number of them have published novels and short stories, even won some awards. My first class was phenomenal: I think nine out of twelve people ended up publishing.

VAN BELKOM: Did you feel any friction from your fellow professors when you were publishing and they weren't.

KINSELLA: Fiction was regarded as something from outer space. When I was first hired everyone came by my office and said, "What's your academic specialty?"

I said, "I don't have one, I teach fiction writing."

One year I published more than the entire English faculty at the University of Calgary.

VAN BELKOM: Was that satisfying?

KINSELLA: Oh, yes. A great deal of writing is, "I told you so," and saying to all the people who've treated you badly over the years, "Look at me, I'm successful, you son of a bitch, and you're still pumping gas." And that's very nice.

VAN BELKOM: Living well is the best revenge.

KINSELLA: It certainly is.

VAN BELKOM: You've had considerable success in Hollywood. *Field of Dreams* was, of course, a very successful movie, but when "Lieberman in Love" was the basis of an Academy Award-winning Live Action Short film, you — the writer — were totally forgotten and went unmentioned when the producers accepted their Oscar. What has your experience taught you about how Hollywood looks upon writers?

KINSELLA: Well, I think it was summed up in Robert Altman's movie *The Player* when these two producers tried to figure out how they could remove the writer from the movie-making process. If there wasn't a writer, things could really work well, and that's sort of the attitude Hollywood has always had.

My "Lieberman in Love," which is a story from *Red Wolf, Red Wolf*, was optioned but no one kept in touch with me or my agent. I didn't even know it had been made, or shown, or nominated. I mean, it was my fault I didn't know it had been nominated because I didn't bother to read the Live Action Short category — it just never occurred to me.

Then on Oscar night I'm sitting with my girlfriend in a motel room in Charleston, South Carolina, watching the Academy Awards, and when this category came up I said, "Hey, that's my story!"

And then I said, "Hey it just won an Academy Award."

And then Christine Lahti gets up, thanks everybody and their dog and doesn't mention me — without whom they wouldn't have had anything to film.

Of course there are precedents for that. The year before, *Forrest Gump* won nine Academy Awards and even the guy who adapted the book into a movie didn't mention Winston Groom. I mean, this is terrible. And I'm told the same thing happened at the Genies this year. I don't have any interest in the Genies, but apparently the film that won for Best Movie was adapted from a book and nobody mentioned the author at all.

VAN BELKOM: When *Field of Dreams* came out, I found it odd that there wasn't a printing of *Shoeless Joe* to tie into the movie?

KINSELLA: The British did one, and, of course, *Shoeless Joe* sells like poison tablets in Britain. It would be like trying to sell a novel about cricket over here, but the British at least had the gumption to put out a book with Kevin Costner and the movie poster on the cover.

I met someone from Ballantine a year or two later and said, "Why in the world isn't there an edition out there with *Field of Dreams*?" And he said, "Well, we consider your book art." And I said, "Fuck art! I want to cash the check." But it didn't do any good.

VAN BELKOM: I was dumbfounded by that because from what little I knew about you, I knew you were pragmatic.

KINSELLA: It should have been, "Now a major motion picture" with the movie poster on the cover and it would have sold a few million extra copies.

VAN BELKOM: One of your very early efforts, "These Changing Times," reprinted in Lesley Choyce's anthology *Ark of Ice*, was a science fiction story. Was there a time when you thought you might write science fiction instead of magic realism?

KINSELLA: Well, there's a blurred line between those two. There were a couple of stories I wrote in high school that I considered

science fiction — "These Changing Times" and "I Walk Through the Valley" — but I don't consider myself a science fiction writer at all.
VAN BELKOM: The natural progression for a writer at your level is to work in film writing screenplays and teleplays. Is that something you'd like to do or are you happy writing stories and novels?
KINSELLA: Well, yes and no. I would prefer to just keep writing novels and let somebody else adapt, but there is just so much money kicking around for screenplays. My agent in Hollywood is dying for me to do something, and I keep coming up with ideas, and he keeps turning them down. The things he wants me to write for Bruce Willis and Arnold Schwarzenegger are completely beyond my ken. I couldn't do that sort of thing at all. So I don't suppose I'm going to do much in that area.

Spider Robinson won the John W. Campbell Award in 1974 as Best New Writer and the years have proven him to be a sage choice for such an honor. Just two years later, Robinson won the Hugo Award for Best Novella for "By Any Other Name" and in 1977 he won both the Hugo and Nebula Awards for Best Novella for "Stardance," which he co-wrote with his wife, Jeanne Robinson. Then in 1983, he won his third Hugo for the short story "Melancholy Elephants."

But awards are just one aspect of Robinson's career. He has been blessed with the good fortune to be able to produce both quality, award-winning fiction, as well as humorous stories and novels that appeal to a large number of SF readers. Robinson's Callahan series began with the story "The Guy With the Eyes," published in *Analog* in 1973, and has stretched out into some eight novels and collections set in Callahan's, Lady Sally's, and Mary's Place: *Callahan's Legacy*, *The Callahan Touch*, *Off the Wall at Callahan's*, *Lady Slings the Blues*, *Callahan's Lady*, *Callahan's Secret*, *Time Travelers Strictly Cash*, and *Callahan's Crosstime Saloon*.

The other parts of Robinson's fiction consist of the Stardance books, co-authored with his wife Jeanne, and some very ambitious and complex novels. Robinson's first novel, *Telempath*, published in 1976, was a continuation of the novella "By Any Other Name." Other novels include *Night of Power*, *Mindkiller*, *Time Pressure* and *Lifehouse*. As with *Telempath*, Robinson's first novel-length collaboration with Jeanne, *Stardance*, was a continuation of their award-winning novella of the same name. Jeanne, a former professional dancer, holds the distinction of winning the Hugo and Nebula award for her very first piece of published science fiction. The Robinsons have since teamed up for two subsequent Stardance novels: *Starseed* and *Starmind*. Robinson has also published two collections of non-Callahan stories: *Antinomy* and *Melancholy Elephants*, the latter first published by Penguin Canada in 1984.

Born in New York City in 1948, Robinson came to Canada and married Jeanne in 1975, settling in Nova Scotia for a time, before moving to Vancouver, where he currently resides.

EDO VAN BELKOM: You've said that you decided to try your hand at writing science fiction after reading a particularly bad example of the genre and feeling you could do better. Was it really that clichéd a beginning, or had you sometimes thought about trying to write SF while reading it in your youth?

SPIDER ROBINSON: Good question. Most interviewers are happy with a short easily-explained cliché. You get the never-before-told Whole Truth — and may God have mercy on your soul.

Sure, I thought about writing SF while reading it in my youth. I also thought about being (roughly in order) a cowboy, a scuba diver, a superhero, an astronaut, a priest (did a whole year in a seminary), a cop, a lawyer, a comic book artist, and a folksinger. Then, at sixteen (I graduated high school at sixteen — long story), I got serious and decided I was going to be an English teacher/pot dealer, and went to college.

Toward the end of my college career I noticed a mimeo poster in the halls soliciting submissions for something called a "science fiction fanzine," edited by three fellows named Jim Frenkel, Lou Stathis, and Norman Hochberg. I was *utterly* innocent of fandom, and in all candor not terribly interested once I did hear of it from Jim Frenkel, who was then a prime mover in the campus Science Fiction Club (I had never been much of a joiner) ... but I had always been faintly curious to know if I could actually imitate an SF writer, and decided to seize the moment. I fired up a bowl of prime Jamaican, and in short order produced a short story called, if memory serves, "The Dreaming Dervish." I also did three black and white pen-and-ink illustrations for it, which were much more interesting to do than the story itself. (I was doing a regular weekly cartoon in the campus paper, then, and modeling for Marvel artist Don "Iron Man" Heck off-campus.) Jim accepted all of it, without perceptible excitement, and "The Dreaming Dervish," lavishly illustrated by the author, saw print — excuse me, saw mimeography — in what I believe was the first issue of his fanzine, *Xrymph*. My (and Jim Frenkel's) best guess as to date is somewhere in the 1969–70 range, which would have made me twenty-one. The circulation was doubtless comfortably in the double digits (Jim claims 250, but then he's an editor).

I waited eagerly for response, and to the best of my recollection there was none whatsoever. Zippo. I got much more feedback and egoboo (certainly more women) from the folksinging I was doing around and near campus then. Jim did ask for another story, but I discounted that: he had space to fill. I believe I did write him a second story, a typographical experiment inspired by the tricks Harlan Ellison had pulled in his immortal "The Region Between," in which the reader was asked to follow both timelines of a time travel story at once, by means of adjacent columns of text that occasionally ran together into one whenever the time machine connected their parallel stories — but I don't at this remove recall its title, or whether Jim ran it. (For some reason I remember that the villain's name was Drun Drun Droon.) Having accomplished what I'd set out to do (prove to myself that I could imitate a writer well enough to fool at least one person), and seeing nothing more to be gained, I forgot the whole thing and went back to being just a reader of SF. (The first book I ever read, at age six, was Papa Heinlein's *Rocketship Galileo*.)

I'm quite certain that it *never* occurred to me — then — that I might put a manuscript in the mail, to someone who might offer me money for it. I don't know why. It seems such an obvious thing to do, in retrospect. But in those days I imagined real SF stories were written by gods, and then judged by surly gods; my own highest ambition had been to play one just long enough and well enough to maybe get laid. It hadn't worked, so I moved on.

Now we jump ahead several years, to 1974. I'm at my first-ever SF convention, a Boskone. At this point I have sold one story to *Analog* magazine, but it has not yet been published. I've also mailed a dozen more stories to *Analog*, one at a time, and they've all bounced — there, and a few other places, too. I don't know a single fan, and the only pro I know — Ben Bova, who bought that first story — isn't at Boskone that year. What I'm trying to say is, the first two days are horror: alienation and confusion and loneliness in the midst of a huge rollicking party. I'm dimly aware that since I'm a published writer (well, about-to-be-published), there are probably many people here who would like to talk to me . . . but I have no idea how to gracefully introduce this into the conversation. Finally I wander past something called a SFWA Suite, and dimly wonder if I'm entitled to enter it. Just then somebody who looks just like me emerges: a skinny, long-haired, bearded freak. He sees my face, comes over and says, "Are you okay, brother?"

So I hesitantly explain my problem, and he turns out to be Jay Haldeman, and he insists on taking me back into the SFWA Suite and introducing me to, like, Gardner Dozois and Piglet Effinger and Jack Dann. You know, gods. And they all tell me not to worry about being slow to sell a second story, that if you can crack *Analog* first time out, you'll do it again eventually. Hours later, royally drunk and happy as a pig in shit, I depart. I wander the hotel for several more hours, and then, just as the elevator doors are closing on me, I suddenly hallucinate a voice calling my name in the distance. I hold the door — to the annoyance of several of the other fans — and yell, "Spider here," and someone even taller and skinnier and longer of beard and hair than me appears and says, "Hi, I'm Ted White, and I've been combing this hotel looking for you since I bumped into Jay Haldeman, because from what he said, you'll probably want to hear that I just bought your second story for *Fantastic*. Nice work. The check's in the mail." And the elevator doors slide closed, and everyone in the elevator stares at me . . .

Anyway, the point of this wandering anecdote is that the story White bought, only slightly revised, was "The Dreaming Dervish," that first-spasm I'd done for *Xrymph*. If it had never been written, I might well have quit the business in despair around then and never had a second sale. (Though I would like to note that of those dozen failed stories I mentioned above, all eventually found a home — usually after I had rewritten them to Ben Bova's suggestions.)

VAN BELKOM: Those early stories, mostly set in Callahan's Place, were quite successful, earning you the John W. Campbell Award as Best New Writer in 1974 and spawning a series of books. But was that success a sort of double-edged sword, with the more Callahan stories you wrote, the more Callahan stories people wanted.

SPIDER ROBINSON: Any sort of success will always be a double-edged sword. I imagine Charles Shultz has dreams of throttling Snoopy. But everybody should have such problems!

Twice now, I've tried to gently nudge the whole Callahan's gang off the Reichenbach Falls. (The first time I used a nuclear weapon. The second time, in *Callahan's Legacy*, I got serious.) Each time it was for the same reason: I had simply run out of bar stories; just for the life of me couldn't think of anyone who could walk in with a new science fiction problem solvable by a bunch of barflies.

The first fiction-annihilation almost worked. As I had expected, Ace Books, assuming I was merely being coy, waved a large amount of money under my nose to tempt me into another Callahan book — and as I had expected, it did tempt me — but I still didn't have any ideas. So, stalling, I said, "How about if I write you a book about the whorehouse Callahan's wife used to run?" They blinked, and asked, "Could we put 'Callahan' in the title?" and when I said "Sure," they forwarded a large check, and that's how Lady Sally's Place was born. I followed it up with a second Lady Sally book . . . and then a dreadful thing happened. I ran out of whorehouse stories.

At about the same time, Ace decided the first Lady Sally book hadn't sold as well as they'd hoped (whether this suggests that sex is less popular than booze, or that the Lady Sally stories weren't as well written as the Callahan stories, or that Ace had recently been acquired by Matsushita Electric and was being micromanaged by clueless suits in Tokyo, is left as an exercise for the reader.) and hinted that they'd like another bar book instead. What luck! During the years of downtime, I happened to have idly dreamed up some more SF stories that could happen in a bar. And if the truth be known, I'd started to miss those rummies. So I invented Mary's Place, and *The Callahan Touch* got sold, written and published.

The next book contracted for was the final book in the Stardance series, my third collaboration with Jeanne. (Throughout my career, I've tried to arrange it so I alternate: a funny book — Callahanian, I guess you'd say — then a serious one — *Mindkiller*, for instance — then a funny one again, and so forth. Nothing kills humor faster than being required to produce it nonstop.) While working on that, I light-heartedly signed for a second Mary's Place book, *Callahan's Legacy* — for several reasons, chiefly that I had just left Ace Books for Tor, bringing with me the by-now-reverted rights for the first three Callahan books as a dowry, and Tor thought a new book would be a swell way to raise interest in an omnibus re-issue of the first three. And you'll never guess what happened. When it came time to write *Callahan's Legacy*, halfway through I ran out of ideas for SF bar stories . . .

Fortunately, I moaned to anyone who would listen about my problem, and a fan named Steve Herman in Montreal listened to me patiently, then put on his most pretentious expression and intoned, "two words: origin stories," and I whacked myself on the forehead (I have difficulty reaching my afthead at my age) and went home and finished the book. And at the end of the damn thing, I took care to have Mary's Place confronted by a force so awesomely potent and hellishly destructive that even technology approaching magic cannot defend against it — an implacable enemy even I can't figure out how to overcome.

And now there's all this Internet fuss, and I find myself wondering if there isn't some way I can undo the catastrophe and revive the place again somehow. I haven't thought of one yet — but watch this space . . .

VAN BELKOM: Creating Callahan's Place helped to make you a favorite of science fiction fans around the world for more than twenty years, but after all that time, I get the feeling that you prefer to keep a low profile where SF fans are concerned.

SPIDER ROBINSON: I don't know that I keep a lower profile than any of my peers. Past a certain point of success, you simply have to start reducing access, in order to get any work done. At conventions, four or five times a year, I'm as high-profile as I can get: I'll listen to anybody, answer any query, indulge any reasonable request, party all night long, sing every tune the Beatles ever wrote, accompany anything you play, and sign anything but a cheque; my only firm rule is that I won't interact with strangers while eating a meal. Then I go home and take about three or four months to recover from the energy drain . . .

Basically what I do is concentrate for a living, and that makes me either a solitary, private chap by custom, or an indigent. The Muse is a harsh mistress.

At present, I get snail-mail only from people bright enough to write me in care of my publishers and e-mail only from people I've personally given my ID to, and it takes me at least an hour of every day just to deal with that, often more. I dare not let my profile get much higher . . . I haven't got that many hours of concentration in me.

Opinion is split on whether Fandom Is A Way Of Life or Fandom Is Just A Goddamn Hobby — those are agreed to be the two options. Well, I've got a way of life: writing science fiction . . . and thus I can't afford a goddamn hobby. A better use of my time is staring at a blank word-processor file until beads of blood form on my forehead . . .

I like success, money, and warm words from satisfied customers. Fame, however, I am wary of. There seems to be a growing consensus these days that if you allow yourself to become famous, you deserve anything you get: your privacy may be invaded with impunity, anyone may libel or slander you, the media are allowed to treat you like a captive pig, and you need bodyguards. The national sport has become tearing down heroes; it seems like a bad time to become one. I'd just as soon be a writer.

The thing I've liked best about science fiction fame is that it is what I think of as "fifty-cent fame." I hope that doesn't sound like I'm sneering at it; I'm not. Those warm words I mentioned go a long way toward making up for the lousy payscale in this racket. What I mean is that if I were set down in any major city in North America, I'm confident that I could locate at least half a dozen people willing to buy me a drink . . . but there's nobody from *People* magazine outside right now going through my trash looking for provocative receipts. I'm hoping it will prove possible to maintain that comfortable level of notoriety, while raising my income.

VAN BELKOM: You moved to Canada after you had sold a few short stories. Was the decision to emigrate made in part because you thought it might be a good place for a writer to live and work, or were there other reasons unrelated to writing behind the move?

SPIDER ROBINSON: I went up to Nova Scotia to visit two old college chums. They'd met and despised each other as freshmen; then I reintroduced them as juniors and they got married; after graduation they worked for Welfare in New York City for awhile, then moved to Nova Scotia to become small-farmers. They invited me up to see their ninety acres on the Bay of Fundy shore.

I'd just quit my job; they'd given me a choice: give up writing that SF crap in my spare time, become a full-time real estate editor with all my heart and soul, and double my salary . . . or quit. That same week, the woman I had been dating came out, to me and the world. So I went up to Hampton, Nova Scotia. Why not?

The Annapolis Valley was a pastoral paradise, spattered with beauty and inhabited by decent, honest people who met your eye. Nobody thought Annie odd for smoking a pipe. My friends had no way to lock their home, would not have dreamed of doing so. When I asked about it, Charlie looked puzzled and said, "Suppose somebody came by when I was out; how would they be able to build up my fires for me?" We went shopping in splendid old Annapolis Royal, and when Charlie had more groceries than he could carry, he set them down on the fender of his truck and walked away. "Won't somebody take any of that?" I asked. He blinked, and said, "People got reputations, don't they?" Our next stop was the drugstore; the pharmacist squinted at Charlie's prescription and said he could sell him what it said there for five dollars or the identical substance in an off-brand for three. What was Charlie's pleasure? I gaped. Two blocks later that pharmacist came huffing and puffing up behind us, freezing in his shirtsleeves; he'd accidentally overcharged Charlie fourteen cents. I was one mindblown New Yorker . . .

Almost everyone in the New York-Long Island area was rich and stark raving nuts, almost everyone in the Annapolis Valley was poor and sane; it looked like a place where one could survive on a freelance writer's income — and sure enough, a couple of grand a year goes a long way if you're willing to cut your own firewood and grow your own food and boo and make your own wine and keep your fires fed and so on. I just wanted to live where your neighbor was a valued asset rather than a smelly nuisance; I had the idea that this would help me write, but I didn't care much if it didn't. I just knew in my heart that going there, then, was a Good Idea.

I didn't know the half of it . . . for it was in Nova Scotia that I met Jeanne, and everything in my life started going Right.

VAN BELKOM: Speaking of Jeanne . . . Your collaborations with Spider have been tremendously successful (winning the Hugo and Nebula award for "Stardance," but after three novels how much has the collaboration process changed from the first "Stardance" novella to the third *Starmind* novel?

JEANNE ROBINSON: As much as my own life.

The original novella was a happy accident. Spider started a story about a zero-gravity dancer and asked me to be his resource person. So I corrected some terminology, and he grunted and fixed it. Then I heard myself say, "She'd never do *that* . . . she's not that kind of a person." Spider stared at me . . . then scratched out the offending paragraph. "What *would* she do?" he asked, and I told him. He turned back to page one, and added my name to the byline.

I thought he was crazy. I was no writer. But he wouldn't let me go . . . and he kept asking me what happened next, and I kept thinking of things, and it started to be fun. Once he'd managed to explain the physics of zero-gee to me, inventing free-fall dance was pure joy. Motherhood had just interrupted my dance career, and I had a lot of choreographic energy backed up. Then it was done and I put writing out of my mind — for good, I thought.

Many months later the story saw print, was a huge success, and was nominated for awards. Our friends started telling us we should pad it into a novel and cash in. We hated the idea. Then one night Spider's friend Gordy Dickson, the best plot-doctor in SF, said, "Don't pad it: *write the sequel.*" Aha. Spider and I talked it over at length and realized there were a lot of important questions we'd left unanswered. So we plotted out the rest of the book together, and sold it to Jim Frenkel at Dell.

But by that time our baby was weaned and I was immersed in dance again. I'd been invited to perform with Beverly Brown's company at the Riverside Dance Festival in New York, so Spider wrote most of the rest of the book in a tiny apartment while taking care of the baby. Each night after rehearsal, I tried to read and critique what he'd written before falling unconscious. We were both pleased with the results — and for the second time, I put writing out of my mind for good. I started up my own dance company, Nova Dance Theatre, in Halifax, and was far too busy to think about writing for over a decade.

Then the roof fell in. My back gave out and I had to stop dancing. A year later my company folded. I was suddenly out of work and heartbroken. We moved to Vancouver, where I hoped to figure out what to do with the rest of my life. Spider was very patient, but finally he said, "Look, do you want to have another baby?" I shuddered. "Fine," he said, "Me neither. Want to have another *book*?"

I stared. "Come to think of it," I said slowly, "we never did get around to explaining why those aliens showed up in the first place, did we?" The next thing I knew, we were writing a book about a forcibly retired dancer . . .

As with making a baby, the conception was the most fun. We talked it out for weeks. Then Spider wrote a first chapter, and showed it to me. I thought it was great, fast-paced . . . a little too fast-paced. "Too much happens too fast," I said. "The reader doesn't know who this woman *is*, yet."

Spider looked stubborn. "Show me where we can wedge in back-story without stopping the story in its tracks," he said.

I couldn't.

That night we went to a local club to hear Johnny Winter. Just as he came onstage, a thunderbolt hit me. I borrowed Spider's pen and notepad, and an hour later the Prologue to *Starseed* was done.

Spider was so impressed with it, we wrote the whole rest of the book sitting side by side at the Mac, arguing about every sentence. For the first time, I started to feel like a full-fledged collaborator, started to believe I was good at it. We'd agreed in advance that in the event of any deadlock disagreement, Spider won, but it never came up. The process of writing it helped me come to terms with losing dance. And then for the third time I put writing out of my mind for good.

"Wow, you know what?" I said a year or so later. "We got so involved in Rain's story, we still never got around to explaining why the aliens came . . ."

This time the process changed again. Spider likes to write until dawn; I can't stay awake that late. And since our last book, I'd taught myself to word-process. So we developed a kind of overlapping collaboration. We'd sit down together at about 10 p.m.; I'd totter off to bed at 2:00 a.m.; Spider would continue on his own until sunrise. Then I'd get up, fiddle with what he'd written, and go on from there for several hours. Each of us had time alone with it and time together. It seemed to give a deeper perspective. *Starmind* was the most fun to write, for me at least. I got to write about my Portuguese ancestors and my beloved Provincetown. And *this* time, we finally got around to explaining the damned aliens . . .

The *Stardance* story is completed now; we don't envision any more books set in that ficton. And I'm currently building myself a new career, as a producer/director of what I call Keepsake Video Productions. But Spider and I *have* discussed collaborating again someday . . . on a mystery novel this time. If we do, we'll probably use the same overlapping method we used for Starmind. It seemed to work well.

VAN BELKOM: At the 1980 World SF Convention in Boston, your hometown, you performed the simulated "Zero Gee" dance "Higher Ground" to an enthusiastic group of SF fans. How close do you think you got to the free-fall dance you've cultivated in your mind over the years?

JEANNE ROBINSON: Well, the point with that piece, "Higher Ground," was not to "get to the free-fall dance I've cultivated in my mind over the years," but to *fake* it well enough to fool civilians in one gee — a wholly different thing. I think I did well at that . . . people seemed to like it . . . but at no time did I feel, onstage, anything like what I imagine it would be like if I were in free-fall.

It was more an attempt to describe the *process* or progression I had undergone of learning to think of dance in those terms — although it did culminate with a pretty good *simulation* of zero-gee dance onstage, with help from lighting devices and a translucent cube, augmented by backscreen-projected trompe l'oeil film footage. I saw an evolutionary progression, from a primitive creature crawling in the primal mud, driven for some reason to stand erect — to Neil Armstrong, and beyond to Shara Drummond. It seemed to me that since dance has been there from the very beginning of that struggle, it is certain to follow us out into the Last Frontier. At least, it started seeming that way once Spider got me thinking about it; before we wrote "Stardance," I hadn't thought of dance in evolutionary terms any more than a fish thinks about water. But the more I thought about it, the more certain I became that the Second Oldest Art (just after Seduction) will be with us all the way across the galaxy. That's what the piece was about: that mental evolution.

Actually doing it, though, dancing in microgravity . . . well, the closest I've ever been myself is probably underwater, and I can't hold my breath long enough to do much there. There *are* now private companies that will put you in simulated zero-gee for up to a minute at a time — much cheaper than NASA's famous Vomit

Comet — but even so they're still beyond my reach. And skydiving doesn't attract me; I like enforceable warranties. And I dance poorly when a planet is rushing toward me; it spoils my concentration.

If I ever find myself in free-fall, though, I have years of theoretical choreography backed up, waiting to be tried out and rethought. As a modern dancer, deliberately trained to spend a lot of time off-axis, I think I'd make the transition okay. For all I know, I'd end up like one of those unfortunates Spider and I wrote about — perpendiculars, who just keep getting confused without a local vertical — but I don't *think* so. My worst problem, I think, would probably be with nausea during the first day or so. I tend to seasickness, despite fishergenes, and I really hate being seasick. Still, they have drugs for that.

VAN BELKOM: You have the rare distinction of not only winning a major awards with your first written work, but of also being the only SF writer ever to be invited into space by NASA. Perhaps you could explain that process and your feelings when the Civilians-in-Space program was canceled.

JEANNE ROBINSON: I've accepted that I'm never going to reach orbit, that I'll never actually get to try out what I've danced in my mind so many times. My last chance went up with Christa McAuliffe and her companions. I couldn't help but think of that when, after the Orlando Worldcon, Spider and I and our friends Evelyn and Don watched the Endeavor make the fiftieth-ever Shuttle launch. But I hope when someone does get to dance in free-fall, they'll remember some of the principles and dance phrases I suggested in the Stardance books. I'm sure they'll make new discoveries every five minutes . . . but I think Spider and I have outlined a lot of the fundamentals. Inertia replaces gravity as the antagonist of beautiful motion; the "steps" will consist of altering vectors in non-obvious ways, using a combination of kinesthetic muscle movement and outside-force devices like thrusters or wings. And so on. Who knows? Maybe they'll even remember our names . . .

The day the Challenger exploded, our phone rang off the hook all day. Most of the callers were journalists, from all over the world, who had found my name in a file of what I'm sure they thought of as Next Victims (the Civilians-In-Space roster), and called to ask how I felt about this Buck Rogers stuff *now*? I spent all day saying over and over, "I'll take the next flight. Statistically safer than sitting in my living room," while Spider fed me statistics on fatalities-per-billion-passenger-miles.

But I don't delude myself that the real tragedy was the loss of zero-gee dance — or even the awful death of all those brave people. It's a shame they killed the only part of the space program that really interested me personally, and also the part that could have ignited the imagination of the whole human race. We might have all gotten *behind* the damned space program, instead of letting it rot, if they'd sent up anyone with whom we, the taxpayers, could identify. Even John Denver, one of the candidates for Civilian-in-Space, had more emotional weight than a test pilot with a golf-cart. We needed poets up there, singers, writers, painters, dancers, and maybe even stand-up comics.

But I *do* confess to a perhaps prejudiced opinion that of all the arts we might have brought to space in my lifetime, dance was the most natural candidate — the one that would have translated best, and communicated most viscerally. Perhaps it was the moment an ape first stood erect that he or she began to envy the birds — or perhaps it goes back even further, to when everything that lived was in free-fall because it was all in water. Maybe it's an echo of the nine months spent floating at the beginning of life.

VAN BELKOM: Thanks Jeanne. Spider, much of what you have written while living in Canada has been set in Canada. *Stardance* begins in Toronto, while *Time Pressure* and *Mindkiller* were both set in Nova Scotia. Was it a way of giving your work an added distinction since Canada was a new landscape for SF stories, or was it merely a function of writing what you knew?

SPIDER ROBINSON: Also *Starseed* starts out on Gambier Island, off the coast of Vancouver, and "User Friendly" takes place in Halifax, and *Lifehouse* takes place almost entirely in Vancouver.

Both the motives you cite were present. I had always enjoyed stories set in exotic locations that actually existed, on this Earth, and I found Canada to be full of such: an exciting and storyful place, largely unexploited in science fiction. And it was right in front of me, readily observable. And I confess there was a third motive: I was told that Canadian settings would greatly enhance my chances of getting Canada Council and provincial grants. Whether this is true or not I could not say, but I have received about fifty percent of the grants I've applied for, and am told this is an excellent hit-rate, so it certainly couldn't have *hurt*. On the other hand, I *have* received grants for works with *non*-Canadian settings, too. Go figure.

As to the editors' reaction, I find that fascinating. There was absolutely none. Not once in twenty years has an editor so much as raised the subject, to the best of my recollection. No, I take it back: one editor said I made Nova Scotia sound like a marvelous place to retire to. Many Canadian writers seem to believe as an article of faith that his/her fiction *must* be set in America, preferably in New York, to have a hope of being published by an American house. I've even heard a few claim they were forced to scrub Canadian references to get an American sale. Nothing like that has ever happened to me, nor been reported to me by any writer I personally know.

From the above, by the way, perhaps I should segue into the question I assume will interest Canadian readers: why have I sold virtually all my work to American houses? Since I moved to this country (years before I got legal Landed status) I have been doing my level best to locate a Canadian book publisher — ideally one that would buy my book and market the American and world rights for me. Result: the square root of bugger-all. Zero interest. Twice I've hired Canadian agents; countless times I've sent out CVs and proposals to Canadian publishers myself; several times I've offered to separate out Canadian rights to a new book I planned to sell in New York. I'm perfectly aware that a Canadian publisher might do a better job of marketing and selling my books in Canada — and that without one I am more or less transparent to the Canadian literary community.

I've been looking for two decades, now. (And by the way, the Canadian agents charged fifteen percent — my New York agent gets ten — and charged extra for phone calls, photocopying and postage, which Eleanor Wood does not.) Not once have I received an offer for Canadian rights that was as much as half of what my American publisher was willing to pay for the same rights, even though they plan to exercise them half-heartedly.

That is: if I withhold Canadian rights on my next book, the New York publisher will pay X dollars less for it — and the most a Canadian house will offer for those rights is .45X — in Canadian dollars! I would love to help support the Canadian publishing industry, and it might well get more of my books to Canadian readers (it might even get me on a Canadian bestseller list, which I have never been yet so far as I know), but I have a family to feed, and rent to pay, and vices to indulge. I simply can't afford that much patriotism. Nonetheless, I have one Canadian-originated book.

New York editors share opinions like viruses over lunch. Some years ago the shibboleth somehow took root that "Sci Fi short story collections don't sell." This is a classic crock, but they swallowed it. It became impossible to sell a collection, even cheap, even with a Hugo-winning story in it. At about that time, Penguin Canada (out of the New York City loop and thus uninfected) kicked off a new Short Story Collection Series . . . and bought the one I sent them in desperation, *Melancholy Elephants*. (They paid beans — and Canadian beans — but they *paid*.) They did a *splendid* job, produced the most beautiful artifact there is with my name on it, and released it simultaneously with collections by Kinsella, Findley, and Levine (which is how I met Bill Kinsella, which is a whole other story) to launch the line, and put us all on CBC for massive and respectful national publicity, and I was just tickled as hell. It's trade paperback sized, and the cover painting depicts an oatmeal cookie suspended in a stormy sky, *that's* how Literary it is.

Then Tor Books in New York, who had previously passed on the collection, saw a copy of the Penguin and inquired whether American rights were available? They paid twice as many beans as Penguin had, small for ten times the market, but Yankee beans after all (which swell as if waterlogged as they cross the border), and they produced a typically garish mass market SF paperback, with an elephant in zero-gee on the cover.

Penguin sold out the first edition and never went back to press; in effect, turned off the money spigot and gave it back to me. Perhaps they caught the New York virus, but I believe they quietly dumped the Short Story Collection Series, even though all of them sold well and the Kinsella became a movie. Tor kept that sucker in print for years; it probably earned more in royalties than Penguin paid for the advance, and only reverted recently.

I *have* to keep selling North American rights to New York — despite the disgusting fact that the New York publishers usually pay me a lower royalty rate on copies sold in Canada than they do on copies sold in the US and possessions. (They have to pay a cut to a

Canadian distributor, you see.) I wish it were otherwise . . .

VAN BELKOM: You have the reputation of being unappreciative of some editor's efforts to tamper with your prose. For example, your limited edition book from Pulphouse is called *Kill the Editor*. Does the time you take to craft a book have a lot to do with this, or has your work been given ham-fisted attention from some well-meaning editors in the past?

SPIDER ROBINSON: Actually, I've had what I'm told is astonishingly good luck with editors. So far I can't say I've ever had a change forced on me that ended up damaging the story in my own opinion. I did once have to resist the successive weight of . . . let me see, six determined editors before I got *Night of Power* into print exactly the damn way I wanted it, with that "artistically unbalanced, narrative-stopping" soliloquy that opens the final chapter. Everybody agreed that was a mistake, but I found I had written the whole damn book as an excuse to write that soliloquy (though I didn't know it until I got there) and I stuck to my guns and got my way. And the book went straight in the dumper; it is now available only electronically from Bibliobytes. So what do I know? And on the other hand, several editors have materially enhanced my work, or saved my ass when I blundered, or suggested profitable clouds to farm — starting with Ben Bova and continuing through to Jim Frenkel today.

My breaking editors' chops is more of a literary convention than anything else, fondly intended. I think they know it, and know that the readers know it . . . or they wouldn't let me get away with it so much. God, I hope I'm right. A good editor is a pearl without price, and our genre is top heavy with them. Typesetters, on the other hand . . . the one at Ace, at least . . . the first two pages of *Time Pressure* are largely spent setting up a ghastly, almost inhuman pun, and in the first couple of hundred thousand copies printed, the typesetter thoughtfully *fixed the pun* for me.

VAN BELKOM: In the forward to *Callahan's Secret* you spend a lot of time denying that the third book in the Callahan series constituted a trilogy, but you have since gone on to write a trilogy of Stardance novels and your most recent book, *Lifehouse*, is the third in the ficton that *Mindkiller* and *Time Pressure* are set in. Do you still feel the same way about trilogies, or have you mellowed on that point over the years?

SPIDER ROBINSON: Well, Callahan's seems to have safely passed into an octology with a vague prognosis . . . and there's no reason to suppose that Jacques LeBlanc's ficton will self-seal at the end of *Lifehouse*. But I have to confess you have me dead to rights on the Stardance Saga. That one, as far as Jeanne and I now know, is complete: it's a trilogy.

I dodge the label because even in my own mind, the term has come to mean "something which if you don't buy all the bits, you're wasting your money" — like a magazine serial, useful only to faithful readers. (And there can never be enough of those.) No book I have ever written or will ever write is a "Sneaquel". . . where you find out only after you've gotten it home and invested precious hours of attention on it that it, uh, isn't done yet — or find out as you begin that it's already in progress and you missed the setup and premise.

But there's no polite way to say in your cover-blurb, "This isn't *like* those other, sucker-trap trilogies my colleagues publish," so I find it more politic to just insist that three guys standing in a row with identical features aren't necessarily brothers. Maybe you're right and it's time to stop the dodging. Give me the statement, officer: I'll sign it. In one short lifetime I have already committed editorship, agentry, criticism . . . and trilogy.

Robert J. Sawyer

As Canada's only native-born full-time SF writer, Robert J(ames). Sawyer takes his Canadian identity very seriously. For example, several of his novels, including the Nebula Award Winning *The Terminal Experiment*, take place in Canada, and his books and stories are generously populated by Canadian characters. As he commented in the *St. James Guide to Science Fiction Writers*, "Although Canadian fantasy writers have often set work in Canada, very little SF has had identifiable Canadian content. I've undertaken to rectify that."

Born in Ottawa in 1960, Sawyer began his writing career as a freelance business journalist. He turned to writing science fiction full-time in 1990 with the publication of his first novel *Golden Fleece*, an Aurora Award winner for best novel. He followed up that novel with The Quintaglio Ascension, a series detailing the intellectual, scientific and sociological ascension of a race of intelligent dinosaurs comprised of the books *Far-Seer* (1992), *Fossil Hunter* (1993), and *Foreigner* (1994). Another unrelated dinosaur novel, *End of an Era*, followed in 1994, and for a while it seemed that Sawyer would be an SF writer who specialized in dinosaurs.

But all that changed with the publication of the near-future thriller, *The Terminal Experiment* in 1995. The book won the Nebula, Aurora, and HOMer Awards for best novel and was a finalist for the Hugo Award. The book also established Sawyer as someone who could write "Crichton-esque" SF/mainstream thrillers, while still able to produce diamond-hard SF for the core readers in the genre. *Starplex* (1996) is a hard SF novel full of "sense of wonder," while *Frameshift* (1997) is another thriller set on Earth. His most recent book, *Illegal Alien*, published in 1997 is an SF courtroom drama.

Sawyer has also written several well-received short stories, most notably "Just Like Old Times," winner of both the Aurora and Arthur Ellis Awards, and "You See But You Do Not Observe," which won France's Le Grand Prix de L'Imaginaire.

In addition to fiction, Sawyer writes a regular non-fiction column "On Writing" for *On Spec* Magazine, and he co-edited the anthology *Tesseracts 6* with his wife, poet Carolyn Clink. He currently resides in Thornhill, Ontario, just north of Toronto.

EDO VAN BELKOM: You've got an arts degree and your background is in business journalism. How did you end up writing hard SF?

ROBERT J. SAWYER: Ever since I was a little boy up until my last year of high school, I thought I was going to be a paleontologist; I wanted to devote my life to studying dinosaurs. But as high school drew to a close, several things became apparent to me. First, I was getting tired of school — something heretical to say in my family. My father was a professor of economics at the University of Toronto, my mother had also taught there, and her father had been a professor at Berkeley. I lived in an academic family but was coming to realize that the academic life wasn't for me. I couldn't imagine spending the next ten years getting a Ph.D. so that I could make $18,000 a year sifting dirt. And, of course, all dinosaur paleontologists are civil servants — they work at museums or universities. This was 1979, but one didn't have to have too much speculative ability to see that the lot of Canadian civil servants was going to get progressively worse as time went by. Finally, there are only three dinosaurian paleontologists in all of Canada — one at the Royal Tyrrell Museum in Drumheller, one at the Royal Ontario Museum in Toronto, and one at the Canadian Museum of Nature in Ottawa — and it didn't look like any of the three incumbents was going to give up his job just because I'd arrived on the scene.

Now, I'd always known I'd write science fiction, but I'd assumed it would be a hobby or a sideline — which is precisely what it is for ninety percent of the members of the Science Fiction and Fantasy Writers of America. But there are only two dozen dinosaurian paleontologists in the entire world, compared to more than a hundred full-time SF writers. And SF writers, unlike paleontologists, aren't on a quota system: a writer can live anywhere, and the fact that Canada already had Spider Robinson and Phyllis Gotlieb didn't have any impact on whether I could do it, too.

Still, I knew it would be an uphill battle; I couldn't

just start being a full-time SF writer straight out of high school. But I did want to make my living writing. I thought about studying journalism, but the only degree program in journalism in Toronto at that time was at Ryerson Polytechnical Institute, and it required high-school history as a prerequisite, something I didn't have; I didn't want to leave Toronto because I was already involved with Carolyn Clink, who would later become my wife. Still, on a tour of Ryerson I was introduced to their wonderful Radio and Television Arts department, which was without doubt the best broadcasting program in Canada. I thought, hey, I could learn script writing — that's a marketable skill. They said they had seven applicants for every spot in the program, so I applied almost on a lark, but I got in.

Ironically, I ended up doing mostly journalism during the 1980s: 200 feature articles for Canadian and American magazines, everything from dollar-a-word stuff for *The Globe and Mail's Report on Business Magazine* to an article for *Sky & Telescope*. I also did a lot of very lucrative corporate and government work for such clients the Ontario Science Centre and Bank of Montreal, and, while I was doing that, I was banking a lot of money. By 1989, my wife and I had $100,000 in the bank — enough so that I felt comfortable quitting the non-fiction work and trying to become a full-time SF writer; I knew I'd never get a novel written if I tried to do it around my commitments to my clients. I'd already sold a number of short works, including a novelette called "Golden Fleece" that was used as the cover story in the September 1988 *Amazing Stories*. Fellow Toronto writers Andrew Weiner and Terence M. Green had both recently expanded short works of theirs into their first novels, and I decided to emulate that. With my short-fiction credentials, I had no trouble landing my first choice of agent, Richard Curtis, and he, in turn, had no trouble selling the novel-length *Golden Fleece*.

VAN BELKOM: Early in your career you were often referred to as a shameless self-promoter because of your efforts to promote yourself and your work. What's your response to that?

SAWYER: "Often" simply isn't true. Early in my career, a few vocal fanboys — jealous wannabe writers who were having no success of their own — saw fit to dismiss the accomplishments of everyone who was enjoying success, not just me. So if Orson Scott Card named my first book, *Golden Fleece*, the best SF novel of 1990 — and he did —

well, it wasn't because it was a good book, but rather, somehow, because I had "promoted" the book. If Terry Green got rave reviews for his short story collection *The Woman Who Is The Midnight Wind* — and he did — well, it wasn't because the stories were brilliant.

Do I appear on Canadian television a lot? Yes — but because the producers call me, not the other way around. TVOntario's *Prisoners of Gravity* phoned me, for instance, because John Rose at Bakka, Toronto's SF specialty store, recommended me to them; I'd never heard of the show when producer Mark Askwith first called, but I ended up being their most frequent guest, making sixteen appearances over the run of the series. I do have a degree in Radio and Television Arts, after all, and am very comfortable on camera or in front of a mike. These days, I crop up a lot on *@discovery.ca*, the Canadian Discovery Channel's nightly science program; I've made eighteen appearances to date. But, again, they came looking for me, and once more it was because I'd been recommended to them as a possible guest, not through anything I'd done.

Do I apologize that I keep getting asked back to *Morningside*, *Canada A.M.*, or *Imprint* in Canada, or by *Sci-Fi Buzz* in the States? Do I apologize that some radio programs have had me on as many as fourteen times? Of course not; I'm a communicator by profession, and I'm successful in that profession because I do it well. Sure, I do some small amount of promotion, but it takes up less than a day a month, and it's just part of the job. If you think Margaret Atwood or Michael Ondaatje do less, think again.

Besides, I've done far more to promote Canadian SF in general than I've ever done to promote myself. Who paid out of his own pocket to fly Donald Kingsbury from Montreal to Toronto so that he could give a free public reading in 1982? Who then got an interview with him into *Books in Canada* and another interview into *Science Fiction Review*? Who got Terence M. Green interviewed by *Books in Canada*? Who was the first person to have Terry Green, Andrew Weiner, or Robert Priest as guests at an SF convention? Who was co-chair of the first-ever conference on Canadian SF, NorthStar, held in September 1982? Who published Tanya Huff's first story, back in 1982? Who interviewed Élisabeth Vonarburg on CBC radio coast-to-coast in 1986, before she'd had anything significant translated into English? Hundreds of people noticed there was no entry on Canadian science fiction in the first edition of the *Canadian Encyclopedia*, but who made sure there was an entry in the second and subsequent editions? Who as a volunteer ran Toronto Hydra, Canada's first association of SF professionals, from its founding in 1984 for the next eight years? Who made sure there were readings by Canadian authors at the National Library of Canada to supplement the posters of Captain Kirk and Superman that were displayed during their exhibition on Canadian SF? Who spent three acrimonious years fighting to establish the Canadian Region of the Science Fiction and Fantasy Writers of America? Who produced the column "Northern Lights: Canadian Achievements in SF" for the newsletter of the Spaced Out Library, and who later turned that into a standalone newsletter? Who, year after year, produces the brochure called "Award-Winning Canadian SF," thousands of copies of which have been distributed by Bakka? And who co-edited *Tesseracts 6* for a fee of less than one percent of what he normally gets for doing a book?

I've done all of that, and more — all for the sake not of myself, but of Canadian SF in general.

VAN BELKOM: Your second novel, *Far-Seer*, was the first in a trilogy you call the Quintaglio Ascension, but since your fifth novel, *End of an Era*, you've concentrated on stand-alone books. Will there be more Quintaglio novels, or perhaps some other series or linked novels?

SAWYER: I found doing a trilogy very constraining. I devoted over two years of my life writing the three Quintaglio books; that's an awfully long time to spend with any one set of characters. I know trilogies or open-ended series are all the rage in SF, but I much prefer doing stand-alones. In fact, when my then-agent Richard Curtis sold the outline for *Starplex* to Susan Allison at Ace, he pitched it as the first book in an on-going series — and it could have easily been that. But as I was writing it, it became apparent that I was holding things back for future books, and I thought that was a cheat. A person buys a novel in a bookstore; he or she should get a complete work.

The Quintaglio trilogy never started out as a trilogy: there was originally only going to be one Quintaglio novel, *Far-Seer*. But my agent suggested I do more, and I agreed. I'd been influenced some-what by the early career of American writer Michael P. Kube-McDowell, who, at the time, seemed poised to become one of the top names in SF, and he'd started out with a trilogy for Ace, the publisher who had done *Far-Seer*. But I actually think, in retrospect, that doing a trilogy was a mistake — at least with the three volumes coming out with no other books in between. I was pigeonholed for a while as the talking-dinosaur guy — and if there's one thing I never want to be as a writer, it's pigeonholed.

That said, I actually have already written what I think of as a second trilogy, after the Quintaglio one. I consider *The Terminal Experiment*, *Frameshift*, and *Starplex* to be a thematic trilogy; they don't share any of the same characters, and *Starplex* — which is an off-Earth, far-future, spaceships-and-aliens novel — is much different in tone from the other two, but they explore related territory, and I think of them as my "Eschatological Trilogy." *The Terminal Experiment*, which deals with the discovery of scientific proof for the existence of the human soul, is about the origin and ultimate fate of individual human beings. *Frameshift*, which explores the discovery of a second level of coded information in our DNA, is about the origin and ultimate fate of the human species. And *Starplex*, which tackles just about every major issue in modern cosmology, is about the origin and ultimate fate of the entire universe.

Meanwhile, the book I just finished, *Factoring Humanity*, and the one I'm just starting, currently called *Mosaic*, also cover thematically related ground — in this case, the nature of human memory and subjective time. Again, they share no characters, but they, too, are parts of a thematic grouping.

VAN BELKOM: You've probably been interviewed in the media more times in the last few years than most northern dreamers will be in their whole careers. Is there any discernible bias against SF as a genre by the Canadian media?

SAWYER: Oh, certainly. It's *de rigueur* at *The Globe and Mail* to take potshots at SF. But, on the other hand, most of the other major newspapers in Canada have been very good not just to me but to SF in general: *The Toronto Star*, *The Ottawa Citizen*, *The Edmonton Journal*, *The Calgary Herald*, and *The Montreal Gazette* deserve particular credit for recognizing SF as a valid art form, and one of the most thoughtful analyses of my career to date was a piece by David Pitt in *The Halifax Chronicle-Herald*. Still, *The Globe* is not alone. I was the subject of a snotty profile in *Toronto Life* in which the self-styled journalist — he made a point of asserting himself as such in the article's first paragraph — decided to review the covers of my books, rather than actually read them. This clown lamented in his article how poorly his own books sell. I find that's often the source of the prejudice against writers of commercial fiction: reviewers and interviewers are often failed writers.

But, on balance, I think we do pretty well. The CBC and Newsworld, for instance, could not be more supportive of the SF field. I appeared on *Pamela Wallin Live* a short time ago with Tad Williams, a bestselling American SF author. He remarked that the CBC treats SF authors with real respect and gives us major exposure.

As for a general prejudice against SF, it's still there, in spades. Terry Green has come up with the best answer for it. When someone tells him they don't like SF, he asks, "What book have you read that led you to form that opinion?" And the answer, of course, is none. So we've got an uphill battle, but it is winnable. Because of the media exposure my work gets in Canada, I've had lots of people tell me that either *The Terminal Experiment* or *Frameshift* was the first SF novel they've ever read, and that it was nothing like what they thought SF was all about. But they also say they're going to continue reading SF now, which is very gratifying.

VAN BELKOM: As you become more successful in the field, do you find that critics and others are tougher on you than they've been in the past?

SAWYER: I really don't pay much attention to reviews. I used to read them myself, but I don't even do that anymore. My wife Carolyn works for me full-time as my assistant, and one of her jobs is to read through reviews, extract any quote that might be useful for the next dust jacket, and, if the reviewer was sufficiently perceptive — that is, if he understood the book — to photocopy the review and send copies to my publisher and agent. But, sure, when you win a major award, there are always some people lining up to take a knock at you. Still, as of right now, I've had two books out since I won the Nebula for *The Terminal Experiment*: *Starplex* and *Frameshift*. And although there have been a few detractors, those two books have gotten some of the best reviews I've ever had.

VAN BELKOM: Several of your novels have been set in Canada and have featured Canadian characters. Obviously you're a Canadian writer, but have you sometimes have difficulty being accepted as a Canadian SF author in your own country?

SAWYER: *Golden Fleece* has a Canadian protagonist, and its only Earth-based scenes take place in Thunder Bay and Toronto. *End of an Era* is set entirely in Canada — in Alberta, at TRIUMF in British Columbia, and in Toronto. *The Terminal Experiment* is set entirely in Toronto, as is the novel I just finished writing for Tor, *Factoring Humanity*. *Frameshift* and *Illegal Alien* are both set in the States, but still have major Canadian content; I had to set them in the States because Canada is just too nice a country for the stories I wanted to tell. In particular, for *Frameshift*, which has a Québécois as its main character, I needed a country that didn't have socialized medicine, and for *Illegal Alien* I needed a country that had capital punishment. In both cases, the US was sufficiently nasty a setting. I've never had any trouble being accepted as a Canadian SF author in my own country. *Quill & Quire* used a wonderful caricature of me as the cover illustration for its May 1993 issue, and when *Books in Canada* did a special Canadian Speculative Fiction issue in March 1993, I was the author they chose to profile. Still, I did have some trouble being welcomed as part of the literary community here. There's a real tendency for SF to be pooh-poohed by the literati. In fact, I got tired of being told that I wasn't literary . . . in large measure because I'd never had a government grant. So I applied for one — the lowest value Ontario Arts Council grant available, which was $500. And I got it, which shut a lot of people up.

But whatever lack of acceptance there might have been in the early years has been overcome. I've read twice at Harbourfront, I was keynote speaker at the 1997 annual meeting of the Canadian Authors Association, I'm profiled in *Canadian Who's Who*, and my books are taught at many Canadian universities in courses offered by departments as diverse as English, Astronomy, and Philosophy. I feel very much a part of the Canadian writing community.

VAN BELKOM: You have dual citizenship and are a Canadian as well as an American citizen. Have you ever considered moving south of the border?

SAWYER: I was born in Ottawa and my father was born in Toronto. My dad married my mother when they were both grad students at the University of Chicago; my mother grew up in California.

I am a Canadian by birth, a Canadian by residence, and a Canadian by preference. In the year I was born — 1960 — my mother had my birth registered with the US consulate in Ottawa as a foreign-soil birth to an American national, and thereby I gained dual citizenship. But I don't actually believe in dual citizenship conceptually; I think citizenship is like marriage: it should be a form of monogamy. Yes, I could move to the United States anytime — I do have an American Social Security number, and all the other paperwork required to live and work there. But I choose Canada.

We Canadians are notorious for embracing our expatriates. Is William Shatner Canadian? Not in any meaningful sense; Canada may have been his birthplace, but it isn't his home — and the former is something he had no choice over while the latter is an act of volition. Shatner, as it happens, is no longer married to his first wife — he divorced her, and he divorced his country of birth. Is writer Sean Stewart Canadian? Some might say yes, because he lived here for a number of years, but he was born in Lubbock, Texas, and now lives full-time in Houston, Texas. If you choose to live somewhere other than Canada, I don't think you have much right to call yourself a Canadian.

Lots of my friends in the arts would kill to have what I have — the freedom to work in the United States. They're desperate to get a green card. But Canada is my home, and, I honestly believe it's the best nation on Earth. In a very real sense, I'm married to Canada; I've never been tempted at all to move away, but, if I do, I'll do so with the understanding that if you're no longer living together, then you're no longer really married.

VAN BELKOM: Several of your novels have strong mystery elements, *Golden Fleece* and *The Terminal Experiment* for example, and you've even won the Arthur Ellis Award for Best Mystery Story for "Just Like Old Times." Have you considered leaving SF for the mystery field, or perhaps writing a straight mystery in addition to your SF?

SAWYER: I've considered a lot of things, but winning the Nebula Award for Best Novel of the Year made one thing absolutely clear: being a science-fiction writer is my first, best destiny. In SF, I've been able to explore an incredible range: I've written mystery stories, love stories, and adventure stories, all in an SF context. I've gotten to do stories about marriages in trouble, such as *The Terminal Experiment*; I've gotten to do stories about contemporary ethical concerns, such as *Frameshift*; I've even gotten to do a courtroom drama (*Illegal Alien*). Some SF publishers do try to pigeonhole you — they want your next book to be just like your last. But there are others, such as my current publisher, Tor, who give you a very wide latitude. I asked David G. Hartwell of Tor when he became my editor what he wanted me to write next, and he said, "Write whatever you're moved to write, and we'll find the best way to publish it." That's music to a writer's ears.

If I'd started out as a mystery writer, I'd be stuck working a very narrow street. Sue Grafton, with her series that began with *A is for Alibi*, embarked on doing twenty-six novels about the same character; that would be absolute purgatory for me. I love the freedom SF gives me, and can't imagine leaving it. Even the so-called "mainstream" is more constraining than SF. I'd make more money and sell better if I wrote nothing but novels like those of Michael Crichton or Robin Cook, but I wouldn't be nearly as satisfied artistically, and that is very important to me. If all I'd wanted to do was get rich, I would have become a lawyer.

VAN BELKOM: You've won major and minor awards for both your novels and short stories and served on the jury for the Philip K. Dick award. What's your take on the awards process and their value to the field?

SAWYER: All award processes are inherently flawed, of course. The whole idea that there's one "best" book or movie of the year is ridiculous. But I've benefited enormously from the fact that all sorts of award-bestowers have admired my work. I've won the Nebula once, been nominated for it a second time, been twice nominated for the Hugo, won the Arthur Ellis Award, been twice nominated for Japan's Seiun Award, won France's *Le Grand Prix de l'Imaginaire*, and won more Canadian Science Fiction and Fantasy Awards ("Auroras") than any other English-Canadian author. Is all of that gratifying? Hell, yes — particularly since so many of them were things that came out of the blue. *Le Grand Prix de l'Imaginaire* is the top SF award in France; I never dreamed I'd win that; an Arthur Ellis Award from the Crime Writers of Canada for an SF story seemed an equally improbable event. But the award wins clearly mean I'm doing something right. Have they helped my career? Damned right. Do I care about awards? No more than I care about reviews — of course, I'm interested in anything that has an impact on my livelihood, but I don't write for reviewers and I don't write for those who give awards. I write for me.

VAN BELKOM: *The Terminal Experiment* was a definite turning point in your career. How much did things change for you after the book was published and won the Nebula award?

SAWYER: Winning the Nebula Award had a major impact. I won it Saturday, April 27, 1996. Greg Gatenby was on the phone to me three days later, inviting me to be part of the Harbourfront International Festival of Authors. Prior to winning the Nebula, my novels had sold in the United States, the United Kingdom, Italy, Japan, and Russia. After winning the Nebula, they were almost immediately snapped up by France, Germany, Holland, Poland, and Spain, as well. My advances in the US and the UK doubled, and my advances in Japan went up 500 percent. As my editor put it, I went overnight from being a promising newcomer to an established, bankable name. My career would have continued without winning the Nebula: I had sold one novel to Tor for hardcover publication, had a second under contract to them, had *Illegal Alien* under contract to Ace, and motion picture rights to *The Terminal Experiment* were already under option. Still, it was a huge boost.

VAN BELKOM: You recently did a stint as an anthology editor. What was it like co-editing *Tesseracts 6* with your wife, and was there anything about the process that surprised you?

SAWYER: "Surprised" is too soft a word. I was stunned by the utter lack of professionalism of most aspiring Canadian writers. They hadn't bothered to learn proper manuscript format; they couldn't spell; they didn't understand basic grammar. We had people submit previously published stories, or stories that had already sold somewhere else, without disclosing that fact — a blatant, and pretty damned unforgivable, violation of the etiquette of the genre. It was a real eye-opener. A number of these people, to my surprise, had publication credentials to cite, but they were all in the genre small-press publications. These days, any joker with a LaserJet can start his own magazine. It used to be meaningful to say, "I am a published author." Now, apparently, it doesn't mean anything; certainly many of these people placing stories in magazines with circulations of 100 or 500 copies aren't writing at a professional level.

We had people e-mail us submissions without our permission, people who sent us abusive letters, people who sent a dozen different submissions on a dozen different days but only one self-addressed, stamped envelope, expecting us to dig through the pile to find theirs. I used to doubt the horror stories editors tell at writers' conferences; I don't anymore. That said, Carolyn and I were very pleasantly surprised by some of the writers we discovered. If you do another edition of *Northern Dreamers* in twenty years, I'll bet you'll be interviewing many of the writers who had either their first, or one of their first, stories in *Tesseracts 6*: Katie Harse, Nalo Hopkinson, Catherine MacLeod, Derryl Murphy, Douglas Smith, Jena Snyder, Hayden Trenholm, and Michael Vance are all going to be big names in 21st-century Canadian SF.

As for working with my wife, it was terrific. We enjoyed it so much that Carolyn decided to quit her job and come work with me full-time. Obviously, if we hadn't had a blast editing *Tesseracts 6* together, that never would have happened.

VAN BELKOM: Where do you see yourself in regards to the SF field say, twenty years from now?

SAWYER: Exactly where I am today: writing novels and stories that please me and hopefully my readers as well. I'm already making a comfortable living, I've already won the field's equivalent of the Academy Award; what more could I ask? I've got the greatest job in the world, and I hope to continue to enjoy every minute of it.

Élisabeth Vonarburg

As David Ketterer aptly put it in his 1992 book, *Canadian Science Fiction and Fantasy*, "French-Canadian SF received a boost in 1973 with the arrival of Élisabeth Vonarburg." Vonarburg was born in France in 1947 and moved to Québec in 1973, settling in Chicoutimi in order to teach at the University of Québec. She became a Canadian citizen in 1976, with her first published SF, "Marée Haute," appearing in *Requiem* in 1978.

The following year was pivotal for Vonarburg as it was the year she organized the first Québécois SF convention, and joined the editorial staff of the Québec speculative fiction magazine *Solaris*, where she would remain until 1990. During that time, she also contributed to the development of Québec SF as a critic, theorist, translator, and SF writing instructor.

But no matter what Vonarburg has done to promote the cause of SF in Québec, her greatest contribution to both Québec and Canadian SF is her impressive body of work, especially her short stories and novels. Vonarburg has published three short fiction collections in French: *L'Oeil de la Nuit* and *Ailleurs et au Japon* in Québec, and *Janus* in France. Her short stories have garnered several awards and have appeared in translation in publications such as *Amazing* and *Tomorrow*, and each of the six *Tesseracts* anthologies.

Her novels have been even more successful. Vonarburg's first, *Le silence de la Cité* (*The Silent City*), was published in France in 1981, winning *le Grand Prix de la SF Français*, and was then translated and published in Canadian, British, and American editions.

In 1992, her second novel, *Chroniques du Pays des Mères*, was published simultaneously in the US as *In the Mother's Land* and in France, winning the *Grand Prix Logidec de la SF Québécois*, and was then published in Canada as *The Maërlande Chronicles* in 1993. A third novel, *Les Voyageurs Malgré eux*, was published in France in 1994 and in Canada and the US as *Reluctant Voyagers* in 1996. Other titles include two fantasy books for young adults — *Histoire de la Princesse et du Dragon* and *Les Contes de la Chatte Rouge* — and a science fiction and fantasy book, *Contes & Légendes de Tyranaël*. Vonarburg's current publishing project is a five book SF series, Tyranaël.

EDO VAN BELKOM: I guess the first and obvious question is, why did you move from France to Québec in 1973?

ÉLISABETH VONARBURG: After his Masters degree in Physics, my then husband didn't want to do his military service in France — a year of doing nothing, earning nothing, and being unemployed when it was over, or a year of doing things he didn't want to do, like work in the nuclear industry. He asked for military cooperation, where you went to a foreign country that had cooperation accords with France (at the time; it doesn't exist in the same form now, I am told). You worked for two years at a puny salary ($400 Canadian a month in 1973), but you got experience, and you might get work more easily on coming back — if you wanted to come back and didn't find work first on site. Which was what happened to him. The University of Québec in Chicoutimi wanted to keep him. In the meantime, I had also found work at the university, as a full-time part-time teacher. Three courses per session, *and* the summer session, and stayed that way for about ten years. It was very easy to stay. The main reason being — we *wanted to*! We were fed up with France, we wanted a change of venue . . .

We never asked for Québec, though. We asked for North-Africa: we had friends there. Adventurous, yes, but not too much! We barely knew Québec existed. Jean-Joël (my then husband) was assigned to Chicoutimi by pure chance, and looking back on it, considering I am (and he is!) still here, I can't only think "serendipity" — as far as I am concerned, that is. I fell in love with winter on the first winter we were there, and from then on, I never really thought I wanted to go back to France on a permanent basis. In the beginning, it was "we'll go back during the summer vacations." I wouldn't have missed a winter for the world . . . And then, I don't remember when exactly, I stopped kidding myself: I didn't want to go back. There are undoubtedly other, more private reasons for that, family things I won't go into (I did, in a way, in *Reluctant Voyagers*); there is always more than one reason we do things. But the fact is, I stayed because I wanted to.

VAN BELKOM: When your science fiction became popular in France, was there a temptation to move back to France and be closer to the biggest market for your work?

VONARBURG: Oh my. "Popular?" On the grounds that my first written and published novel won an award? "Market?" This is so . . . hum, North American of you, my dear. You imply I must have been seeing writing as a "career," stories as marketable products, stories as *books*! I didn't. I still have some trouble doing so. If you want to describe it in those terms, writing was more of a hobby for me! Except this "hobby" was, is, like breathing to me. If I don't do it, I suffocate (which happened to me during the year when I was a full-time teacher in France).

French SF in France was not, and is not, what American SF is in the States; more like what Canadian SF is still in Canada: a curiosity at best, a publisher's category and cheap popular hackery at worst (I'm talking about the public's perceptions here, of course). Having a book published, and being successful in that very small milieu, was definitely not a reason for me to go back. The thought never even crossed my mind. *The thought that I could become a published writer and make a living out of it* never crossed my mind! Only when I separated from my husband and when full-time temporary work at the university began to appear less than a sure thing did I begin to consider it.

No, no, French SF people had, and many still have, a different outlook on things. You cannot make a living being a science fiction writer in France. A few (and I mean few: two, perhaps) did make a living writing in the "popular" genres and a very, very few do *now* in SF in France. That was not my first published book, either. I had already published a short story collection in Québec, which had won an award too (albeit a regional one). I had reasons a plenty to stay: I could do things here I could never have done in France. I was singing semi-professionally, doing radio, television, I was an active member of the nascent Québécois SF milieu (had been since 1974). In 1982, I knew full well that I would never go back willingly to France.

VAN BELKOM: Do you consider yourself a French science fiction writer, a Québécois SF writer, or a Canadian SF writer? And does the term "feminist writer" figure somewhere in the picture?

VONARBURG: Let's see . . . I am a woman born and raised in France, who writes science fiction in French in Chicoutimi, Province of Québec, Canada. And yes, "feminist" figures in the previous sentence if you know where to look. Which is to say my real "place" is my native tongue; it colors and orients everything else, I believe. The other places (and corresponding cultures) are parts of my identity as a person and as a writer, of course. But after all these years, I have come to the above conclusion about my native tongue being my only "place."

As for the F-word, I have trouble thinking one can be a woman and not be a feminist. Perhaps because my feminism is of the home-grown variety, not acquired and developed through the Canon (more through SF, for that matter!) or membership in this or that feminist organization. If *others* want to describe me as "a feminist writer," I have no problem with that — as long as it is a description and not a definition. I hate boxes.

VAN BELKOM: What sense of accomplishment accompanied the translation of *Silence de la Cité* into English for publication in Canada? Was it another breakthrough when the book was published by a mainstream mass-market publisher in the United States?

VONARBURG: Well, one entertains fantasies. In my moments of shameless megalomania, I had this fantasy of seeing one of my stories translated in English, and thus accessible — potentially, at least — to people I admired. For me, a story is a transaction between a writer and a reader. I received a lot from English-speaking SF writers, I'd like to give some of me in return. That dream became reality, with a vengeance as far as I was concerned, when Judith Merril accepted one of my stories, "Home by the Sea," for the first *Tesseracts* anthology. I didn't see it as a "professional" breakthrough, mind you — now, in retrospect, yes, but not at the time. It was an almost unbelievable honor to be read and accepted by *Judith Merril*, one of my legends, wow, I could die, now. You could say that seeing *Le Silence de la Cité* translated and published in English in Canada was sort of anti-climactic!

But seriously. I was happy, of course — but not thinking "career," thinking "communication." I was even happier when it got published by The Women's Press in the UK, since I am a "feminist writer" — the book might now reach some of its intended readership. The publication by Bantam . . . well, the circumstances were so weird, so unlikely, so incomprehensible (even now), that it somehow tainted my pleasure, still does.

I knew by then it was a "breakthrough" in communication as it would certainly reach a much wider audience and might become a "breakthrough" in professional terms. Fortunately, my potential delusions of grandeur got a reality check when I saw the first royalties statements and the abysmal sales (about a third of the 30,000 print run, as it has been for each of the three books published by Bantam). It helps keeping a perspective on things! All in all, I was, and am, very skeptical about that whole American adventure of mine. I saw it as a fluke from the very beginning — albeit a hilarious one, like a big cosmic joke, so beyond anything I had dreamed of — a purely circumstantial happenstance. Considering how it turned out, where I am now (no American agent or publisher, back to publishing my novels in French only, even though I've had a few more short stories published in the States, not even sure the new novels will ever be translated and published in Canada), I tend to think I was right: flukes all around! Very unprofessional attitude, eh? Maybe I don't have the make-up of the true, go-getter SF pro (that is, American-style) because I come from a culture where, as I said earlier, you can't make a living writing SF, you cannot think "career" and "SF" in the same thought. Or perhaps it's just me.

I'm grateful for the opportunity the translations gave me, though. I finally got to *meet* those writers I admire and who inspire me, thanks to the translations and the short stint that followed in American publishing. Some of these people even read my books. And that's what I really wanted.

The annoying thing about all this, of course — I can feel my annoyance while I am answering you — is that darn American (and English) tropism of mine. It's hard not to think "traitor" . . . I often catch myself thinking or even saying my "true readership" is there in the States. (There are more potential readers, that's for sure! And as far as the feminist thing is concerned, undoubtedly the readership is more . . . organized and aware in the States than in France or even in Québec). But as if the States were the Mecca of SF! Annoying American SF: can't live with it, can't live without it, have to write with or against it — but it is never out of the picture . . . And living so close to the US, it's too easy being contaminated and subscribing to the "American SF is The One and Only True SF" American dogma . . .

VAN BELKOM: What can you say about the translations of your work done by Jane Brierley? Is it a strange experience reading your work in English knowing that someone had a hand in interpreting and shaping your vision?

VONARBURG: Jane Brierley is a very good, Canadian award-winning, translator — one of those translators who is also a writer. A would-be writer when we first met in the mid-1980s, and I don't know if she will go on with her plans, but nevertheless: translation is an art, not a science, or as much an art and science as writing, and when a bilingual writer gets a writer-translator, and both are in sync, one thanks the Goddess or whomever. I know I have been very lucky that Jane liked my stories and wanted to translate them.

All the translations have been about 50/50, and we've always discussed them at length. They have my *imprimatur*! Working with Jane taught me more about English and French — and about how and why I write — than years of Academia! It was fun teaching her how to translate science fiction, too.

It is a strange and wonderful experience reading one's stories in another language that you know well. They are the same and yet not the same, your voice, but as if coming from . . . a parallel universe. Two languages never really coincide, of course. There are shifts in focus, rhythms, sounds, colors, texture . . . double vision. It is fascinating, like visiting another world without moving, like being someone else while retaining all your memories of yourself.

I happen to love the English language, and my eternal regret is that I will never be able to write fiction directly in English, as some of my more fortunate Québécois colleagues are able to do — Yves Meynard, Jean-Louis Trudel. But I am happy enough that I am able to work on the translations, and even, sometimes, to translate my stuff myself and do a respectable-to-good (I'm told) job of it. I like my English voice, that third voice I hear when I read the novels, for instance, neither exactly mine, nor Jane's. It is more spare, more laconic, often closer to my character's persona. Of course, it loses a lot of its . . . poetry, as far as sounds and rhythms are concerned.

VAN BELKOM: You've done translations from English into French. How well do the languages translate? Is it a help or hindrance being a writer yourself, and do you sometimes feel tempted to try and improve something?

VONARBURG: As to how well the languages translate, it depends on what you are translating. Science fiction is a bitch to translate into French. All that techno-babble comes so naturally to the English-speaker/writer who has always been allowed to *invent* words, to boot! That's one of the reasons English is so successful, I guess — its adaptability. You take a name, make a verb out of it, an adverb, an adjective, whatever. You can be "Spielberged" in English (I'll let you guess what that means . . .) but definitely not in French. Fantasy also is a bitch, for different reasons. In fantasy, a lot depends on the writing, style, poetry, mood, etc. You can't just do a "serviceable" translation; it must be a powerful recreation for it to work — that's what all translations must be, of course, but I feel it is much more important in fantasy.

So, obviously, I believe being a writer is a big help when you do translations. But here, too, it depends on what kind of writer you are, or more accurately what kind of person, perhaps, when it comes to the editing, revising, rewriting. All translations, as I said earlier, are recreations, adaptations. You have to translate not merely the letter of the text but its spirit — that of the author, and the "genius" of her native tongue.

All of which is why I like translating: it is as close as a non-writing writer can come to writing — at least you don't get rusty while earning a (meager) living! You learn a lot by scrutinizing other writers' works in this light (and sometimes it is heart-breaking: you loved the story as a normal reader, but reading sentence by sentence, word by word, you realize the author . . . just is not a good one!) Also . . . do you know that some very successful writers, in Europe, and especially the Eastern ones, consider it a duty to translate foreign writers? Not for money, but for the sake of literature and communication between cultures. Well, I know there are a lot of SF & F writers whom I would just love to translate almost for free . . . if I could afford it. I've been lucky so far: I've mostly translated authors that I like, or even admire. And some of these books I first recommended to publishers and it worked: I got to translate them.

Nowadays . . . well, not really. The French publishers' tastes and mine haven't evolved in the same directions!

VAN BELKOM: Would you ever feel comfortable enough to write in English, or is there even a benefit to doing so at this stage?

VONARBURG: As I said earlier, I *cannot* write fiction in English. There is a level of expertise, mastery, er . . . nimbleness, that I do possess in French — in droves — but can never hope to achieve in English, simply on the linguistic level. And that is far from being the only relevant level — the basic one, yes, but there are other, more important levels piled up on it afterwards! A language is a culture. English culture is not, and never will be, my culture, however interesting it may be and however well versed I can become in it. I've been living for twenty-four years in Québec; they do speak French here, and that is not, will never be, my culture either!

After twenty-five years here, when I go to Europe, I know that I feel rather alien over there, be it in France or anywhere else. Each time I go outside Québec, to the rest of Canada, it is very easy to get the same feeling. And when I go to the States, I realize I will never be a North American either. Distinctions blur — "Québec," "Canada," "the States" . . . "the Americas," "the New World" — it's all an imaginary place for me, all of it, even as I live there.

Mind you, being an "alien" has its advantages. Helps you see some things more clearly, even while it blinds you to some others. It puts questions of "nationality," "belonging," "group," in an entirely different light. I even think it helped me being more aware as a woman, since women are the Alien, aren't we?

Anyhow, that's why I said earlier that today I feel my only place is French, the language. And writing in French. France has taken leave of me as much as I did her, Europe too. Québec, Canada, North America all have seeped in somehow to replace most of it. But still, basically, I am at home nowhere. Except in my language.

As to writing in English being a benefit at this stage . . . at this stage, of what? Of my "professional career?" Oh, it sure would help me trying to publish in the States, but it wouldn't guarantee I would be published. After all, we had a nice gig going on, what with the translating being done in Canada, then the publishing in both countries; but it didn't make Bantam desperately cling to me, did it?

I don't have "a professional career" in the States. I have something like a "professional career" in French, though, and a rather well established one. It would be silly for me to let go of the prey for its shadow, wouldn't it? Especially since, as I said earlier, there is no chance in hell I can ever be as proficient in English as in French.

VAN BELKOM: For over ten years you worked as editor/fiction editor of the Québec SF magazine *Solaris*. What impression did you have of Québec SF when you began in 1979 as opposed to the one you had when you gave up the editorship of the magazine in 1990?

VONARBURG: I was fiction editor from 1979 to 1990, and editor only for three years or so. When I came on board *Requiem* in 1974 (it became *Solaris* in 1979), it was already one year old. For five years I was merely a reviewer and essayist among others. I saw the Québécois SF milieu coalesce around the magazine during these years. Being part of the Birth of a Fandom is one thing Québec gave me which I could never have had in France, where the milieu, and fandom, were already two generations old, institutionalized and rather monolithic.

VAN BELKOM: You spent a lot of energy promoting SF in Québec and did much to foster the Québec SF scene. Did it need much nurturing, or just a slight nudge in the right direction?

VONARBURG: I really don't know, I am not the person to answer that question. Yes, I spent lots of time promoting and fostering. But perhaps I was just playing my own little drama on my own little inner scene, you know, just "found a cause." It was fun doing whatever I did, though, it gave me a sort of legitimization.

Now, nudge or kick . . . Seems to me SF-Québécois (SFQ) was quite strong from the very beginning. And I am certain that Norbert Spehner and the rest of the original *Solaris* gang — Daniel Sernine, Luc Pomerleau, Claude Janelle, for instance — did as much as me and more to promote and foster. Not to mention the other magazines, *Pour Ta Belle Gueule D'Ahuri* — which didn't stay the course but was important at the time for graphic artists — and *Imagine* . . . — its board of editors and its director.

As to "the right direction", what would that be? Québécois SF didn't die off, it's still very much *there*, changing, evolving, that's enough for me. It has about half-a-dozen professional writers (in terms of quality and regularity of output), which is more, proportionally, than France can boast about — and some of these writers have access to the wider SF world through translations.

There are a dozen younger writers growing in the wings; SFQ is a strong presence in the YA market; it has two professional magazines and a current Renaissance of fanzines; a specialized publisher (ALIRE); one juried award (Le Grand Prix), one Readers' Award (Boréal); an annual convention; a writing workshop; third generation writers . . . We are getting a better exposure in France now that it is undergoing an SF Renaissance of its own, with three semi-pro or pro-zines and a slew of fanzines. After exhausting years of promoting and fostering on our part, we even managed to keep *some* relations with the other SF milieu, i.e. the English-Canadian one. Some stories get translated into French, some into English; Québecers go to a few conventions outside of Québec (or to Con*cept, in Montreal); some of us are both on the SFFRANCO and SFCANADA electronic discussion lists . . . The fact is, Québécois SF is going on, which is the surest way to go *somewhere*, isn't it? As to where it is going . . . well, SF writers are not in the business of making predictions.

VAN BELKOM: One of the recurring themes in your work — both in novels and short stories — is metamorphosis. Does this particular theme hold special interest for you as a writer, or did the stories you wanted to write simply require that science fiction trope in order for them to be told?

VONARBURG: It does hold a special interest for me as a writer — and as a person, since I tend not to compartimentalize. Each one of us, and I don't mean merely writers, has a central metaphor, a personal myth — their handle on things, if you will — that expresses itself in every aspect of their life. Mine is metamorphosis: life, death, being reborn as Other and yet the Same, continuity in change, the possibility for neverending life — and its corollary: what is the price we pay, and who pays it? It is such a neat metaphor for so many things, from writing to the way the universe works . . .

I am a closet mystic, too, and so this satisfies me both on the aesthetic and the spiritual level. I tend to think now that's what attracted me to science fiction. Not only the "sense of wonder," although it is a big part of it, but *change* as well. Not change all by itself but change in a dynamic relationship with immutability, or rather our desire for change not to happen. We don't want to get old, we don't want to die, we don't want things to decay, "go bad." There is a very hubristic side to science fiction, a lot of recurring stories about immortality, eternity, getting rid of matter and time and their constraints.

Perhaps because I am European born, perhaps also because I am a woman, what I've always noticed the most is *resistance to change*, and how changing — metamorphosis — is hard, terrifying even. The inevitability but difficulty of change, the need not so much to *control* it but to understand how it works in order to ride the wave, to understand what the consequences might be in order to choose among them, the different ways we can live with change, adapt to it . . . That's what I am interested in, as a writer and as a person.

And certainly science fiction has allowed me to tell stories I don't think I could ever have told otherwise, so the answer to the second part of your alternative would also be yes!

VAN BELKOM: Do you have plans for setting more books in the world of *The Silent City* and *The Maërlande Chronicles*?

VONARBURG: I have a love-hate relationship with the trilogy, more-than-one-bookology syndrome, both as a reader, and as a writer. When a book is just one long intricate novel cut in several parts (as C.J. Cherryh's books tend to be, for instance, or Gene Wolfe's), I love it. When it is a one-book novel (or worse, a short story!) abusively stretched on the rack, I hate it — like everybody else, I suppose: it's just bad literature. Of course, I tend to see my own more-than-one-bookologies as the "long, intricate novel" which evil publishing constraints force us to present as separate books. It is only the case for the publication of my vast, five-volume, two-thousand page saga, *Tyranaël*. Conversely, *Silent City*, *The Maërlande Chronicles*, and the would-be third book are really three separate novels which happen to take place in the same universe.

But I love mind-traveling. A well-realized other world, with all the trappings, is one of the things which also attracted me to science fiction — I mean, the writers as Gods & Goddesses Inc. I have always found the demiurgic aspect of fiction writing very seductive. And science fiction is so much more satisfying than mainstream for world-building.

VAN BELKOM: You've recently branched out into young adult

science fiction and some fantasy. How are you finding it? And will you be trying your hand at fiction outside of the speculative genres?
VONARBURG: I didn't as much "branch out" as I was drafted/grafted! I'd written a short story for my adult collection *Ailleurs et au Japon*, titled "Histoire de la Princesse et du Dragon," which was a loving (and feministly twisted) homage to fairy tales. The then-editor at Québec/Amérique asked me, "What if we took it out and published it in our YA line?"

I said "Why not?" — one more published book is always a good thing in a publishing milieu where there are no advances and you rely only on royalties; plus I knew the YA market to be a good, reliable one in Québec (my friend and SF colleague Daniel Sernine almost makes a living out of it). The story was not intended for kids (the vocabulary and such), especially in the age bracket it was labeled for (seven and above), but to my unending surprise it worked very well: parents and teachers loved to read the story to/with their kids.

The next year, I asked for a writing grant for two YA novels. Had it been refused, I would not have written them, perhaps. But it was accepted. One book was *Les Contes de la Chatte Rouge*, a (again rather twisted) fairy tale. The other was *Contes de Tyranaël*, myths and legends which the inhabitants of my invented planet, Tyranaël, tell their children to please and educate them — fantasy in a science fiction frame. And both books were very well received, both almost winning YA awards in France and still selling pretty well after about five years.

I love writing fairy tales and such. I can't really say "writing for children." What children? The age categories used by publishers are so meaningless. When I meet my young readers and they tell me what they think of the books they just defy all expectations. So I write, in this as in everything else, for myself — the child in me, as they say. I am very much in touch with my inner child, I assure you!

Curiously enough, I haven't really written science fiction for kids yet. It's as if the requirements of science fiction, for me at least, got in the way. I need things to be plausible in SF, but I hate lengthy explanations, and they're certainly a no-no in children's books. I feel much freer with fairy tales. But, conversely, I haven't written fantasy for adults yet, and don't know if I ever will.

I would like to try writing "real" fantasy for adults, though. Problem is I can't really afford to *play* at writing nowadays, to experiment for the sake of experimenting. If I had a day job or a wealthy old mecene, perhaps . . . Also, I need to be motivated by other reasons than just play, or money which comes really last, and by a long nose. . . (Such an elitist, artsy attitude, eh? Well, I've learned to live, or survive, with it.)

If a story really grabs me, means something to me, and it happens to be a fantasy story, then I will write it. Same thing for a — heavens! — mainstream story. A fantasy story is much more likely, I suppose. My imagination just doesn't run to mainstream stories. If I tried my hand at non-speculative genres today, it would be mostly for the joke, the nose-thumbing at the "Why don't you write serious literature?" people: "I can do it, so there and so what?"

Hardly enough of a motivation for me. But I try never to say never.

Andrew Weiner

Andrew Weiner has been writing accomplished SF short-fiction for more than twenty years, but as his entry in the *Encyclopedia of Science Fiction* points out, he "is yet to gain an appropriate reputation." But whether people are noticing or not, Weiner continues to write well-crafted, ambitious science fiction that consistently appears in the most prestigious of the genre's publications.

For example, Weiner's first short story sale was to none other than Harlan Ellison, who bought "Empire of the Sun" for his *Again, Dangerous Visions* in 1972. After that auspicious start, it wasn't until 1978 that Weiner's second story appeared. However, when "The Deed" was published in *The Magazine of Fantasy and Science Fiction*, it signaled Weiner's arrival in the genre. He published a story in *F&SF* again in 1979, then went on to publish some thirty stories through the 1980s in such publications as *Proteus, Quarry, Interzone, Leisure Ways, Rod Serling's The Twilight Zone Magazine, Isaac Asimov's Science Fiction Magazine, Chrysalis 10, Night Cry, Borderland, Amazing Stories*, and *Full Spectrum*. Appropriately, Weiner ended the decade with a collection, *Distant Signals* published by Porcépic (now Tesseract) Books.

Weiner's first novel, *Station Gehenna*, an expansion of a novelette previously published in *F&SF*, was published in hardcover by Congdon and Weed in 1987 as part of their "Isaac Asimov Presents" series. Also worthy of note is that two of Weiner's stories, "Distant Signals," and "Going Native," were made into episodes of the American television series *Tales from the Darkside*. In addition, "Distant Signals," likely his best, has been reprinted seven times, most notably in *The Norton Book of Science Fiction* and *Northern Stars: The Anthology of Canadian Science Fiction*.

Weiner was born in London, England, in 1949, and came to Canada in 1974. He holds an M.Sc. in social psychology from the London School of Economics. He has written six non-fiction books, and his articles have appeared in numerous periodicals, including *Maclean's, Toronto Life*, and *Reader's Digest*. He lives in Toronto with his wife and son.

EDO VAN BELKOM: Your first short story, "Empire of the Sun," was published in *Again, Dangerous Visions*, edited by Harlan Ellison. That must have come as a shock because up until then you hadn't sold to any of the major markets.

ANDREW WEINER: It was even more of a shock because I'd never even submitted to the book. I had submitted the story to the English SF magazine *New Worlds*. The editor I'd sent it to, James Sallis, was American. Unknown to me, he had gone back to the USA taking a bunch of stories with him, including mine, which somehow found their way into Ellison's slushpile.

VAN BELKOM: After that sale there was a gap of six years until another story appeared. What do you attribute that to . . . Were you still writing and submitting?

WEINER: Not for most of that time, no. "Empire of the Sun" was one of a bunch of short stories I wrote in the late 1960s while I was still at university — very experimental stories, very derivative of J.G. Ballard's "The Assassination Weapon" and the rest of the UK New Wave. I never submitted any of these stories to the American magazines — I didn't even read them at the time — just to *New Worlds* (which never did buy one). And I'm sure they would have been unpublishable in any American market in any case. I didn't look upon writing SF as a career at that point, it was just something that interested me, something I did when I had some spare time. Actually, I still don't look at it as a career. After I got my undergraduate degree I worked as an advertising copywriter for a couple of years, then went back to school to do a Masters. Any spare writing time I had went mostly to non-fiction — writing music and film criticism for *New Society*, *New Musical Express*, and other publications. It wasn't until after I moved to Canada, in 1974, that I began to make even sporadic attempts to write and sell fiction for the US markets. By then I was writing something closer to conventional North American SF.

VAN BELKOM: You say yourself that you weren't going to

make a career of it, so is it safe to say you've made a hobby of writing science fiction?

WEINER: I'm a professional writer. I've made my living writing for more than twenty years. But I'm not a professional science fiction writer. A professional SF writer, as I see it, is someone who earns the majority of their income from SF. There are very few people who meet that definition. And personally, it's not something I've ever aspired to. You know, the late John Campbell Jr., editor of *Astounding/Analog*, deplored the professionalization of the SF field. He much preferred to buy stories from gifted part-timers — usually scientists — than slick full-time hacks. This is one of the few points on which I ever agreed with Campbell. One of the big problems with SF is too many professionals!

VAN BELKOM: I sense from you that you have a fascination with writers who make their living writing full-time, especially pulp-era writers that produced large amounts of work to keep themselves fed. Is that true?

WEINER: Well, I have a great admiration for Philip K. Dick who once wrote twelve novels in one year — first draft, a lot of them, judging by the way they read — and yet several of them were among his very best. I was at one point quite fascinated with Barry Malzberg who used to knock off a novel on a weekend, but I couldn't imagine writing at that pace myself.

VAN BELKOM: Your short story "Waves," published in 1987, makes mention of e-mail, so you must have seen it on the horizon as part of everyday life in the future, but here we are today and I don't think you're on the Internet.

WEINER: It's funny you should say that. I've had a CompuServe account for about seven or eight years, but I've barely used it the past few years. My son's been using it, but I haven't. I used to have a GEnie account, and I would occasionally browse the SF forums, but never found anything to interest me there, just a bunch of people patting each other on the back and sounding off endlessly. And I never used e-mail. But I have finally begun to use it because I'm on this year's panel of judges for the Philip K. Dick Award, and this is the easiest way to communicate with my fellow judges. So, I am now online.

VAN BELKOM: Did you not think it was of value or were you

intimidated by the technology?

WEINER: I've been working with computers since the mid-1980s, so I'm not intimidated by technology — I just didn't have a real need to use e-mail until now. But I'm discovering that it is a very efficient means of communication when you need to circulate information rapidly.

VAN BELKOM: The characters in your stories tend to be psychologists or artists. Is this a case of writing what you know or are these the kind of people you find most interesting?

WEINER: I have a Masters in social psychology so, yes, I have known a lot of psychologists and I do like to use them as characters. And a lot of my stories evolve around the human mind, dreams, mass-psychology, identity, boundaries between self and universe, and so on.

VAN BELKOM: What about artists?

WEINER: I've written a number of stories about musicians, which draw on my background as a rock writer, and one or two others about visual artists. I suppose some of these stories are to some extent about the creativity process, which is something that interests and puzzles me.

VAN BELKOM: Are you looking at yourself trying to figure out how to become more inspired?

WEINER: I'm sure I am, at least to a degree. I still don't know where my stories come from — what makes me write them, or stops me from writing them.

VAN BELKOM: A lot of your stories feature aliens who find earth and its culture incredibly interesting. Do you really think aliens would find us so fascinating or are you just using aliens as a metaphor?

WEINER: I have no interest in aliens other than as projections of our own minds. Which is, of course, exactly what they are, whether in print, or in movies and TV shows. We made them up! They're a projection of out hopes and fears. I like to use aliens as tourists, basically — inscrutable observers, able to make comments on aspects of society. But I have no interest in trying to possibly imagine what a real alien would look like. The alien is by definition the other, and therefore unimaginable.

VAN BELKOM: You write SF, you don't mind being called an SF

writer, but in a lot of your essays you dismiss SF?

WEINER: I'm not thrilled to be called a SF writer because most people have a very low opinion of SF and with good reason because most SF is terrible. Realistically, I am an SF writer because I write stuff that is published as SF. I accept that. Life's too short to worry about these labels.

VAN BELKOM: Whether you consider yourself an SF writer or not, you do spend a lot of time criticizing the genre and breaking it down. Many of your essays say there isn't any science in science fiction, it's all fantasy. So, on the one hand, you write science fiction, and, on the other, you downplay it's importance.

WEINER: I wasn't so much downplaying the importance of SF as trying to pinpoint what the difference between SF and fantasy is. And what I concluded was that, psychologically speaking, they're identical — they're both equally irrational, and neither one can claim to be more realistic. Personally, I've always preferred SF as a medium, although lately I've been writing some stories that fall right on the border between the two.

VAN BELKOM: You've published over forty short stories, all to top flight markets, and yet you've only had one collection published. The entry on you in the *Encyclopedia of Science Fiction* says you've yet to gain the appropriate attention. Do you agree with that?

WEINER: I don't think that's really for me to say. I'm writing at the margins of what is already a very marginal literary genre. I'm not a crowd-pleaser, and I don't think I ever will be. So I can't expect to gain that much attention and I'm not sure that I would really want it.

VAN BELKOM: When your novel, *Station Gehenna*, came out did you have high hopes for it?

WEINER: I hoped it would be reasonably well received, but I didn't think it was going to be a bestseller. I guess it was received maybe a little better than I expected because the book earned out its advance, there was a paperback, and a movie option, although it wasn't exercised. So the book did fine. I guess I would have hoped that it would make it easier for me to sell my next book, but it didn't.

VAN BELKOM: You've published in literary magazines in Canada. Did you find the reception of your stories there any different from when they are published in the genre magazines?

WEINER: The reception of all my stories is pretty much the same. A couple of people will say, "I saw your story, nice story," and then that's it. Maybe it'll get reprinted in Poland, or somewhere. But otherwise, it's gone. You don't get letters. I've only had two very peculiar letters over the years from people who have read my stories. You don't get any feedback. It's like throwing your stuff out into a void. It's a message in a bottle. Somebody gets it, but who knows who, or what they make of it?

VAN BELKOM: How frustrating is that for you? You've been producing for twenty years and you might think that you've produced something of quality, and then you send it out into the void. If there was more of a response would it be easier for you to write?

WEINER: As I said, I don't understand creativity. I don't know what makes me write or not write. Although I'm pretty sure I don't do it for the money! For the past few years, I haven't been writing much of anything, because I gave up smoking and I've been massively blocked ever since, although I am just starting to work on a few things now.

VAN BELKOM: So there's a correlation between smoking and the creative process?

WEINER: Oh, definitely for me. Norman Mailer wrote that when he gave up smoking he had to learn how to write all over again. I'm not comparing myself to Mailer — but it has taken a couple of years for my concentration to even start to come back.

VAN BELKOM: Have you ever thought of writing for the mainstream, leaving SF behind?

WEINER: I've thought of it. But most of my ideas fall inside the genre rather than outside of it. I'd like to write a really dark, noir-y psychological thriller — but I suspect that it would end up very close to SF or dark fantasy. I have no interest in writing a straight contemporary novel of character. There are a lot of people who can do that better than I could.

VAN BELKOM: You've had two of your stories filmed as television episodes of the series *Tales from the Darkside*. How did that come about and how did it feel to have your work transferred to another medium by someone else?

WEINER: Anything to do with film is basically like winning the lottery. You can't write a story with the expectation that it will be filmed. *Tales from the Darkside* was a low-budget show that sought out stories that could be filmed cheaply, with a minimum of sets. The stories of mine they bought met that requirement — both were set in modern-day North America. They did a nice job on filming "Going Native," my story about an alien observer in group therapy. I didn't find "Distant Signals" as cohesive, although it had some nice actors in it.

What I liked best about was the way they were able to use big chunks of my dialogue, almost unchanged, in their script. Until then, I had always worried that my dialogue was stilted and unnatural. But it worked fine on TV, so I realized that maybe people do talk like my dialogue.

I talked about the alien as metaphor before: the alien in "Distant Signals" isn't really an alien at all. What he is, is a fan. A nostalgic, obsessive fan. He's the dead hand of the past, squeezing the life out of the present. At least, that's how I always understood the story, but who am I to say? Orson Scott Card, when he reviewed my short story collection, thought it was about the enduring power of art.

VAN BELKOM: What is your impression of SF fandom? You don't seem to be someone who cares to be a part of it.

WEINER: I do identify with that wing of fandom that is very literary, like the people who run *The New York Review of Science Fiction*, but that's such a small part of fandom — in Canada it's virtually invisible. In my experience, most fans aren't really interested in written SF, they are either interested in media or they're interested in other fans, and that's fair enough. Why should they read science fiction? Most of it is terrible anyway.

VAN BELKOM: Thomas Disch said "Dressing up in a costume is not an appropriate response to literature."

WEINER: Right. I mean, look at *Locus*, the SF newsmagazine, a very sober, serious magazine. But once a year, they have their Worldcon Report, with page after page of people dressed up in costumes. And you think, *this* is the secret heart of SF, fans dressing up in ludicrous costumes. You can forget the serious sober book reviews, the interviews, the reams of publishing data — because *this* is what it really comes down to.

VAN BELKOM: Where does the satisfaction for you come from in writing SF? What is the little germ of satisfaction that keeps you doing it, why haven't you thrown up your hands and said the hell with it years ago?

WEINER: It's like the slot machines in a casino. Why do people play them? Because once in a while it pays off. Behavioral psychologists call that a variable reinforcement schedule. Now and again I come out with a story that I think is good. A lot of the time I come out with stuff that doesn't really satisfy me at all, but I know that I've just got to move on.

VAN BELKOM: It would be safe to say that the person you're writing for is yourself.

WEINER: Well, me first. Hopefully, some editor will like it enough to want to buy it. And eventually some other people will read it. But first of all, I write for my own amusement. I suppose my most successful story, judging by the number of reprints and foreign sales, is "Distant Signals." But it's not my favorite story by any means. If I knew what the appeal of it was, maybe I'd be able to write another one like it. Or maybe I should novelize it! But really, I think, once you start trying to second-guess the market, you're dead. So it's probably better that I don't understand the appeal.

Michelle Sagara West

Born in Toronto in 1963, Michelle Sagara West has worked at the Bakka science fiction bookstore in Toronto since 1986. Like (another DAW author) Tanya Huff before her, she served as the store's manager for several years. She currently works there on a part-time basis.

Her first appearance on the Canadian fantasy scene came as Michelle Sagara, the author of a four-book series from Del Rey called The Book of the Sundered. The first volume in the series, *Into the Dark Lands*, was published in 1991 and was followed each year by another in the series: *Children of the Blood*, *Lady of Mercy*, and *Chains of Darkness, Chains of Light*. Her four-book debut in the fantasy field earned her a Campbell nomination in 1991, a feat she was able to repeat the following year.

In 1995, she changed publishers, moving from Del Rey to DAW Books while changing her pen name from Michelle Sagara to Michelle West by adopting her husband's surname. With DAW, she has published The Sacred Hunt duology, which includes *Hunter's Oath* and *Hunter's Death*. She has apparently found a home at DAW with another series underway. The Sun Sword is her first trilogy and includes the 1997 title *The Broken Crown* and the forthcoming volumes *The Uncrowned King* and *The Shining Court*.

Sagara West has published numerous short stories, all commissioned for themed anthologies, usually co-edited by Martin H. Greenberg. Her first story was "Birthnight" in *Christmas Bestiary*, published by DAW Books in 1992. Since then she has published some twenty other stories of fantasy and science fiction. In addition to Martin H. Greenberg, some of the other editors she has penned stories for include Mike Resnick, Katherine Kerr, Richard Gilliam, Mercedes Lackey, A.R. Morlan, and Lawrence Schimel.

Sagara West is also a book reviewer. She has written both the "Guilty Pleasures" and "Musing on Books" columns in *The Magazine of Fantasy and Science Fiction*, and has reviewed books for *Contacts*, a monthly supplement to the Barnes & Noble web page. Sagara West is married and has one son.

EDO VAN BELKOM: You worked at the Bakka science fiction bookstore in Toronto while Tanya Huff was manager there. What effect did Tanya's success have on your writing?

MICHELLE SAGARA WEST: The most important thing that Tanya's success did for my writing was make success seem accessible. I saw that she worked, and worked consistently, at her craft; I saw also how that work played out. Tanya had already sold her first couple of short stories by the time I started working at Bakka; she sold her first novel while we were working together, so I also saw her go through the first novel editing process. It made the whole process seem, if not mundane, then at least par for the course. It also gave me early warning that "hurry up and wait" is a publishing rule of thumb.

The only negative thing about this was that I thought if Tanya was successful, the method that Tanya used — and at that time she was much more structured about her outlines — was the only successful way to finish a novel, so I struggled a lot to conform to her process before giving up entirely and just doing what worked for me.

VAN BELKOM: Later, when Tanya became a full-time writer, you took over as manager. How did managing an SF bookstore help — if at all — your writing career?

SAGARA WEST: Immeasurably.

First of all, it was Tanya, then managing and buying for the store, who told our Ballantine Del Rey sales rep, Gord Davis, that I'd written a book that was terrific and that his company should publish. I had already sent it to Del Rey at that point, where it was in the slushpile, and he told the editor to pull it and read it. So she did. That would have been in August of 1988. In December of 1991, my first novel was published by them, after several overhauls and rewrites.

I think that every writer, every would-be writer, should spend a few years working in a bookstore. Before I started working at Bakka, I worked at the now defunct Classics chain, and it was there I learned how books are treated in the retail environment: bestsellers, frontlist midlist, and backlist; hardcovers, trade paperbacks, and mass-market paperbacks. I learned about returns, strip-lists (head-office would send a list of books that had past their best-before date, in a manner of speaking, and we would be responsible for stripping the new release quantities we had and paring down the title to backlist quantities, etc.), front of store displays, etc.

Bakka gave me access to sales reps. Talking with the reps — and reps are generally both intelligent and friendly because they're in the business of building a long-term relationship with a buyer that will benefit both bookstore and publisher — gave me a window into the publishing world that I hadn't seen at all: how books are presented and what effect a sales force can have on projected print-runs.

What does this have to do with writing? Nothing directly. But if you've had experience of that nature, editors expect you to be clear-eyed, and they tend to speak to you as if you're a bookstore person and not a writer. They don't have to explain returns. They don't have to explain why the incredibly beautiful painting on so-and-so's literary novel just plain wouldn't work for your high fantasy. They don't have to justify their shipping numbers — or rather, they don't have to explain why you are not Stephen King — and they can assume you know how sales conferences work.

If you don't know these things, it takes a fair amount of time to explain them — and in this day and age, editors are so over-worked that they're not likely to have that time. However, giving a writer facts out of context can be damaging to the editor-writer relationship, so very often, facts are put to one side until you know which ones to ask for.

VAN BELKOM: You still work part-time at Bakka and are around books all the time. Have you noticed a trend in SF publishing, and do you have any thoughts on where the field seems to be headed?

SAGARA WEST: Not really. I think the one thing I've noticed is how many writers of this generation seem to be having dialogues with writers that influenced them heavily, and I think any genre is going to change because of that. But as far as predicting a trend of any sort, no. I've seen various things wax and wane in popularity — *Star Trek* books, for example, have had their highs and lows — but nothing shocking or revolutionary.

VAN BELKOM: Wasn't your first novel originally to have been published as part of the Del Rey Discovery series? What happened?

SAGARA WEST: This isn't entirely accurate. My first novel was published before the Del Rey Discovery program was started; it was published at the end of 1991, and the Del Rey Discovery program started publication with Carol Severance's *Demon Drum* in 1992. My *second* novel, *Children of the Blood*, was considered for the Discovery line, but they decided against it because it was a second novel. And, I think, because they couldn't make the cover that Lester chose work with the Discovery banner.

VAN BELKOM: After your first four novels were published by Del Rey, you moved to DAW Books and changed your name from Michelle Sagara to Michelle West. What happened and why the name change?

SAGARA WEST: Two things, but the most significant was this: I had a child.

No, really. I had a child. I realize that this is something that people the world over do and survive, but it was such a shock to me to go from managing a bookstore — and the whole of my life — to having control of so very little of anything. That and the sense of isolation made everything that I did have seem very, very important to hold on to.

Lady of Mercy, which was my third Del Rey title, went out of print a few months after its initial release (it had a pub date of June '93, which means an in-store date of May '93). I had been told that the books would be kept in print until the fourth book had at least been published, and in fact my editor told me that a reprint of the third book was pending — but it stayed pending; it never happened. My son was born at around the same time, and I thought, I could lose my only publisher. I owed them two books at the time, so I could have confidence in those — but really, that wasn't enough. I wanted what you can't really have in this business: security.

And there was no question that I could lose the publisher; I'd worked in a bookstore for long enough to see those patterns emerge. I love both the editors I had at Del Rey, and I would work with either of them again in a second — but the realities of *publishing* are separate from the realities of *writing* in many significant ways.

I wanted my books to be somewhere where they would STAY

IN PRINT. That was the most important thing to me at that time. But, being an unrealistic person, I *also* wanted them to go to some- one I liked enough to work with (I can think of two other editors that I would be happy to work with, but whose control over in-print decisions is really controlled by numbers), and that really left only one company: DAW books. But of course, I was being published by someone else.

I go insane if I don't actively *do* something constructive — or worse, I become somewhat self-destructive — so I wrote four sample chapters and three outlines for what I assumed would be a trilogy (I'm terrible at actually judging the length a story takes to tell), and I sent it to Sheila Gilbert at DAW. She read it and agreed to buy it. The name change came about at that time; it was a mutual decision.

VAN BELKOM: What was the basis for the mutual decision made by yourself and Sheila Gilbert surrounding your name change?

SAGARA WEST: At the time that I made the sales to DAW, we didn't have a clear idea of what the numbers for the series were, although about two years later, we knew that they weren't good. We had shipping numbers for books one and two of The Sundered, which were neither terrific nor hugely terrible, but not for *Lady of Mercy*. But because I wanted to continue to publish with Del Rey, and really didn't — at that time — want to have to explain why I was writing for someone else, and as I wasn't confident in either numbers or future, I was perfectly willing to start again. DAW was actually will- ing to go either way because — and I owe Mike Resnick for this, indirectly — Sheila loved the short fiction that had appeared in DAW anthologies and didn't think the shipping numbers for the first two books were bad enough to merit a forced name change.

As it turns out, the shipping numbers on the last two were bad enough to merit it. But that's hindsight.

VAN BELKOM: If you owed Del Rey two books after your third book went out of print, that means you only delivered one of them. Did you buy back one of the books and resell it to DAW? I had been led to believe that you'd been "dis-published" by Del Rey and you had changed your name from Sagara to West in order to get a fresh start with booksellers for your DAW titles.

SAGARA WEST: The fourth book of The Sundered was delivered before *Lady of Mercy* saw print, so I owed them two titles, *Hunter's*

Oath and *Hunter's Death,* which later were published by DAW. I bought back both of these titles and sold them to DAW when *Lady of Mercy* went out of print, and I remember this because my editor at that time was on vacation, but I *really* needed to pull the books, so we pulled them and then I phoned her and told her why in a very apologetic way. As I said, I really liked her, and it made things very complicated; there was nothing at all that she could really do to address the issues of concern for me.

DAW bought those two books as well, so I theoretically owed them five books before the first book was published. I sold them the duology that was to follow the *Hunter* books as well, and I don't think I've ever owed them less than five novels . . .

DAW has (a) kept the books in print, and (b) put terrific covers on all of them, and (c) shipped more copies of the book, which leads to (d) sold more copies. So I imagine I'll be at DAW quite *happily* for a very long time.

I don't much like change.

VAN BELKOM: All of your novels have been parts of larger series. Do you enjoy doing series novels, or would you prefer to write standalones?

SAGARA WEST: Obviously, I enjoy writing on a larger canvas. I've written short fiction, but I consider myself to be a novice at that form; it's the longer form that I love because it has space and time to explore things — structural nuance, character nuance, detailed and complex senses of *place*. If books could be 2,000 manuscript pages long, then I'd write standalone volumes. I would actually use the words "multi-volume" as opposed to "series," because a series book is one — to me — that stands alone but builds on previous volumes, and nothing I write stands alone in that fashion: book one is part one; book two is part two, etc. Bujold, for instance, writes series books, and good ones — and that takes its own peculiar skills, has its own demands.

I've been very lucky in some ways; I've never been asked to write something other than what I want to write, what I feel very strongly about writing. Sheila Gilbert is wonderful in that she sees very distinct strengths to my writing, none of which she feels would translate well into writing I personally felt less strongly — I'm tempted to say passionately, although perhaps that's too over-used a word — about.

VAN BELKOM: You had a child a few years back. How difficult has it been to continue writing while raising a small child?

SAGARA WEST: I'm glad that I'd published two novels before the baby was born. Having a small infant was vastly more daunting than writing a novel, and it made the process of writing a novel, and the agonizing one does over it, seem trivial by comparison, although I lose that sense of perspective as things get easier at home.

I foolishly assumed that children basically slept a lot during the first year of their life, so I'd set up a writing schedule that forced me to start writing again when my son was three months old. I would get up between two and five in the *morning* to work because it was the only time he'd be guaranteed to actually sleep for a three hour block. I was constantly exhausted, and if it weren't for the fact that my parents live close by, I wouldn't have gotten any writing done at all.

I learned to grab time as he started toddling; my parents would come over and I'd rush up to my office to type away until I was needed; it was hard to juggle, and I got more writing done working full-time at the bookstore than I did being at home almost full-time with a child. This says something about the relative difficulty of either job.

But as my son has gotten older, it's gotten easier. I now write in the mornings while he's at junior kindergarten, and the two and a bit hours feels like eternity.

VAN BELKOM: You've done a lot of short fiction, but most or perhaps all of your stories have been commissioned pieces for themed anthologies. Is that the only kind of short fiction you've done?

SAGARA WEST: All of my short stories have been commissioned pieces for themed anthologies. No exceptions. I've written some other short fiction, but, aside from one short story — my first attempt at writing anything — nothing intended for publication. I'll write short stories as gifts for people that I'm close to, if I have something to say to them that fits the confines of a short piece.

My first four novels started as a short story, and they were my second attempt. After that, I've always worked under contract, and especially during the last four years, it's been very hard to find the time to finish the novels I owe. I consider people who write short stuff on spec to be particularly brave — I'm not — and confident about their work. I generally don't submit to anything I'm not asked to submit to. I write commissioned short works because I'm terrible at saying "No" and because I'm pretty sure, given that I've been asked for a piece, that there's a market for it. The guidelines I'm given are so general I can write a piece that's *mine* while at the same time conforming to the theme of a given book. I've been told that my short fiction is more accessible than my longer work, for what it's worth.

VAN BELKOM: How would you describe the kind of fantasy you write?

SAGARA WEST: I think the closest question to this I've ever been asked is "What's this book about?", an occupational hazard when you work in a bookstore. I'm not sure how I'd describe it. High fantasy, I think, although as time goes on I become interested in some of the complexity and nuances of historical fiction, and I think I use some of what I consider to be historical fiction's strengths in the context of a purely fantasy environment.

High fantasy to me implies the use of archetypes and is almost always informed by the concept of justice, of a just outcome to a situation; in its barest sense its about coming of age, about struggling for justice, about how the one and the other are interconnected. I think that as the genre changes and grows, it becomes muddier, more complicated by the question of what justice is, but that's fair; it's a reflection of the society that creates it.

VAN BELKOM: Have you ever tried writing in other genres, like science fiction or horror?

SAGARA WEST: Not really, no. I've written alternate history short stories, and I think those come under the umbrella of SF. I've written short stories that I've been told are essentially horror, but I don't really classify them that way, and in fact have always felt that I *can't* write horror because the way I distinguish horror from contemporary fantasy is probably unique to me.

VAN BELKOM: Which of your novels are you most proud of and why?

SAGARA WEST: That's almost like asking "which of your children do you love best and why?" but it's a fair question, and I've thought about the answer for a while now.

I think that I would have to say I'm proudest of my most recently published novel, *The Broken Crown*, because I set out to do something in that book that I had never done before: to create a culture that was real enough to shape the emotional reactions and all of the nuances of the characters who were born into it.

I've long admired those writers who are able to create an *immersive* sense of culture, of otherness, that rivals a well-thought out, well-researched historical, because it gives a book a sense of the organic that doesn't otherwise quite exist in a created environment. But having said that, it's one of the things I've found most difficult to do. It's not enough to *know* about the details and the world, the economic system, euc., etc; it's not enough to build worlds. You have to stitch the world into its people, because it's only knowing the people that the place becomes so real (at least, for me as a reader, this is true). I think in many ways I succeeded in my goal with *The Broken Crown*.

I have to add, though, that in many ways *The Broken Crown* seems to be a step backwards in terms of accessibility; I didn't get one bad review for *Hunter's Death*, the novel previous to it, but I've gotten a couple now for *The Broken Crown*, and I think part of the reader reaction has to be the opacity of the culture itself.

I hope to address some of that in the next book; I always try to do things that I haven't done before in every book I write. I think, sometimes, I bite off more than I can comfortably chew, but you almost have to do that.

Robert Charles Wilson

Born in the United States in 1953, Robert Charles Wilson moved to Canada with his family at the age of nine. He has lived in Nanaimo and Vancouver, but currently resides in Toronto. Wilson has consistently mined one of the classic themes of Canadian literature in both his novels and short stories. According to the *Encyclopedia of The Science Fiction*, "He expresses with vigor and imagination the great Canadian theme (for the sense of being on the lonely side of a binary has sparked much of the best Canadian SF) of geographical alienation."

Wilson is probably best known as a novelist who made his debut in 1986 with *A Hidden Place*. His second novel, *Memory Wire*, was published in 1988, with the rest of his novels following roughly at the rate of one per year: *Gypsies*, *The Divide*, *A Bridge of Years*, *The Harvest*, *Mysterium*, and *Darwinia*. *Mysterium* won the Philip K. Dick Award (an award for distinguished works of science fiction published in a paperback original) in 1994, and both *Harvest* and *The Divide* — a novel set in Toronto — were selected as Notable Books of the Year by *The New York Times Book Review*.

Wilson's first short story sale was "Equinocturne" to *Isaac Asimov's Science Fiction Magazine* in 1974. He did not publish any more short fiction until the 1980s when several stories appeared in the genre magazines, including "Ballads in 3/4 Time," which first appeared in *The Magazine of Fantasy and Science Fiction* in 1987 and was reprinted in the anthology *Northern Stars*. In the mid-1990s, Wilson made a return to short fiction with the novelette "The Perseids," published in *Northern Frights 3*. That story won the Aurora Award and was a Nebula nominee the following year. Other publications featuring Wilson's recent output of short fiction include *Realms of Fantasy*, *Tesseract 6*, *Northern Frights 4*, and *UFO Files*.

Wilson has been compared by more than one reviewer to the likes of Theodore Sturgeon. *Books in Canada* has said of him, "With each new novel, Robert Charles Wilson adds to his reputation as one of the best SF writers of his generation."

EDO VAN BELKOM: You're a native of California and you came to Canada at the age of nine, but for some reason I think there's still a lot of what I would call the classic Californian in you. You know, laid back and easy going. Do you think there's truth in that?

ROBERT CHARLES WILSON: Well, I'll try not to take it personally . . . Yeah, I guess so. Coming to Canada was interesting because not being a native you feel a certain discontinuity, and when you're nine years old, you know you're not one of the gang. I came up here at a time when there was a lot of Canadian nationalism happening so I knew what it was like to be different. I've lived here most of my life and I feel more Canadian than American, but it's not really fair for me to say because I don't know how much Californian baggage I carried with me.

VAN BELKOM: Your first short story, "Equinocturne," was published in *Asimov's* in 1974, at the ripe old age of twenty-one. With such early success, why did it take another twelve years for the novels?

WILSON: I was nineteen when I wrote that story. I think it was just a lucky shot basically. I was at that stage of writing when you flail around and mail all sorts of garbage to all sorts of magazines. I managed to place one story with Ben Bova, which was a thrill for me, but it wasn't something I could do at will. It took another ten years of writing — and of not writing — before I could write publishable material consistently.

VAN BELKOM: Whenever someone sells their first story there is always the thought, "Let's see if I can do it again." In those ten years did you ever think you couldn't do it again?

WILSON: Of course. Yeah, sure. I spent many of those years thinking that. I spent a lot of those years not writing, too, because I felt I didn't have any control over what I was doing. It really was a case of flailing in the dark and I didn't like that, and it meant that most of the time I spent writing was wasted. It took me an awful long time to get a grasp on what you do when you write, what story structure is, and what voice is . . .

VAN BELKOM: Did you do that all by yourself, or were you working with other writers?

WILSON: No, I did that mostly by myself. It probably would have been helpful to have other people to go to for advice, but I just couldn't bear it. I didn't like what I was producing myself and I certainly didn't want to show it to people.

VAN BELKOM: What did you work at before becoming a full-time novelist?

WILSON: For a few years I was a transcriptionist at the Ontario Human Rights Commission, which was an education in itself, and which was great for learning how to write dialogue, too, because most of what I was transcribing was conversations between caseworkers and people who came off the streets with human rights complaints. I learned an awful lot about how people talk and what it looks like on paper.

VAN BELKOM: Did you enjoy that work?

WILSON: I hated going into the office every day. I hated physically being there, being chained to a desk doing secretarial work essentially, but I learned a lot from it.

VAN BELKOM: You've lived in Toronto, moved to Vancouver Island, and are now back in Toronto. Why the moves, and what's the basic differences between lifestyles in Toronto and the West Coast?

WILSON: Well, there were all sorts of reasons for the moves. I wanted to explore the west coast a bit. We lived in Nanaimo on Vancouver Island, and also a little more than a year in Vancouver proper. But unlike the vast majority of Canadians — and I know it is virtually treason to say this — I seem to prefer Toronto to Vancouver. When I went to get a new library card when I moved back to Toronto, I told the guy I had been in BC for several years and he said, "Well what are you doing here? I thought we were all supposed to be moving out there." It's pleasant out there, and a unique environment, but I just feel more at home back east.

VAN BELKOM: How much do you think your moving around has affected what you write about since in many of your stories your characters are looking for a place to belong, or fit in?

WILSON: Yeah, I think that's an honest reflection. A lot of my characters are looking for a place to call home, and I guess that's what I was doing for a lot of that time. And it's reflected in my work in others ways. If you look at the small town in *Mysterium*, the experience I've had of a small town is essentially Nanaimo, a town of 50,000. As an experience of the way people work and interact in that kind of environment it was really useful.

VAN BELKOM: Are you settled now in Toronto?

WILSON: I certainly hope so. Unless the city becomes uninhabitable.

VAN BELKOM: Drugs play a prominent role in your fiction, and I'm wondering how much of a part they play in its creation?

WILSON: In its creation, I would say, relatively little. The only really writing-related drug experience I had was overcoming writer's block using psychedelics. It was a specific experience I designed around that. I was having enormous trouble finishing anything, starting anything, knowing where I was going or knowing what I wanted to do. I had been reading a lot of the old literature about how people used psychedelics as problem-solving substances. And I sat down to an LSD session with the intent of confronting and try-ing to understand what was making it so difficult for me to work. I know it's probably not fashionable, or maybe even a good idea to say this, but it was enormously successful and a lot of stuff came out of that that I'm still working through.

But as for getting inspiration from drug experiences, apart from that one specific case, I can't say that I have. It's not that I'm taking a lot of drugs, it's just that I've experimented with different things. And I don't think inspiration comes out of a pill or out of a plant. The most you can do is rearrange the contents of your own mind, and as helpful as that sometimes is, that's not where my ideas comes from, that's not where the impetus to sit down and work comes from. Very little inspiration comes from that source and, of course, ninety percent of what we do is perspiration.

VAN BELKOM: You mentioned rearranging the contents of your mind. That seems a natural considering that the SF you write deals a lot with alternate and parallel worlds.

WILSON: Perhaps subtly, but not in any obvious way. I think that's one of the great virtues of science fiction. It gives us a way to stand apart from what is familiar and look at it in a new light. I think I was getting that from science fiction long before I ever had any kind of drug experience.

VAN BELKOM: Do you think you'll continue mining the theme of alienation, or are you ready to move in another direction?

WILSON: Well, yeah, I'm always ready to move in another direction and I always perceive myself as moving in another direction. But I think any writer voluntarily or involuntarily returns to familiar themes. You write out of your own life experiences so you find yourself coming back to certain ideas. But I like to think I'm finding new approaches to what I write about. To me the constant struggle is to understand what I'm doing and why, and then do it better, do it more precisely.

So I can't say that I'm leaving behind the theme of alienation, but certainly I'm trying to find new approaches to it.

VAN BELKOM: What's the starting point for you when you write a short story or novel? Is it a basic premise, an image of some parallel world?

WILSON: Usually it's some combination of idea and image, some striking image combined with some striking idea, and if they meld in some unusual way then obviously there's a germ there. And then you begin looking for characters — what kind of characters would be illuminated by the thing.

VAN BELKOM: How much of the story do you have when you begin, and how much is discovered by you as you go along?.

WILSON: I have most of it when I begin. There are endless acts of discovery when you write something, but I don't want too many major surprises. I like to know where I'm going, and to have a thematic resolution in mind because I think it helps you get where you're going.

I'll usually sketch out key scenes, key developments. It's sort of like having a rough map of unfamiliar territory so you know where you're going and you know approximately how you're going to get there, but the pleasure is what you discover along the way.

VAN BELKOM: In 1996, your story "The Perseids" won the Aurora Award. What do you consider that story to be about?

WILSON: I guess when you come right down to it, it's about the experience of being "separate" — I wouldn't say alienated — the inevitable separation we feel from other people. As close as you can get to other people, you're born alone and you die alone and I wanted to force that perception onto a character. There's a sort of paradoxical thing in there about the character because it's his "separateness," his fear that he's actually different from other people in some fundamental way that insulated him from the terrible things that are happening around him. It confers on him an immunity, but it separates him utterly.

VAN BELKOM: That story seems to have opened the short fiction flood gates and you've now got stories in *Northern Frights 4* and *Tesseracts 6*. Will there be more short stories?

WILSON: It's really interesting coming back to short stories after a long gap. Initially, I wrote stories even though they weren't my favorite form of SF — I was always a novel reader. I wrote short stories essentially as a way of entering into the field and they met with a fair reception, but they're not work that I'm especially proud of, it's not the work that I want held up as an exemplar. And so I gave it up for a some years for novel writing. Coming back to it, I actually feel I have more control over the form, that I can do more of what I want to do with it, and that there's a little more latitude. I'm really enjoying it, so I guess there probably will be more in the future.

VAN BELKOM: Do you approach the writing of short stories differently than novels. Most of your stories are fairly long, and it seems to me that people who write short stories first are very conscious of condensing and getting it down to the bare minimum. You seem to take your time enjoying the scenery, and if it turns out to be a novelette or novella, well then, so be it.

WILSON: The story finds its own length, and I was conscious in those stories of relaxing a little bit. I like to think of these stories as being idea dense. It pleases me to get a lot of things done in a relatively short volume, but they all seem to come out to novelette length and it's tough writing anything shorter than that.

VAN BELKOM: Do you think you could write a 3,000 word short story?

WILSON: Yes I could. Now, could I write a good 3,000 word short story? I don't know about that.

VAN BELKOM: Your novels have been coming out one-a-year since *A Hidden Place* in 1986. Does it take you a year to write each one?

WILSON: Yeah, except for the last one. It took a couple of years all told.

VAN BELKOM: Is that something you'd like to change, or is it a comfortable time period for you?

WILSON: A book that's easy to write is a book that's faster to write, and a book that's more difficult to write takes longer — I don't think it necessarily means that one is a good novel and one is not a good novel. Some books are just more problematic, and I can't tell when I sit down to start writing a novel whether it's going to run into difficulty. But a year seems a comfortable pace for me.

VAN BELKOM: You have a beautiful and flowing writing style that's very easy on the eyes. Did it take a long time for you to develop that or was it something that came to you naturally?

WILSON: My problem wasn't stylistic. I always felt that I could write a very nice sentence and a half-decent paragraph. It was past that point that I was having problems. So my problems were with structure, continuity, foreshadowing, suspense, theme, and resolution.

VAN BELKOM: You've been well-received by critics and reviewers, but you haven't seemed to have garnered large numbers of readers. Does that sometimes bother you?

WILSON: If it doesn't change it will bother me. It's kind of a crap-shoot I think. Writing is a crapshoot, whether your work comes to the attention of a lot of people or not. I don't think there is any particular reason my work couldn't be more popular than it is, but I'm not complaining either. Any writer wants a larger audience, but a lot of that is out of your control. I mean, some of it is in your control and you can attract a larger audience and you can bring your work to the attention of people, but some of it's also a crapshoot. So we'll see what happens.

VAN BELKOM: Has their been any movie interest in your work?

WILSON: Yeah, I've had options periodically and there is some stuff going on right now that may or may not turn into anything.

VAN BELKOM: Which of your novels are you most pleased with?

WILSON: Well, I'm not completely pleased with any of them. But I guess *The Harvest* stands out in my mind as a solid piece of work. It achieved a lot of what I set out to do with it. You can't always say that. It was also relatively easy to write and I think it succeeded on a number of levels.

VAN BELKOM: Which do you think is the poorest?

WILSON: *Memory Wire*. No question. It is the one I don't reread. It was a second novel. It was just out of my control. So much of the writing was "Cross your fingers and hope for the best."

The thing that was a real problem for me was a terrible reluctance to expose my own inadequacies on paper and show it to people. The trouble was I had a well-developed critical sense and I knew what I was writing was crap . . . I just didn't know what to do about it. And part of overcoming that was just being willing to let people see work that was only as good as I could make it, and *Memory Wire* was only as good as I could make it at the time. It's not something I'm enormously proud of, but a lot of people have told me they liked it and that's fine. It was educational.

VAN BELKOM: If there's one way you'd like your work to be remembered, how would it be?

WILSON: Well, on one level, it's satisfying to have these things around, to have my books in the Library of Congress and so on. And to know that my great grandchildren, if they so desire, could pick up one of these things and read it. That's satisfying in itself.

But I was pleased with "The Perseids" and the other Toronto stories I've been doing — I think of them as a cycle of Toronto stories. I've done another one for Don Hutchison (*Northern Frights 4*) and for *Tesseracts 6* and even another story I'm doing for an anthology in the US. And I sort of envision this work being put together at some point as a volume of Toronto stories. I think that would probably be my most impressive body of work.

Edo van Belkom made an auspicious debut in the speculative fiction field when his first short story sale "Baseball Memories" was an Aurora Award nominee and reprinted in *Year's Best Horror Stories 20*, edited by the late Karl Edward Wagner. Since that first sale in 1990, he has published more than 120 other stories of science fiction, fantasy, horror, and mystery in such magazines as *Palace Corbie, Parsec, Storyteller, Haunts, On Spec* and *RPM*, and in the anthologies *Northern Frights 1, 2, 3, 4, Shock Rock 2, Deathport, Fear Itself, When Will You Rage?, Hot Blood 4, 6, Dark Destiny, Seductive Spectres, Truth Until Paradox, Alternate Tyrants, Demon Sex, Brothers of the Night,* and *Robert Bloch's Psychos.* In 1997, his story "The Piano Player Has No Fingers" was both an Aurora nominee and a finalist for the Crime Writers of Canada's Arthur Ellis Award for Best Mystery Story of the Year. Twenty of his stories are gathered together in the collection *Death Drives a Semi*, published by Quarry Press.

His first novel, *Wyrm Wolf,* published in 1995, was a *Locus* bestseller and a finalist for the Bram Stoker Award for superior achievement in a first novel, presented by the Horror Writers Association. Other novels include *Lord Soth* and *Mister Magick.*

Born in Toronto in 1962, van Belkom graduated from York University with an honors degree in Creative Writing. He then worked as a daily newspaper reporter for five years before becoming a full-time freelance writer in 1992. He currently serves as the Horror Writers Association's Canadian membership representative and as the Canadian Regional Director of the Science Fiction and Fantasy Writers of America. He is a contributing editor to the *SFWA Bulletin.*

As a teacher, he has taught short story writing for the Peel Board of Education, been an instructor at Sheridan College, and has lectured on horror and fantasy writing at the University of Toronto. In 1997, van Belkom was Toastmaster of the World Horror Convention in Niagara Falls, New York. He lives in Brampton, Ontario, with his wife Roberta and son Luke.

His web page is located at www.horrornet.com/belkom.htm

Edo van Belkom

Science Fiction, Fantasy, Mystery, and Horror Books
from Quarry Press

Death Drives a Semi $19.95
by EDO VAN BELKOM

King's Cross $19.95
by D.G. COURTNEY

The Orient File $29.95
by DOUG HALL

Out of This World: $19.95
Canadian Science Fiction & Fantasy Literature
edited by ANDREA PARADIS

Trapdoor To Heaven $16.95
by LESLEY CHOYCE

Available at your favorite bookstore or directly from the publisher:
Quarry Press, P.O. Box 1061, Kingston, ON K7L 4Y5, Canada.
Tel. (613) 548-8429, Fax. (613) 548-1556, E-mail: order@quarrypress.com.

Name _____

Address _____

_____ Postal Code _____ Telephone _____

Visa/Mastercard# _____ Expiry Date _____

Signature _____   Your books will be shipped with an invoice
                                          enclosed, including shipping costs, payable
                                          within 30 days in Canadian or American currency
                                          (credit card, check, or money order).